STUDIES IN ECONOMICS

Number Five

OREGON STATE MONOGRAPHS

STUDIES IN ECONOMICS

Charles B. Friday

Consulting Editor

John R. Commons

his assault on laissez-faire

Foreword by WAYNE MORSE

JOHN R. COMMONS

Corvallis, Oregon
OREGON STATE UNIVERSITY PRESS

his
assault
on
laissez-
faire

By LAFAYETTE G. HARTER, JR.

OREGON STATE UNIVERSITY PRESS, CORVALLIS, OREGON

Library of Congress Catalog Card Number: 62-63219

Printed in the United States of America

JRC

FOREWORD

By WAYNE MORSE

ALL OF US who attended the University of Wisconsin and pursued any of the courses in economics during the 1920's could not help being influenced by John R. Commons. I was not among those who took course work from him directly. But among my own professors were some of John R.'s most notable students, including the late Selig Perlman and Edwin E. Witte. Professor Commons frequently lectured to us in the courses taught by Perlman and Witte, and I attended many informal round-table seminars conducted by him, Perlman, and Witte.

John R. Commons virtually founded a school of thought of his own in the area of the economic institutions of the United States and their relations to each other. More than that, he saw—what few academicians ever see—his ideas tested out at state and national levels. To me, his greatest contribution was the assumption on which he worked and which he fostered that theorizing about economics was not enough—that the academic world must communicate with makers of public policy and put their theories to the test of practice.

vii

The result was that starting in Wisconsin and spreading to other states and eventually to the national government, a series of advances in industrial relations was brought about.

Unemployment and accident insurance, public utility regulation, social security, civil service and administrative law as we know them today all may be traced in one degree or another to the work of this academic statesman of political economy. These will be detailed and described in the following pages. While most were fought tooth and nail at the time of their adoption, they have largely produced the era of "enlightened capitalism" which we enjoy today.

A second great contribution of Commons which many of us absorbed from him was his insistence on following where the facts lead. Commons worked and wrote in direct opposition to the type of economics which is based on pure logic. Today, it is perhaps hard to understand how remote from practice and practicality much of our academic thought in the social sciences really was at the turn of the century, and how novel his approach of fact finding was.

Every student of Selig Perlman has heard him tell how he came to the United States as a young man for the purpose of showing how American labor fitted into and buttressed the Marxian concept of class warfare and revolution. He told Commons this was his objective, and he wanted to study under Commons to prove that the American labor movement fitted into Marx's dialectic.

Commons' reply was that he would hold Perlman to only one requirement, and that was that his conclusions must be based upon carefully researched facts, no matter where they led. Distorting the findings to fit a preconceived theory would not be allowed. Perlman accepted the requirement and held to it. Out of his study, Perlman showed American labor history as disproving Marx, rather than supporting him. Instead of seeking control of production by wresting it from capitalists, American labor sought rather a fair share in the fruits of capitalist productivity.

This kind of direct investigation into corporation functioning and the day-to-day operation of a labor organization was not the general practice at that time. Commons was a great intellectual pioneer in bridging the considerable gap between social theories and social practice. He not only did it himself, but he trained a generation of scholars in the same technique.

The interest in political economy which he aroused in his students and the intellectual demands he instilled in them have flowed out to thousands of others.

Commons' anniversary fully deserves this observance. He changed much of our academic procedure and he contributed enormously to the betterment of our economic life.

Senate Office Building
Washington, D. C.
June 13, 1962

JRC

ACKNOWLEDGMENTS

I WISH TO EXPRESS my appreciation for the aid and inspiration given by Professors Melvin Reder and Moses Abramovitz of Stanford University. They supervised the version of this book which I submitted as my doctoral dissertation. I also wish to thank my friend, Hale Champion, for his suggestions. A number of Commons' students also gave me clues to his life and work. During the two summers I spent at the University of Wisconsin, I talked with Professors Edwin E. Witte, Selig Perlman, Don Lescohier, Martin Glaeser, Elizabeth Brandeis, and Kenneth Parsons. For the changes from my thesis version I am especially grateful for the detailed criticisms of the late Professor Witte. In the last weeks of life, despite his poor health, he carefully read the entire manuscript and made many suggestions. However, I assume full responsibility for errors and limitations. To my colleagues both at the College of Marin in California and at Oregon State University I owe thanks for patience and support. Also I am grateful to the staff of the Oregon State University Press. To our senior Oregon Senator, Wayne Morse, goes my appreciation for joining me in this tribute to John R. Commons. Most of all, I thank my wife whose aid and encouragement made this work possible.

Oregon State University   LAFAYETTE G. HARTER, JR.
Corvallis, Oregon
July, 1962

JRC

CONTENTS

JRC

INTRODUCTION

JOHN R. COMMONS' books collect dust on library shelves. Except for brief mentions in histories of economic and social thought, few books mention his name. Each year the ranks of his former students thin. Although they continue to honor him, he is almost forgotten by others. Few laymen ever have heard of him; even the younger economists are a little hazy as to what he represented.

Why should anyone take the trouble to write a book about such a man, and why would anyone wish to read it? The answer lies in Commons' extraordinary career and its influence. Nominally he was an economist—but of the institutional school. Like others of this school, he rebelled against the prevailing doctrines of his day. But more important than his economic protestantism was the fact that he was a reformer. His impact as a theoretical economist has remained small, but the reforms in which he participated have become important institutions. They, more than his or any other economist's theories, have contributed to a radical change in American thought. Because the reforms were incompatible with the prevailing conceptions of the social order, they slowly undermined it.

At the turn of the century, economists, lawyers, and political scientists as well as the general public were behind the times. Neglecting the changes brought on by industrialization and urbanization, they thought in terms of an individualism more appropriate to America's rural past. In their eyes each individual had complete responsibility for making his own decisions and for accepting the consequences. Although local governments did provide care for the destitute, such aid was held to a minimum, because it was inconsistent with the doctrine of individual responsibility. The state and federal governments were supposed to refrain from such activity.

The role of government, in the eyes of the turn-of-the-century thinkers, should be limited to that necessary for maintaining law and order. It was held that regulation of economic activity not only was wrong, but also was unnecessary. Competition regulated the economy more effectively and justly than could any government. Without any need for governments to interfere, the competitive system operated to gauge the community's needs in type and quantity of goods. It provided protection for the consumer, an efficient allocation of resources in production, and a just distribution of income. Governments could afford to follow a laissez-faire policy.

Although this conception still was widely held at the turn of the century, it overstated the amount of competition that actually existed. Growth of trusts and large corporations threatened to stifle competition in many industries. In some, such as in railroads and public utilities, attempts to provide competition produced serious problems without protecting consumers effectively.

Unequal bargaining power between employers and their employees also cast doubt that distribution was as just as was supposed. Even when workers combined in unions they were unable to bargain effectively.

The greatest shortcoming of thinkers at the turn of the century was that most of them gave insufficient attention to instability in our economy. Periodically, large numbers of workers were thrown out of work long enough to exhaust their savings. Such savings provided, at best, only a postponement of destitution. Those who had no savings were not much worse off. Not even superior workmen were immune from this suffering. During depressions that periodically plagued the U. S. economy employers were forced to dismiss even their best workers. Clearly, through no fault of his own, a man could be reduced to destitution. Although he worked hard and well, lived prudently, and saved part of his income he had no assurance that he would escape the effects of unemployment.

Commons believed that the concept of society prevailing at the turn of the century was outmoded as well as unjust. Even at that time he felt an urge to create a new concept to fit existing conditions. More important to him, however, was the need to solve some of the problems caused by changing economic conditions. Most of his life he worked on these problems; and finally, late in his life, he published his version of the economy and social order. It did not change America's conception of its society, because reforms on which he had worked already had done that. Furthermore, his theoretical formulations were not well received by other economists. Ignored more than rejected, his theories have had limited influence. But his reforms profoundly affected American thought.

His career was allied with the progressive movement in Wisconsin. Because Wisconsin was a pioneer state in social legislation, he had unusual opportunities to participate in reforms. This state's university, where he was a professor of economics for many years, was, in a very real sense, part of the state government. Governors, legislators, and other officials turned to the professors for expert aid in many fields. Being an intimate friend of Governor Robert M. LaFollette, Sr. (later Senator), Commons played a frequent and an important role in drafting legislation for state officials.

Commons went to the University of Wisconsin in 1904 after serving for two years as a labor conciliator for the National Civic Federation. The acceptance of this organization by respected individuals was the first nationwide recognition of the legitimacy of labor unions. As such, it was an admission that individual bargaining no longer was adequate. Commons continued, through his teaching at the University of Wisconsin and through his writing, to spread the word that labor unions were both respectable and necessary. However, they were not the entire answer to the workers' problems. Some of these problems required governmental action.

Commons sponsored so many important proposals for social legislation that he has been called "the intellectual origin of the movement toward the welfare state."[1] In the movement to perfect safety laws and to introduce compensation for injured workmen, he was the outstanding leader. Not only did he draft the safety law adopted in Wisconsin, but also he traveled widely to explain the program to officials of other states. To aid in the spreading of this and other proposals he was instrumental in organizing the Ameri-

---

1 Boulding, p. 7. See BIBLIOGRAPHY.

can Association for Labor Legislation. This organization brought together economists, social workers, and officials charged with administering labor laws. After serving as its secretary for several years, he installed his student, John B. Andrews, in his place. Through this organization he was able to extend Wisconsin's experience in labor legislation to many other states.

Among other labor laws for which Commons was responsible were Wisconsin's minimum wage law for women, its improved child labor law, and its unemployment compensation law. He also strongly backed health insurance, but the campaign for it failed. Of the labor laws, his unemployment compensation law was the most significant. After Wisconsin adopted the bill he and his students drafted, his students carried on the campaign until the federal government made unemployment compensation nationwide.

He took an interest early in the organization and administration of governments because his reforms were dependent on them for implementation. Soon after he went to Wisconsin he drafted its civil service law. Like Robert M. LaFollette, Sr., for whom he drafted the bill, he was concerned with the power of machine politicians to frustrate the enactment and administration of progressive laws.

His greatest contribution to government was his share in the development of the administrative commission. Although today such commissions are ubiquitous, they were radical innovations at the turn of the century. Because their powers included those usually distributed among the legislative, judicial, and executive branches of government, it was claimed that their use violated our traditional form of government. Conservatives insisted that such commissions were unconstitutional and that the regulation they attempted was unnecessary and harmful. But because none of the three older branches of government could regulate economic activity effectively, the administrative commission was developed and introduced into one field after another. Commons played a significant role in this process.

In 1907 he drafted the Wisconsin law that later was used as a model in numerous states to create commissions to regulate public utility companies. Yet his contribution in the development and use of administrative commissions would have been comparatively slight if it had been limited to the public utility field. Far more important was his extension of their use to the administration of labor laws. When Commons drafted the law creating Wisconsin's

Industrial Commission in 1911, he revolutionized the administration of safety laws. By transferring the function of making safety regulations from the state legislatures to a commission equipped with experts, he made it possible for such laws to be kept up to date.

The commissions also served as comprehensive agencies to administer other labor laws such as those concerning child labor, women workers, minimum wages, maximum hours, and accident and unemployment compensation. They also could provide such services as those offered by employment offices, mediators, and conciliators.

From the first, Wisconsin's Industrial Commission has been a success. So well did Commons draft the law creating it that it has been copied by numerous other states. The widespread success of these commissions has made them the principal means of administering labor laws.

Commons did more than create administrative agencies to regulate economic activity; he helped to staff them. As a university professor he trained numerous economists skilled in research techniques. While other economists were skilled at developing and explaining theories, these Commons-trained people were skilled in the digging up of facts crucial to the success of any economic regulation. Because persons who could do this work were in demand, many of his students found jobs in government. A surprisingly large number of them gained prominence as administrators. Their knowledge and influence contributed in large measure to the success of the reforms Commons sponsored.

Troubled by a belief that the U. S. economic system worked injustices on the consumer and the worker, Commons worked on many reforms. He offered regulation of public utilities for the consumer, greater bargaining power, and a system of social security for the worker. Yet such protection meant the abandoning of the old concept of each individual being responsible for his own welfare. It meant replacing laissez-faire with many of the administrative features of the welfare state.

The lack of appreciation for John R. Commons' contributions should be remedied. Until his influence is placed in its proper perspective the history of reform in America is incomplete. Although nearly 17 years have elapsed since his death in 1945, as yet no one has written a book about his influence. Perhaps one out of the rapidly thinning ranks of Commons' students will honor him yet with such a book. Such a student would be familiar not only with institutional economics, but also could give firsthand information about Commons' life and personality.

Commons' many writings reveal traits of his personality, but its main force can be felt only by reading and listening to what his students have said about him. From their descriptions he can be pictured as a small, thin man with a furrowed face and unruly hair. Apparently, he gave the appearance of being reserved and shy, but there must have been sufficient warmth in his personality to make even a stranger comfortable in his presence. His speech was slow—sometimes painfully so to the impatient—but those who knew him did not mind. His intelligent questions revealed a genuine interest in whomever he interviewed, no matter how humble that person might be. Commons' interviewing technique has been described as Socratic, but with gentleness and warmth. Everything his students say about him adds to the image of a kind, generous, and sympathetic person. Besides admiring him as a great scholar, they worshipped him as a man.

David Saposs declared:

> Closest to us of course was Commons, or "John R." as we worshipfully referred to him. In his bearing, appearance, manner, and casual relations he was the extreme opposite of the exuberant, extrovert type. His shabby and ascetic appearance and his obviously reserved air would be likely to discourage and even unintentionally repel those not aware that this forbidding exterior sheltered a sensitive genius who warmheartedly overflowed with inspiring ideas and sympathetic appreciation of the trials and tribulations of novitiates.
>
> His happy technique of launching his assistants and students on a project by outlining some general ideas and permitting them the joyful experience of working on their own, with only occasional guidance, was a remarkable procedure in developing initiative and firing scholarly imagination.[2]

Perhaps the reason why no student of Commons has written a book about him is that they loved him too well. Perhaps they fear no book will give him full justice. Furthermore, they find it painful to accept anything but the highest praise of him. So far their inhibitions have prevented them from putting an end to the serious neglect of Commons' part in social and institutional reforms.

With full consciousness of my own limitations, I offer this book as an introduction to Commons. May I be among the first, but not the last, to make such an offering.

---

2 David Saposs, "The Wisconsin Heritage and the Study of Labor Works and Deeds of John R. Commons," an address at the Selig Perlman Memorial Dinner at the University of Wisconsin on November 20, 1959.

PART I | BACKGROUND
AND
LIFE

JRC

1

PERSONAL BACKGROUND
AND EARLY YEARS

John R. Commons was born October 13, 1862, in the little town of Hollandsburg, Ohio, on the western border of the state. Soon his parents, John Commons and Clara Rogers Commons, made him into a Hoosier by moving a few miles to Union City, Indiana. Although a few miles to the north of Hollandsburg, Union City is just over the line in Indiana. In Indiana, Commons was raised in a small-town atmosphere, where the center of social activity for the male inhabitants was the general store. There the men sprawled in their chairs and drawled their witticisms between squirts of tobacco. They loved to expound on politics and science; and the boy, John R. Commons, loved to listen to them.[1]

Commons' home influences

Originally, Commons' father operated a harness shop in Union City, but when his friends asked him to edit a local political paper, he freely gave of his time. Finally, after working for a while without compensation, he decided to make editing a paper his business. By swapping his harness shop he acquired the *Union City Times*. Afterwards he made several more such trades so that at various times he had in his possession three hundred acres in the unsettled Red River Valley of Minnesota, thirty acres in the pine forests of

---

1 Commons, *Myself*, p. 8.

Florida, and another newspaper, the *Winchester Herald*. Unfortunately, he never could operate any of these enterprises profitably. John R. Commons declared that his father had never made the transition between the barter economy and the modern one of money and credit.[2] He tended to spend too much time writing articles, poetry, and making pictures.

In spite of his literary bent, the elder Commons failed to achieve the same success of that Hoosier journalist of fiction, John Harkless.[3] Like Booth Tarkington's hero, Commons' father devoted much space in his newspaper to local politics; however, he never could collect from his customers or manage the business end of his paper. At one point, John R. Commons and his brother offered to relieve him of the financial and mechanical responsibilities if he would concentrate on editorial writing and newsgathering. He refused to make this admission of failure, even though the business continued to worsen.

Although John R. Commons' father was not a successful man, apparently he was intelligent. With only a country school education, he managed to be a "studious reader of Milton, Shakespeare, other poets, and of history."[4] His particular enthusiasm was Herbert Spencer, who at the time was popularizing Darwin's theories on evolution. How much the elder Commons understood of Spencer's extensive philosophy only can be conjectured, but even his interest in the subject displayed an interest in intellectual currents of his day.

Charles Darwin had upset many men's thinking when he published his *Origin of Species*.[5] Particularly hard hit were the theologians who had contended previously that they could see a Divine design for the universe. Evolution with its changing forms seemed to deny there was any such design. In fact, it seemed even to deprive God of his role of Creator. If man had evolved from lower animals how could it be said that he was created in God's image, if created by God at all? Later most theologians were able to accept the concept of evolution but not without some reluctance and changes in their thinking.

Even scientists found Darwin's theory startling.[6] Such an outstanding naturalist as Louis Agassiz rejected it to his death in

2 *Ibid.*, p. 11.
3 Tarkington.
4 Commons, *Myself*, p. 12.
5 Darwin.
6 Hofstadter, *Social Darwinism In American Thought*, p. 5.

1873. Even President Barnard of Columbia, a distinguished scientist, wrote in 1873 that "the existence of God and the immortality of the soul could not be maintained if organic evolution were true."[7] Yet most scientists did accept Darwin's work. Evidence by other men in geology, biology, and paleontology had been casting doubt on the concept that species had been fixed at the time of the world's creation. Darwin's *Origin of Species* provided a theory that could explain previously puzzling facts.

If scientists found the concept of evolution a controversial matter at first, laymen did even more so. Many of them viewed with horror the idea of having an ancestor who was " . . . a hairy quadruped, furnished with a tail and pointed ears, probably arboreal in habits." They preferred to keep Adam in the role of ancestor and to believe in the Biblical version of creation. Only someone willing to defy public sentiment would defend the theory of evolution in those first years after its publication. Commons' father was that sort of man.

Although Darwinism certainly symbolized an unconventional outlook, the extensions of it into the social field were conservative in their implications. When Herbert Spencer coined the phrase, "The survival of the fittest," he was describing the rugged individualism of a highly competitive economic order. He and his followers, who were called Social Darwinists, believed that competition weeded out the unfit and permitted the fit to rise to the top as economic rulers. To permit such competition to function, they insisted governments should adopt completely laissez-faire policies. There is no indication as to whether the elder Commons was aware of the conservatism of Spencer's doctrine.

Conservative though Spencer's beliefs might be in their social implications, the idea of evolution certainly was very radical for a little Indiana town. People there tended to be highly religious. Anyone entertaining such thoughts about evolution was thought to be flirting with eternal damnation. The four leading churches of the region, Presbyterian, Methodist, Baptist, and Christian, were ultra conservative.[8] A fifth church, with its numerous Quaker Friends, added to the soberness of the community. John R. Commons' mother was a devout Presbyterian. His father was of Quaker origin.

John R. Commons described his home as one with a rift.[9] He did not mean that it was marred by quarreling or lack of harmony.

7 Quoted in Curti, p. 549.
8 Carmony, p. 22.
9 Commons, *Myself,* p. 8.

Rather he referred to the strong contrast between his father and his mother. His father, an impractical man with a speculative mind, was quite different from his sober-minded, ambitious, and responsible mother. Commons thought these differences were significant in his development, and he probably was right.

The elder Commons and his tobacco-chewing cronies might enjoy the titillating experience of discussing dangerous subjects, but his wife, Clara, held tenaciously to her Presbyterian faith. Although she taught her children tolerance of others' views, including those of their father, she strove to impress upon them the necessity for maintaining religious orthodoxy. For a long time she clung to the ambitious hopes that John R. Commons would become a minister. She failed to realize these hopes, but she did succeed in making him into a reformer.

The Calvinistic religion his mother planted in John R. Commons did not guarantee salvation if a person performed good works and tried to live a good life. Only God could predestine man with Grace that would bring salvation. Furthermore, no man could be sure of having been given Grace. If he had, he undoubtedly would perform good works, lead a good life, and be strong in resisting temptation. Yet even the best man must have felt some shadow of doubt; in the privacy of his mind he must have admitted the existence of at least some evil in his life. The obviously damned could go about their ways, but the good never could be complaisant. Each man felt he should work hard to prove to himself that he was of God's elect.

This early religious training, along with the sober example of his mother, seems to have left an imprint on Commons' character. In his autobiography he describes himself as a product of Puritanism.[10] He demonstrated his fervor by abstaining from use of liquor and tobacco for twenty years after he entered college. Perhaps his greatest demonstration of Puritanism was in his adoption of his mother's industrious habits.

Not only was Commons' mother industrious; she also was educated. She had attended Oberlin College when it was the only coeducational college in the country, graduating in the class of 1853.

Those who had known Commons' mother at Oberlin had expected her to go far; however, marriage ended her career as a

---

10 *Ibid.*, p. 15.

school teacher. Eventually she became the breadwinner for the family, but not by teaching. When her children reached college age she moved to Oberlin to operate a rooming and boarding house for students. The father remained for a while in Indiana continuing to publish his newspaper, but finally he gave up this losing effort so that he could rejoin her.

Because Clara Commons had to forego a career of her own, she was determined that her children would receive college educations. In this desire she was only partially successful. She suffered from poor health before she could help all three of them get educations. Only the eldest, John R. Commons, managed to finish college. The other two, Samuel (Alvin) and Clara had to withdraw in the middle of their college careers. Thus, John R. Commons, chief beneficiary of his mother's sacrifices, became the principal carrier for her ambitions. No matter how subtly applied, the pressure was on him to succeed.

Commons' educational difficulties

Commons did not attend college immediately after graduating from high school at Winchester, Indiana. Instead he spent three miserable months trying to teach in a country school. When he lost disciplinary control over his pupils he resigned, vowing never to teach again.[11] He then tried selling subscriptions to Henry Ward Beecher's *Christian Union,* but was unsuccessful. After these two failures, he worked for his father on the *Winchester Herald.*

Since his mother saw no future for him on his father's paper, she scraped up her savings and sent Commons to Oberlin College in 1882. Because of the limitations of his small-town high school education, he was required to spend the first year in the college's preparatory department.

Finally in 1883 he entered Oberlin as a freshman. He had a choice of two curricula, literature or the classical studies of the department of philosophy and arts. Commons, like all but one of his fellow male freshmen classmates, chose classical studies. (They left the literary course to the women.) Hence, instead of taking a seemingly watered-down version of a classical education, Commons struggled with the more orthodox version.

At the time Commons entered Oberlin most colleges in the U. S. emphasized training for the ministry. The majority of col-

---

11 *Ibid.,* p. 28.

lege presidents, including President Fairchild of Oberlin, and many college faculty members were clergymen.[12] Consequently, they stressed Latin, Greek, logic, rhetoric, and mathematics. At Oberlin the curriculum included only as much science as might be taken today by a typical liberal arts major. Elsewhere offerings were even more meager. Although a certain amount of choice was permitted, the number of elective courses was not extensive. Except for Harvard, which had adopted the elective system soon after Charles Eliot became president in 1869, college courses tended to be standardized.

The distinguishing feature of the older type of college, however, was not its curriculum, but the attitude of its professors. They believed in dispensing knowledge, not extending it. Commons' description of his education does not include information about the attitude at Oberlin, but other accounts show the general attitude elsewhere. Commons' colleague, E. A. Ross, devoted a chapter in his autobiography to his own undergraduate days at Coe College. Although Ross tended to praise his undergraduate training, his description does disclose some of its limitations:

> In college days we were by no means ill-taught. As freshmen there were fourteen of us, as seniors only six. We followed one course of study and each was called on in every class session . . . Coe's professors at $1,200 a year (say $2,700 today), were not masters of their subjects, still less builders, but they were men of parts who put a good text into our hands and saw that we mastered it.[13]

G. Stanley Hall, who was a few years older than either Commons or Ross, was even more complete in his account of his education at Williams. After describing the limitations of Williams College in the field of the sciences, he went on to generalize as to the professors' methods. He maintained:

> Most, if not all, of the professors covered nearly the same ground, with the same authors, year after year, and but few of them aspired to authorship of any kind or were known to the outside world; yet the institution was by no means "mono-hipic." The exceptions were Professor A. L. Perry, who was one of the pioneer apostles of free trade; Professor Bascom, who had published several books of a philosophical character and afterwards printed more; and of course, chief of all, the president, Mark Hopkins, who was also "professor of moral and intellectual philosophy."[14]

---

12 Thirteen of 49 faculty members at Oberlin were clergymen. See *Catalogue of Officers and Students of Oberlin College, 1883-4.*
13 Ross, p. 13.
14 Hall, p. 156.

Commons' teacher, Richard T. Ely, received his undergraduate education at Dartmouth during its period when it was also under religious influence. Ely described its president in these words:

> The Reverend Asa Smith had been head of a Presbyterian church in New York and his method of discipline was decidedly of the old school. When he became President of Dartmouth, he immediately restored the marking system, prescribed rules of conduct which were signed by faculty and students, distributed prizes for composition and history and put back into the curriculum the full quota of dead languages of his day.[15]

When Reverend Smith became president of the college, he found its financial condition distressing. Although he wished to effect a number of reforms, he was unable to raise sufficient money. Consequently, many of the college's facilities remained inadequate. Ely's description of the library displays this condition and the general caliber of the college in that day. He said:

> The college library, for example, was a sad reflection of the poverty of Dartmouth at this time. The few volumes were poorly catalogued and contained a good deal of duplication. The library was unheated in spite of the severity of the winters, but this made little difference, since it was open only one hour twice a week.[16]

Ely's description of Dartmouth's library corresponds closely to John William Burgess' remembrances of Columbia's in the late 1870's:

> The library of the college, as I first saw it, was a very great disappointment to me. The college was already more than a hundred years old, and its library did not consist of more than twenty-five thousand volumes, few of which were rare and none of which were modern . . . It was housed in an old tinder-box building with no conveniences for studying or reading. It had nothing but a very inadequate author-catalog; and it was administered by a single person as librarian, the Rev. Beverly R. Betts, who crept up to the building about eleven o'clock in the morning and kept the library open for drawing of books about one hour and a half daily.[17]

Oberlin combined an atmosphere of religious orthodoxy with radicalism in politics and social relationships. Before the Civil War, in the days when Commons' mother was a student, abolitionists made it a headquarters. Not only was it the first to admit women, but it also was the first to admit Negroes. Later it became a prominent center for temperance activities.

---

15 Ely, *Ground Under Our Feet*, p. 28.
16 *Ibid.*, p. 29.
17 Burgess, pp. 174-175.

Commons' career at Oberlin was not particularly successful. His difficulty seemed to stem from the fact that he could not study in the conventional manner, as would be expected from someone studying the classics. For example, in even a subject of a different nature, biology, he spent all of his time trying to find the heart beat of a little waterbug that came to life in the roadside ditches before the ice melted.[18] Instead of tentatively accepting what he was taught, at least long enough to gain a general view, he stubbornly plodded along, refusing to accept each step until it was proved to his satisfaction. In the meantime, the other students completed the study of all specimens included in the course. Commons confessed he believed that his stubborn curiosity earned him a passing grade, although he had otherwise failed his biology examination. He complained that he could never verify any of the pictures he saw in scientific publications which his professor hunted up for him. Such a failure, he claimed, caused him to be skeptical of all scientists.

Commons' first great crisis came in connection with his study of Greek.[19] As with biology, he refused to follow the prescribed program. Instead, he insisted on hunting up everything he could find on the letter Omega. Consequently, he fell so far behind that he was not prepared for his examination.

Some of Commons' scholastic difficulties at Oberlin might be traced to the very formal nature of the courses he took. Because of his practical nature, some of what he was taught might have seemed to be remote from experience in the world he knew. His dissatisfaction with the lack of correspondence between his biology textbook pictures and the actual specimens tends to illustrate this feeling. If he had been willing to accept what he had been taught, without stubbornly following his own course, he would have been far more successful as a student.

Commons' scholastic failures resulted in what he described as a nervous breakdown which came in the spring of 1885. He explained:

> Coming out from a Greek examination, a fierce blow from outside seemed to hit inside my head. I could hardly walk home. Then I spent three months wandering through the woods about Oberlin, until the end of the school year.[20]

---

18 Commons, *Myself*, p. 27.
19 *Ibid.*, p. 26.
20 *Ibid.*, p. 26.

When the semester ended he started on a hike to join his brother, Alvin, at Au Sable, a small town in northern Michigan. His brother got him a typesetting job, but he could not settle down to work. Consequently, he decided to go back to Winchester to stay with his older (half) sister, Anna, and her husband. There he raised chickens until his nerves and his digestion were restored.

Meanwhile, Commons' father and brother Alvin had gone to the thirty acres they owned in Florida. For part of the following winter, after Commons had joined them, the brothers worked at printing, and in their spare time, they planted orange trees on their farm. By spring Commons' health was fully restored, and in April he left Florida to go back to Oberlin.

In the course of a baseball game played shortly after he arrived, Commons was "beaned" and he suffered another spell of indigestion. As a result, he was unable to finish his senior year; however, in 1888, he was allowed to take oral makeup examinations. Although his professors said his responses were poor, no one wanted to stand in the way of his graduation.

Whatever may have been true of his other courses, it is clear that Commons found his course in economics satisfying.[21] It was taught by a Professor Monroe, who had come to Oberlin after spending thirty years in public life as a Republican Congressman, and later as a Consul in Rio de Janeiro. His rich store of experiences enlivened his courses in political science, economics, and modern history, which proved particularly interesting to Commons. On the basis of this experience, he decided to go to graduate school at Johns Hopkins University.

Monroe did more than encourage Commons to go on with his education. He induced two of the trustees at Oberlin College to lend Commons money for his first two years. On one of the loans Commons was required to pay 10% interest, but on the other his benefactor declined to accept interest. (It was not until fourteen years later that Commons was able to pay off these two loans.)

Commons at Graduate School

John R. Commons chose Johns Hopkins University largely because of his admiration for Richard T. Ely.[22] Originally, the idea of going to graduate school came from Commons' friend, Toyokichi Iyenaga, an Oberlin classmate, who planned to go (and

21 *Ibid.*, pp. 38-41.
22 *Ibid.*, p. 40.

went) to Johns Hopkins. Commons had learned of Ely from an editorial by Simon Newcomb in the *Nation,* attacking Ely's newly published book, *The Labor Movement in America.*[23] Newcomb found the book objectionable because of its sympathy to labor. He declared Ely's work to be similar to the ravings of an anarchist or a socialist, and asserted that Ely was seriously out of place in a university chair. This attack, instead of dissuading Commons, only increased his desire to study at Johns Hopkins. From his own experience in working in a unionized print shop during his Oberlin days, Commons knew that Newcomb's charges against Ely's labor sympathies were groundless.

The founding of Johns Hopkins University in 1876 marked the emergence of the modern university in America. Before this time, a number of institutions used the name university, but their only claim to such usage was the possession of special departments for medical, legal, divine, and other professional training. But Hopkins was primarily a graduate school, although it did include some undergraduate education. It brought together on its faculty a group of eminent scholars whose primary function was to advance knowledge in their respective fields.

When Commons arrived in Baltimore in 1888 to begin his graduate studies, he found that Ely was teaching economics in a manner quite different from that to which he, Commons, was accustomed. At Oberlin, Monroe had made occasional digressions from academic material to recount his experiences, but adhered largely to the conventional subject matter. Ely, however, set his students to field work, without much attention to formal training. (Commons' first assignment was to visit building and loan associations in Baltimore; and later he became a "case worker" for a charitable organization.)

As Ely taught it, political economy at Hopkins included sociology and political science, in addition to what we now generally consider economics. Commons readily accepted this combination of fields and later confessed that he could never reconcile himself to their separation. Another of Ely's beliefs that Commons adopted concerned the value of firsthand research experience. Just as Ely had set Commons to study charitable organizations and building and loan associations, Commons later urged his students to take jobs in industry, where they could learn labor problems from the worker's point of view.

---

23 Ely, *The Labor Movement in America.*

Commons did very well as a student with Ely. As a result, when Ely was writing his *Outlines of Economics*,[24] he hired Commons to work as an assistant at ten cents per hour.[25] Although Ely used only a few pages from the many kinds of material Commons wrote for him, he generously acknowledged Commons in the preface. This taught Commons the value of giving credit to one's students; he knew from experience what an important encouragement it could be.[26]

Ely also let Commons substitute for him as a lecturer in his course on John Stuart Mill. Commons confessed that the boys "floored" him in discussion and so he considered himself a "disaster."[27] However, this did not greatly lower Ely's opinion of him. A few years later, in 1894, when he wrote an introduction for one of Commons' books, he said, "It is a time when we need vigorous thinking, clear thinking, and a right spirit; and all these are found in the works of Professor Commons."[28]

Despite Ely's good opinion, Commons' scholastic shortcomings once more arose to plague him in his second year of graduate work. He failed a history examination, destroying his hopes for a fellowship for his third year.

Although they would not award him a fellowship, his teachers at Johns Hopkins recommended Commons in the summer of 1890 for an instructorship in economics at Wesleyan University in Middleton, Connecticut. On the strength of this position, which paid $1,000, he married an Oberlin classmate, Ella (Nel) Downey.

Commons' early teaching experience

At Wesleyan Commons tried to lecture in the orthodox traditions of economics, but without success. Three months before the end of the school year the president notified him that he would not be rehired for the following year because he had failed to interest his students. The news came during his wife's first confinement. He soon received another blow when he discovered that he could not complete his third year at Johns Hopkins without spending another year in residence. He had been under the impression that he needed only two years of residence there, and could spend the

---

24 Ely, *Outlines of Economics.*
25 Commons, *Myself*, p. 44.
26 *Ibid.*, p. 44.
27 *Ibid.*
28 Ely, "Introduction," in Commons, *Social Reform and the Church*, p. viii.

third year elsewhere. What he now learned was that he was required to spend the *last* year in residence in Baltimore. Consequently, his dream of a Ph.D. " . . . was given a final bang."[29]

Upon learning of his dismissal from Wesleyan, Commons
sought the assistance of his old teacher, Monroe, who helped him
get an associate professorship at Oberlin. By this time (1891) it
had become necessary for Commons to share with his brother,
Alvin, the burden of taking care of their parents. (His brother was
then a printer in the iron regions of northern Michigan.)

In addition to his courses in economics, Commons' courses at
Oberlin included one in sociology and one in the history of American institutions for the history department.[30] His economics
courses included one on the history of economic theories, a public
finance course, and the beginning economics course. Professor
Monroe continued to teach the advanced economics courses. If
Commons had remained at Oberlin for another year an even
greater part of his teaching would have been devoted to sociology.

After remaining at Oberlin only one year, Commons reluc-
tantly resigned to go to the University of Indiana.[31] Although he
felt ashamed to leave after all that had been done for him at Oberlin, the $2,000 offered by Indiana was $800 more than he had been
getting at Oberlin. The extra money made it possible for him to
support his father and mother in a little house nearby for the last
years of their lives.

When Commons went to Bloomington in 1892 he found the
University of Indiana had a remarkable young faculty. It had been
recruited by its former president, David Starr Jordan, who had
left to take over the presidency of Stanford University. Commons
declared that his and his wife's life among the young faculty members and their wives was like getting back to his graduate days at
Johns Hopkins.

The University of Indiana listed Commons as professor of
economics until the year 1894 and 1895, when his title was changed
to professor of public finance. At that time he was joined by Frank
Fetter, who was given Commons' former title. At Indiana Commons' trend toward sociology became even more pronounced. Not

---

29 Commons, *Myself,* p. 48.
30 *Catalogue of Oberlin College,* 1891-1892, issued May 21, 1892.
31 Commons, *Myself,* p. 49.

only did he offer more courses in sociology, but even the description of his elementary economics course showed its influence.[32] When Fetter joined the faculty Commons turned over to him most of the economics courses except those in public finance and the history of thought. Thus, for his last year at Indiana, Commons taught chiefly sociology.

He resigned voluntarily from the University of Indiana, but evidence exists that the authorities were glad to see him go. After critics had labeled his book, *Distribution of Wealth,* as disguised socialism, the university officials began to question his fitness.[33] As a result, when he informed the president that he had an offer from Syracuse University for the fall of 1895, he was told to "accept it at once."[34]

However, before accepting a position at Syracuse, he warned the chancellor that he was a "socialist, a single-taxer, a free-silverite, a greenbacker, a municipal-ownerist, a member of the Congregational Church."[35] To this facetious warning, the chancellor, who was a three-hundred-pound Methodist minister, replied that he did not care as long as Commons was not an "obnoxious socialist." Commons, believing that he was not one of the obnoxious kind, took the position only to discover later on that he had been mistaken in supposing his "socialism" was not obnoxious.

At Syracuse (where he taught ethnology, anthropology, charity organization, taxation, political economy, municipal government, and other courses described as sociology), he ran into more serious trouble than he had at Indiana. The nature of his courses provided him with a vehicle for expressing his dissenting views, which no doubt disturbed the university officials. But it was his extra-curricular radical activities that finally induced the Board of Trustees to abolish his chair in the spring of 1899. By organizing a co-operative, he antagonized local business men. When he defended Sunday baseball, religious people demanded his dismissal. Finally, when he startled the members of the American Economic

---

32 "Economics and Statistics. A general introduction to the science of political economy, in which writers of various schools are studied and compared, and the history and present conditions of industry and social questions are developed. The main living social problems are touched upon, and their place assigned in the systematic study of sociology . . ." (*Annual Catalogue of Indiana University,* Bloomington, Ind., 1893-1894. Also 1894-1895.)

33 Dorfman, 1865-1918, Vol. III, p. 285.

34 Commons, *Myself,* p. 52.

35 *Ibid.*

Association with seemingly radical statements, his reputation was made.[36] Upon firing him, the chancellor explained that his presence deterred would-be donors from making gifts. Furthermore, the chancellor declared that at a meeting of college presidents, " . . . all had agreed that no person with radical tendencies should be appointed to their faculties."[37]

Commons had little time to speculate over his prospective un-employment. Two weeks after he had received news of his dis-charge and while he still was on the university payroll, he received an unexpected job offer. The offer was from George H. Shibley, who had heard a speech by Commons on proportional representa-tion.[38] Being an advocate of bimetallism, Shibley believed that the gold policy of the government continually had been depressing prices. To test this hypothesis, he offered Commons a two-year contract, at a salary of $2,500, to construct what was then unavail-able, a weekly index of the movements of wholesale prices. Com-mons accepted the offer and moved to New York City to do the work.

In about a year Commons had the components of his index sufficiently well in hand to begin publishing a weekly index of the movements of wholesale prices.[39] Each week, after the first re-lease in July of 1900, the index number showed a fall in prices. Commons' backer, George Shibley, who was by then the economic adviser of the Democratic National Campaign Committee, was enthusiastic over this confirmation of his opinions on the gold standard. With Shibley the Democratic Party, which was warm-ing up to another campaign for Bryan and bimetallism, was search-ing for a campaign argument. But unfortunately for Commons and the Democrats, the series stopped falling about the middle of August. By September it began to rise in reflection of the Mc-Kinley prosperity. The propaganda value of Commons' index dis-solved, and with it went his job. Although willing to pay Commons until he found another job, Shibley asked that he begin looking for other employment.

---

36 "Today it is Henry George and Karl Marx that have the large influence, because they represent the radical classes that are acquiring political power . . . Economists have not lost influence as a whole—only those who stand for a class which has passed the day of its political power." From "Discussion on the President's Address," *Report of the Eleventh Annual Meeting of the American Economic Association,* New Haven, Conn., Dec. 27-29, 1898, pp. 111-112.

37 Commons, *Myself,* p. 53.

38 *Ibid.,* p. 63.

39 *Ibid.,* p. 65.

Within two weeks Commons received an offer, which he accepted, from a former student he had taught at Oberlin.[40] This former student, E. Dana Durant, was secretary of the United States Industrial Commission which had been appointed by President McKinley. For a salary of $3,000 per year Commons was to finish a report on immigration.

This position marked a turning point in Commons' career. Until then his interests were too broad for him to be considered any sort of specialist. Among his interests had been the study of labor problems, about which he had written an extensive series of articles for the American Federation of Labor publication, the *American Federationist*.[41] However, his knowledge of the labor movement was very limited. Through Commons' position with the Industrial Commission, he was able to broaden his knowledge of the labor movement and its leaders. For, although his share of the work involved studying the effects of unlimited immigration upon American labor, it gave Commons an excellent opportunity to observe many phases of unionism.

Commons wound up his work with the commission with intensive report writing. As a result of this pressure he had another neuro-intestinal breakdown that compelled him to take an extensive vacation in Manassas, Virginia. Financed by his friend, William English Walling (a millionaire radical), Commons went to live with his cousin's family until he felt able to work again.

Ralph M. Easley, secretary of the National Civic Federation, at one time had told Commons to see him if he ever needed a job. Consequently, when he recovered from his illness, Commons went to Washington to see Easley. True to his word, Easley gave Commons a position, paying $3,000 per year, as his general assistant (in 1902).[42] At first Easley set Commons to work on taxation problems, but soon changed his work to labor relations.

Although the National Civic Federation did concern itself with other civic problems, its primary function was that of labor conciliation. In a day before governments were active in the field it endeavored to bring together employers and union leaders to preserve industrial peace.

---

40 Commons, *Myself*, p. 67.
41 Commons, "A Comparison of Day Labor and Contract System on Municipal Works," *American Federationist*.
42 Commons, *Myself*, p. 82.

When Commons joined the Federation in 1902 it was in its most effective period. Although only two years old, the organization's services had been used during some extremely crucial strikes. In 1901 its services had been used in an unsuccessful attempt to settle the United States Steel Corporation strike. During the next year its officers tried to settle the historic strike in the anthracite coal fields. In the negotiations for settling these and other strikes, Commons' role involved contact with the union leaders while Easley worked with the employers.[43]

Much of the effectiveness of the Federation came from the cooperation of eminent business and labor leaders. Within the organization were such industrialists as its president, Marcus A. Hanna, and such labor leaders as Samuel Gompers, its vice president. These men were able to exert pressure on their respective colleagues to bargain collectively. They had some initial success in their peace-making efforts.[44] Hanna's death (in 1904) and the National Association of Manufacturers' open shop drive destroyed the Federation's effectiveness. Consequently, after 1907 the Federation turned to campaigning for social legislation. During and after World War I, the organization became hopelessly distracted by its efforts to combat radicalism, and it disappeared in the 1920's. However, between 1902 and 1904 while Commons was Easley's assistant, it was at the peak of its effectiveness.

On the basis of his experiences as a labor conciliator for the Federation and his work with the Industrial Commission, Commons received in 1904 an offer to teach the labor economics courses at the University of Wisconsin. The offer came through his old teacher, Richard T. Ely, who by this time was head of the economics department there.[45] For a number of years, Ely had been nursing along a project of writing a history of the labor movement. Having written one book on the subject in 1886, he wished to bring his work up to date and to add considerably more material. By 1904, he had collected much material, but the book was yet unwritten. Rather than go on with it, he brought Commons to Wisconsin to finish it. So began Commons' career as a labor economist.

---

[43] Commons dates his participation in the negotiations for the steel strike as of 1902. See *Myself*, p. 86. Yet presumably the strike was over by then. See Perlman and Taft, *History of Labor*, p. 107. Gompers dates the strike as of 1904. See Gompers, *Seventy Years of Life Labor*, Vol. II, p. 128. Memories of old men are sometimes faulty.

[44] Green, p. 69.

[45] Commons, *Myself*, p. 92.

JRC
2

COMMONS' OUTLOOK

JOHN R. COMMONS always sought answers to every problem he studied. Economics to him was not an intellectual exercise, but a study that had very practical results. Although he conceded the value of the pure theorist, Commons preferred working on immediate problems requiring solutions. This was one of the attractions social reforms had for him.

Commons' practical nature was reinforced by the intellectual currents swirling around him. America's anti-intellectualism, its pragmatism, and its empiricism, as expressed by Ely and others, suited his temperament and capabilities. His one attempt at theoretical economic analysis during his earlier years turned out to be a failure.[1] Not being a systematic thinker or a skillful writer, he was most successful when he concentrated on practical problems. Thus, a variety of factors operated to give Commons a "practical" outlook.

Pragmatism and anti-intellectualism

Commons was a pragmatist in several senses of the term. First of all, his conception of philosophy was an adaptation of the

---

[1] Commons, *The Distribution of Wealth*.

pragmatism of Charles S. Peirce and John Dewey.[2] In his *Institutional Economics* Commons acknowledges his use of their philosophies.[3]

Yet long before Commons knew of such philosophers, he was a pragmatist in the sense that he believed that practical experience often is a better source of knowledge than words of authority. Furthermore, through his thinking ran a strong anti-intellectual strain. Although the pragmatic philosophers were not all anti-intellectual, many of them clearly exhibited this tendency.

In using the word anti-intellectual, it is necessary to point out that it does not suggest repudiation of rational thought or the pursuit of knowledge.[4] Nor does it connote the nonintellectual's contempt for the more educated. It is not a derisive term; rather the word anti-intellectual indicates doubt in the ability of anyone to construct a line of analysis sufficiently comprehensive to cover all possible variables. Especially in the social science field, the anti-intellectual stresses the multiplicity of factors that may render prediction impossible. Furthermore, he adds that prejudices and desires of a thinker are likely to influence this reasoning, especially when no laboratory confirmations are possible.

The anti-intellectual is suspicious of theories, although he may employ them as a working hypothesis. He prefers drawing conclusions from a large number of cases rather than reasoning deductively from generally accepted premises. Often he repudiates such premises or declares that reasoning often is dependent on implicit assumptions that may not be true.

Because truth often is highly complicated, the best way to find it may not always be by formal reasoning. A man working with practical problems in a field may, through experience, acquire insights that are more fruitful than the theories of an expert who lacks practical experience. The practical man's thinking may be muddy, but it often approaches the truth, while the theorist's deductions, unless checked by observations, may lead him astray.

An anti-intellectual may be a sophisticated thinker or he may be a romantic revolting against systematic thought. The former may reach his position by attempting to reason so rigorously that he becomes dissatisfied with his efforts, while the latter may be

---

2 See Chapter 8, "Commons' Approach To Economics."
3 Commons, *Institutional Economics*, pp. 150-157.
4 Brinton, p. 223. Morton White prefers the term "anti-formalism," White, p. 12.

either intellectually or tempermentally unfit for developing a systematic line of thought.

Among the less sophisticated, the anti-intellectual's method of thought may be a defense against the glib claims of the unscrupulous. The shrewd but uneducated man very sensibly may conclude that although the salesman's patter may sound plausible, it may not contain the whole truth. In the same way, the claims of politicians may be accepted only with considerable reservations. Such skepticism may extend not only to the truthfulness of the persuader, but even to his ability to know the whole truth. Even though he may not be able to refute an intellectual's argument, a "practical" man may insist that truth is more complicated than his opponent can understand.

America's traditional anti-intellectualism stems in part from the existence of a frontier. In pioneer days the practical man experienced in the ways of the frontier held a distinct advantage over the newcomer. Although the newcomer might be highly educated, his ability to survive depended on his ability to make a living under primitive conditions.

In a limited way, what was true of the frontier continued to be true of farm communities, for some time. Practical knowledge and skills continued to be more important than any provided by formal education. Particularly in the days before the widespread extension of scientific methods to agriculture, farmers followed traditional methods taught them by their fathers. Academic knowledge, even of matters concerning agriculture, was less important than sound work habits and useful skills.[5] Furthermore, the long hours required for the successful operation of farms left little time for intellectual pursuits.[6]

Their contacts with those more intellectually sophisticated than themselves left farmers distrustful of the fruits of education. The man of learning was forever telling him what he wanted was "unsound." For example, when a farmer advocated increasing the nation's money supply, the economic experts frowned on such a proposal as the ideas of a crank. When the farmer saw regulation of railroads as the only possible relief from high freight rates, the economists warned against interfering with free enterprise. To the farmer the ideas of the experts did not seem in accord with agricultural needs. If he could not find the logical arguments to

5 Hofstadter, Richard, *The Development of Higher Education in America*, p. 38.
6 Curti, pp. 265-270.

refute the theories of the experts, he would reject all theorizing as impractical. By clinging to his own practical reasons in the face of authority he displayed (at least some of) the characteristics of the anti-intellectuals.

Even when rural communities developed into towns and cities, a formal education did not greatly aid many of the inhabitants in making a living. In the growing communities the successful tended to be the shrewd, resourceful, practical, and hard working. Fortunes were made without their owners possessing the advantages of superior education.

Those who made fortunes set the standards for the others. It was true that the successful often gave lip service to culture by providing opportunities for their wives and children. Yet education and culture were only ornaments with secondary values, forms of conspicuous consumption. The standard advice was to acquire the practical skills necessary for financial success. Then, and only then, would intellectual pursuits be worthwhile.

If the community valued the practical man more highly than the intellectual, it is not surprising that it also preferred his judgments. To rationalize such a preference, the community had to adopt at least some of the arguments of the more sophisticated anti-intellectuals.

Thus, the intellectual became associated in the popular mind with an "ivory tower," which insulated him from the experience of the men of practical affairs. His glib theories became over-simplifications that could not be trusted. The college professor personified the absent-minded dreamer who expounds theories without practical value. Even the scientist with proved practical discoveries appeared in the eyes of the public as a quaint character pathetically out of place a few feet from his laboratory.

To some extent the attitude of Americans toward intellectuals may be the result of emphasis on the equality of men. Refusing to admit inferiority, Americans decide that the expert does not know the truth after all.[7] Any disputes among intellectuals can be used as proof that their knowledge is a matter of opinion. When pushed into an intellectual corner, many persons may resort to the anti-intellectual argument that hidden complications, if known, would vindicate them. Since often no easy way exists to bring out

---

7 Commager, p. 12.

such complications immediately, disputes must end as stalemates without conversion from either side.

At the time Commons was growing up the anti-intellectual influence in Indiana was strong, although perhaps the small towns in which Commons lived were not so hostile to culture as Edward Eggleston painted in his *Hoosier School Master*.[8] Undoubtedly, Union City and Winchester in Commons' day were culturally superior to Eggleston's Flat Creek. Yet they were a part of rural Indiana where the Hoosier dialect defied the English language. Although such writers as James Whitcomb Riley, Kim Hubbard, and George Ade certainly were expressions of culture, their use of homely expressions and situations displayed interests other than intellectual. Even in modern times their cracker-barrel Hoosier tradition has been carried on by humorist Herb Shriner. Such Hoosiers often strike a pose. As John Martin declared, "Perhaps at some time or another everybody from Indiana has protested that he is a rustic unused to city ways, but probably he never met a city slicker he did not secretly believe he could outdo."[9] Exaggerated as such claims may be, they do suggest a tradition with anti-intellectual influences.

As did most Americans, the Hoosiers of Commons' youth placed the value of the successful practical man above that of an intellectual. Commons recalled with pride that two of his high-school debating rivals, James E. Watson and James P. Goodrich, became U. S. senator and millionaire governor, respectively.[10] Perhaps his memory of their good times at the swimming hole and at other outings was made a little pleasanter by their success. At least he thought his readers would be interested in his successful boyhood friends, and throughout his biography he described with pride his relations with influential and wealthy friends he met later.

In spite of the emphasis on nonintellectual values, Commons did become an intellectual. Although such a course would not have been chosen by most of his contemporaries, it would be respected if he succeeded. If the intellectual could use his brains and education to achieve financial success, he too would gain prestige. Yet without some outward sign of success he would earn only toleration and perhaps even contempt.

---

8 Eggleston.
9 Martin, p. 109.
10 Commons, *Myself*, p. 13.

As was explained earlier, Commons' father was something of an intellectual who failed to achieve any tangible success. Instead of attending to his business he spent his energies reading literature and philosophy. Consequently, his family was supported much of the time by Commons' mother.

A faintly apologetic attitude towards his father is evident in Commons' autobiography. At the same time, Commons shows considerable admiration for his mother. He pictures her as a woman whose considerable promise had to be sacrificed for her family. This little family drama might well illustrate the futility of the impractical intellectual.

Although Commons did not explicitly criticize his father, he did express contempt for certain intellectuals in the labor field.[11] On the other hand, he had high praise for the labor leaders who had been schooled by the practical experiences of being workers, contrasting them favorably with their more intellectual opponents within the labor movement. Commons ascribed the errors of the latter to their lack of experience. Because intellectuals had not shared the worker's experiences they did not actually know how he felt. Consequently, they would misjudge his attitude at critical times. Such mistakes could prove disastrous to unions.

In line with this general attitude, Commons also maintained that economists should never take the leadership of a union.[12] The academic man might be a valuable aid to a union when he served it as a hired expert. Yet his contribution should not include the taking of responsibility for the affairs of a union. Such responsibilities should be left with labor leaders who had grown up in the service of their unions.

Commons' attitude toward the role of intellectuals in the labor movement followed closely the attitudes of the labor leaders themselves. Even today Wilensky reports the prevalence of this attitude among union leaders.[13] Although Commons acquired this attitude from his contacts with union officials, it fitted in very well with his generally anti-intellectual orientation.

Despite Commons' admiration for practical men, he certainly did not deny the value of learning. He aspired to be a first-rate scholar, both in and out of his field of economics. But he believed that the scholar should do more than learn economic theories. Al-

---

11 See chapter on "Commons, Student of the Labor Movement."
12 *Ibid.*
13 Wilensky, p. 265.

ways he urged his students to acquire practical experience in industry as an aid to the understanding of economic reasoning. Such experiences were to serve as a basis for their own theorizing, and as a check upon their own theories and those of others.

Commons' temperament

Commons' anti-intellectualism and pragmatism not only tied in with his background, but they also suited his capabilities and temperament. Being a hard worker, he could dig out vast quantities of material, but his organization of it tended to be unsystematic. He frankly confessed that his lectures were not systematic. In describing his lectures, he said, "Every class meeting or lecture was something unexpected, and they [the students] didn't know what was coming next."[14] Further evidence of his difficulties in organizing material can be found in his writings, particularly the long, theoretical works. Whenever his subject matter was limited or had a natural organization, he managed to write very clearly, but when he was expounding a theory, he had difficulty in making himself comprehensible to his students. Although he had other intellectual difficulties, his ineptitude at exposition was outstanding and aggravated the others.

Commons, with his inability to be completely systematic, found pragmatism more suitable to his nature than any other philosophy. Yet he was not completely comfortable with it. At times he seemed to be searching for its opposite, a secure absolutism. He looked for such a truth to be found through experience, rather than by faith or logic. In college he tenaciously studied a single water bug instead of working with all the specimens scheduled for the class.[15] While studying Greek, he concentrated on the single letter, Omega, trying to learn all he could about it. Always he seemed to think he could find the real truth if he could gather enough facts, make enough observations, or have enough experiences.

The German Historical School and empiricism

Commons' natural inclination to emphasize the practical aspects of learning was reinforced by his experiences with his teachers. At Oberlin Professor Monroe intrigued Commons with many stories of his life as a congressman and a diplomat. Such "practical" experiences provided Monroe with unusual qualifications as

---

14 Commons, *Myself*, p. 47.
15 See Chapter 1, "Personal Background and Early Years," p. 16.

a teacher of political science and economics. Furthermore, he encouraged Commons to study aspects of economics not usually included in college curricula. He even permitted Commons and a friend to lecture on Henry George to his class.[16]

At Johns Hopkins University the influence of Richard T. Ely on Commons was antitheoretical. Not only did Ely send Commons on extensive projects as a caseworker for charitable organizations, but he also encouraged him to study problems from an historical approach. Thus, finding "facts," whether historical or in the immediate situation, became the focus of any study. Supposedly, the analysis would come automatically later.

Richard T. Ely had studied economics under Karl Knies in Germany. From him he brought back some of the ideas of the German Historical School. Ely became an exponent of the inductive method of studying economics, as contrasted with the deductive method which had been used by the English and American economists of his time. Explaining these methods, he said:

> . . . deductive is applied to that political economy which, taking its ultimate facts, its premises, from other sciences, from common and familiar experiences or from the declarations of consciousness, proceeds from these and from definitions to evolve an economic system without any recourse to the external world, save perhaps as furnishing tests of the validity of the reasoning.
> . . . The term inductive, on the contrary, is to be applied to those writers who do not start out with *all* their premises ready made, but who include the induction of premises within the scope of their science and proceed to use these premises deductively. The inductive political economist, for example, gathers together particular facts relating to the division of labor upon production, or facts respecting government and private banks; and observing particulars in which these facts agree with themselves, separates out these similars and forms what we call a generalization. This serves him in the future for a major premise in economic reasoning. The inductive political economist compares his conclusions with external facts, not simply for the sake of testing the accuracy of his reasoning, but also in order to ascertain whether the generalization itself was made on sufficient grounds.[17]

Ely actively battled the economists of his day to get them to adopt the inductive approach. He declared that he and a number of younger economists "felt the urgent necessity for uniting into a solid group in an effort to break the 'crust' which had formed over economists." As a part of their efforts they organized in

---

16 Commons characteristically chose to present the statistical side of the subject.
17 Ely, *Johns Hopkins Studies In Historical and Political Science*, p. 8.

1886 the American Economic Association.[18] Although many others embracing other views joined the association, it did serve as a forum for those who complained that "economics" until then had been too "deductive" or "unrealistic." They insisted that historical, statistical, and other studies accumulating "facts" should be given more attention. Then, armed with facts, the economists could reason more realistically and more scientifically.

Richard T. Ely and his contemporaries carried on their controversy as to the relative merits of the "inductive" versus the "deductive" methods just before and for some time after Commons was a graduate student. They were the "progressives" challenging the hide-bound conservative economists whose "unrealistic deductions" merely defended the status quo. In contrast to the stern laissez-faire policies which forbid government from interfering with the harsh consequences of individual action, Ely and his friends argued for a more humanitarian approach. They believed that government does have responsibility for the welfare of all of its citizens.

Although economic theory had been making progress during the early and middle parts of the nineteenth century, many of the older American economists of Ely's day taught a brand of economics not significantly different from Ricardo's. They did not bother to adapt their thinking from the English to the American scene. Although economic institutions were changing before their eyes, they reasoned as though their economics would be valid in any nation, in any age, and under any conceivable conditions. Not even the rapid technological changes of their time could alter their reasoning.

Arthur L. Perry, the author of a popular text on economics, declared:

> The natural laws of Production are *inexorable* in their operation. It is best for men to find out what these are, and then to conform to them their own economic action. If custom or legislation thwart these laws, they will take their revenge without pity, and lapse of time will only exhibit transgressors more clearly as firmly held in the grip of violated law.[19]

Perry as well as the other prominent American writers, such as William Graham Sumner, Charles Dunbar, and Simon Newcomb, insisted that the only economically sound policy for govern-

---

18 Ely, Richard T., *Ground Under Our Feet*, p. 121.
19 Perry, p. 196.

ments to follow is that of laissez-faire. Even the serious depression of 1873 did not shake their beliefs.

Neither did ideas introduced from other sciences greatly influence them. To some the new idea of evolution was an influence, but a minor one. The concept of "the survival of the fittest" was merely another way of describing the beneficient workings of competition under laissez-faire. It reinforced their own stern conservatism by relegating progress to an automatic process with which men should not tamper. Those unfit to survive were to be denied merciful aid or even sympathy. In Sumner's words, ". . . if we do not like survival of the fittest, we have only one possible alternative, and that is the survival of the unfittest."[20] Such an alternative, he said, was the law of anticivilization.

Simon Newcomb warned against giving in to generous impulses out of pity for the poor. He recommended:

> What we really ought to do is to train, persuade, or compel every person to earn his living under penalty of starvation. The fundamental idea of current charity is the wholly incompatible one of enabling the favored few who chance to excite our sympathies to get a living without earning it. Just so far as we can free ourselves from this benevolent impulse and turn our efforts in a rational direction, so far may we hope that charitable effort may yet be beneficial to the race.[21]

This doctrine of the nonsurvival of the unfit was not any harsher than the "Iron Law of Wages," or the Malthusian positive checks to population increases. In effect, the evolutionary doctrine did not significantly change the recommendations of the conservative economists.

Yet the economists who were willing to use ideas borrowed from biology to support their previously established view failed to take into consideration the possible effects of these ideas on their static theories. They neglected to consider that if plants, animals, and men slowly change, then perhaps theorizing based on assumptions of an unchanging world is not justified.

John R. Commons adopted both Ely's inductive approach and his humanitarian attitudes. His training under Ely reinforced his tendency to stress the practical aspects of economics. He could dig up material, collect facts, and trace historical relationships better than he could reason deductively. When he worked on prob-

---

20 Sumner, William Graham, p. 225.
21 Newcomb, p. 533.

lems involving reform, he found a use for this type of empirical research. At the same time he was following Ely's humanitarian approach. But Ely did not change Commons: he merely reinforced Commons' "natural" bent.

Reaction to a failure

Commons agreed with Ely that economics should be rewritten with a more "realistic" approach. Yet for his first book, *The Distribution of Wealth,* he tried to combine this approach with the abstract theories newly imported from Austria.[22]

In the introduction to this book Commons began by attempting to explain the theory of value in terms of marginal utility. He then went on to explain distribution in terms of a marginal productivity theory. However, his main emphasis was upon the failure of distribution to follow marginal productivity norms. Although he agreed that the wages of labor and interest on capital tend to equal their marginal products, certain owners of monopolies apparently get more. These monopoly owners are able to limit the supply of what they own, while workers and the owners of investment funds find it difficult to raise their prices by limiting what they offer.

Rather than attempt to restore perfect competition, Commons advocated safeguarding the interests of nonmonopolists in other ways. The workers could be protected by increasing their bargaining power. Commons even went so far as to insist that every person should have the right to be employed. To enforce such a right, he advocated creation of courts of arbitration. In his words:

> The new courts that shall enforce the right to employment are courts of arbitration, created by the government, and empowered to compel employers to submit to investigation and to suffer punishment for violating the right of employees to work. No man is to be discharged for any cause except inefficiency and dishonesty. Wages, hours of labor, conditions of labor, are to be adjudicated by the courts.[23]

Apparently, Commons would allow for discharge for reasons other than inefficiency and dishonesty, because a few paragraphs later, he advocated:

> This displacement of labourers by machinery and by trusts can be remedied by government through employment bureaus and public works.[24]

---

22 Commons, *Distribution of Wealth.* See chapter on "Commons' Approach to Economics," p. 274.

23 *Ibid.*

24 *Ibid.,* p. 84. Later on, in other writings, Commons' method of guaranteeing employment became less drastic, and he completely repudiated compulsory arbitration.

These passages set the tone of the book, and determined its reception. Other passages, whose meanings are less clear, heightened the radical tone by seeming to challenge the institution of private property.[25] In others, human rights were made to appear in conflict with the rights of property.[26]

Professional critics were unkind to this maiden effort. F. W. Taussig refused to review it because he considered it an "unbaked" performance.[27] A. T. Hadley, in the *Yale Review,* complained that Commons ". . . based his whole theory on the fallacy that men, as a rule, make money by hurting society."[28] Hadley was more gentle than the other two reviewers, Richard Mayo-Smith of Columbia and A. C. Miller of the University of Chicago. Both of these reviewers mistakenly implied that Commons was less than completely candid. Miller declared, " . . . the whole essay might not be improperly regarded as a disguised attempt to found a scientific basis for a theory of socialism."[29] In the same vein, Mayo-Smith insisted that ". . . the elaboration of the theory of distribution demands perfect impartiality . . . with no hidden purpose underlying the argument, if the author wishes to command the best attention of his readers."[30] Commons' bias, he went on to say, was observable throughout the book. Furthermore, he said:

> This *Tendenz,* as the Germans would call it, whether conscious or unconscious, is unfortunate, because the mere agitator will believe that his practical conclusions have scientific support, without troubling to understand the argument; while the scientific reader will hesitate about accepting many statements which need elaboration.[31]

In any case, Mayo-Smith maintained, Commons should have been frank with his readers.

Commons' reviewers, preoccupied with the radicalism of his proposals, completely overlooked his analysis. What he had was a theory of profit maximation for monopolists.[32] Cournot previously had done the same thing mathematically, but most American economists, including Commons, had overlooked this work.

---

25 *Ibid.,* p. 110.
26 *Ibid.,* p. 80. However, in the end, we find that he would tax in such a way as to " . . . leave capital and labour and business ability free and untrammelled, but endeavor to widen and enlarge the opportunities for their employment." (*Ibid.,* p. 258). Yet even this reassurance for free enterprise was part of a radical proposal of the day, the single-tax.
27 Dorfman, p. 284.
28 Hadley, A. T., *The Yale Review,* pp. 439-440.
29 Miller, pp. 462-464.
30 Mayo-Smith, pp. 568-572.
31 *Ibid.*
32 See chapter on "Commons' Approach to Economics."

If Commons' work (or for that matter, Cournot's) had been understood by his contemporaries, monopoly theory might have taken a prominent place in economic literature much earlier than it did.

This book contained a number of flaws, both of organization and analysis. Consequently, even if the reviewers had tolerated his radicalism, they still might have picked the book to pieces. The mistakes in analysis were minor,[33] but the book's style was so clumsy that no one recognized the contribution it might have made. As a result, the bad reviews buried it. A few authors of books on distribution listed it in their bibliographies, but otherwise it exercised no influence in the field.

After this failure Commons never again wrote anything in which he attempted to use this type of formal analysis. According to his student, Professor Selig Perlman of the University of Wisconsin, Commons' disappointment with his first book provoked him to try to rewrite economics from a broader base.[34] Eventually, this effort resulted in his *Institutional Economics,* which he finally published in 1934, after years of continual rewriting.

In the meantime, Commons turned to the practical side of his nature, as suggested by Ely. Here Commons found a milieu within which he could work successfully. Most of the time these problems involved reform.

Commons and reform

Throughout Commons' life, he was engaged in one reform movement after another. Although he did not fulfill his mother's wish that he enter the ministry, he did share her enthusiasm for reforms. At Oberlin he and his mother were instrumental in the founding of the Anti-Saloon League. They began an antisaloon publication and agitated for "local option" prohibition. This was the first in a long sequence of reform efforts that absorbed Commons' energies.

Reform activity gave Commons an outlet for his energy without requiring that he be systematic. If he clung tenaciously to one problem until he felt satisfied with his efforts, such single-mindedness was all to the good. Above all, reform movements gave him practical problems on which to work. To become a reformer

---

[33] Commons, *Distribution of Wealth,* pp. 148, 154.
[34] Personal interview, July, 1952.

one merely needs to join with others of similar intentions. Reformers usually welcome anyone inclined to join them, and Commons was a prodigious joiner.[35] He joined numerous important reform movements in America from the time of his college days until the early days of the New Deal.

Commons' outlook made reform activity congenial to him. As a result of his graduate work under Ely, his thinking was a combination of sociology and economics rather than economics alone. During the eighties and early nineties, the subject of sociology, although new, was offered by an increasing number of colleges and universities. Even a number of theological seminaries began to offer such courses as Christian sociology, ecclesiastical sociology, or social ethics.

The spread of these courses was due in part to the recognition of social changes stemming from rapid growth of industries and cities. With a change from an essentially rural nation into an industrial urban one, such problems as unemployment, poverty, slum conditions, crime, and social unrest intruded into the public consciousness. But the interest in sociology was also due to the rise of a liberal religious movement, which began to attract converts in the 1880's. Shortly after the Civil War, a number of liberal ministers began directing the attention of their churches to social problems. By the eighties, the efforts of these religious leaders congealed into a movement described as the Social Gospel.[36]

Those following the Social Gospel movement declared that the Kingdom of God is to be on earth. Christians' efforts should be directed towards perfecting society rather than concentrated on securing individual salvation. Recognizing the concept of evolu-

---

35 Commons helped found a local Anti-Saloon League, The American Institute of Christian Sociology (Christian Socialism), The American Association for Labor Legislation, The American Safety Council. He held the following offices: Assistant to the Secretary of National Civic Federation; Secretary, The American Association for Labor Legislation; President, The National Consumers' League; President, The National Monetary Association; director, National Bureau of Economic Research; President, American Economic Association; Grand Master of the Order of Artus, Omicron Delta Gamma (an honorary economic fraternity). He flirted with Populism, but decided its subtreasury plan was unsound. At times he backed single-tax proposals, civil service reform, proportional representation, workmen's compensation, national health insurance, unemployment insurance, minimum wage laws, monetary control by the Federal Reserve System, limitation of immigration, worker's education, and encouragement of unionism. Politically he voted as a Prohibitionist, a LaFollette-Republican, a LaFollette-Progressive, and as a New Deal Democrat. His public offices included: expert, for United States Industrial Commission of 1901; commissioner, Wisconsin Industrial Commission; commissioner of United States Commission on Industrial Relations, 1913-1915; member, Wisconsin Minimum Wage Board; staff expert for Congressional Committee investigating the Federal Reserve System; and expert for the Associated States Opposing Pittsburg-Plus.

36 Hopkins. See also Quint, pp. 103-141.

tion, the followers of Social Gospel believed that social order is gradually improving. In time it will evolve into the Kingdom of God on earth. But this evolution should not be left to automatic forces. Each change for the better in working conditions or labor legislation was cited as a step towards the Kingdom. Men could and should work to bring it into existence.

The Social Gospel movement rejected the orthodox Christian position that man is innately sinful. It maintained that human nature is essentially good. Evil results from a corruption of that nature under external pressure from a corrupt society. Hence, to improve society one should attempt to reorganize and reform the social order in a way that will permit the better side of human nature to emerge. Such a process would not require a revolution or sudden change; rather, it would require the efforts of Christians in the spreading of good will among all people.

Richard T. Ely was prominent in the Social Gospel movement and wrote a number of works on social problems for ministers.[37] Following his teacher's example, Commons joined one of the subgroups of this movement, the Christian Socialists.[38] During his teaching year at Oberlin Commons taught sociology to theological students. In the same year he compiled and published *A Popular Syllabus of Sociology,* intended for ministers and general readers.[39]

When Commons taught at Indiana he and Ely helped found the American Institute of Christian Sociology. He served this organization both as its secretary and as an associate editor of its publication, *The Kingdom*. In addition to attending a number of other conferences for the organization, he directed its summer conference at Oberlin College in 1894. To study "Causes and Proposed Remedies for Poverty," Commons took the exceptional liberty of inviting socialists and labor leaders as well as economists and ministers as speakers. Among the speakers were: Thomas J. Morgan, socialist leader from Chicago; Samuel Gompers of the American Federation of Labor; Professor J. B. Clark, an eminent economist; and Washington Gladden, a prominent minister.

37 Ely, Richard T., *Social Aspects of Christianity,* (New York, N. Y.: T. Y. Crowell, 1889); *The Law of Social Service,* (New York, N. Y.: Eaton & Mains, 1896); *The University and The Churches,* (reprint of address delivered at Thirty-first Convocation, Senate Chamber, Albany, 1893); *Religion as Social Force,* (reprint of address delivered before Education Congress at World's Fair, St. Louis, Mo., 1897); "Amana: A Study of Religious Communism," Harper's Monthly.
38 Dombrowski, p. 72.
39 Commons, John R., *Popular Bibliography of Sociology.*

At about this time, Commons wrote a book entitled *Social Reform and The Church.*[40] In it he declared that ministers and other educated persons have definite responsibilities for promoting reform. Crime and rejection of religion both result from poverty and miserable living conditions. He argued it was the duty of ministers to learn about conditions in such places as slums, alms-houses, workhouses, and jails, and to work toward their improvement.

These activities increased Commons' reputation for radicalism. He was accused of favoring socialism, the single-tax, free trade, and Populism. When Ely warned him that he should be more prudent, he replied:

> . . . I believe fully in what you say regarding the timeliness of ex-
> pressions of advanced views, and I recognize than on some occasions
> I may have seemed needlessly to have aroused antagonism. It is diffi-
> cult to combine opportuneness with exposures of injustice, but I
> believe that I am getting more cautious.[41]

Despite this statement (made in 1895 while at the University of Indiana), he persisted in the same type of writing and activities. As a result, he endangered his university positions. As explained in the previous chapter, he was encouraged to resign from the University of Indiana and was dismissed from the University of Syracuse.

Commons and the doctrine of Meliorism

Despite his lurid reputation (circa 1895-1900) Commons was always a gradualist and not a revolutionary. In this he was typically American. With the exception of the issues which led to the Civil War, Americans generally have been able to resolve their problems by negotiation and persuasion. The lack of class barriers also has prevented the development of the European-type intellectual, who, without a real stake in the social order, would have been willing to risk all in a revolution. Americans of ability and education tended to find too many favorable opportunities for personal advancement within the social order for them to take much interest in trying to destroy it.

The reform movements in which Americans have been interested have aimed at preserving or extending the opportunity for individual advancement.[42] From the very early days of our nation

---

40 Commons, John R., *Social Reform and The Church.*
41 Dorfman, Vol. III, p. 285.
42 Parrington, Vol. III, p. xxiv.

most of the demands for reform have centered on attacks on monopoly, demand for public education, and for a fair distribution of public lands. The reforms did not object to the existence of the wealthy. Many of them aimed to become rich themselves some day, but they did insist that the doors of opportunity remain open.[43]

Even labor leaders tended to remain within the American tradition of reform. In the early history of the labor movement labor leaders also emphasized programs purporting to maintain equality of opportunity. They campaigned for public schools free to all children, cheap or free land for settlers, equality of citizenship, as well as for higher wages and shorter hours. Many of their efforts were directed against what they considered monopoly. They wished to keep open the possibility for workmen to enter self-employment by making credit available to them.[44] Later, when the dream of large numbers of workers becoming self-employed faded, many in the labor movement turned toward producer cooperatives. Even when labor leaders finally came to realize that the wage system could not be eliminated without a revolution, they continued to advocate working within the social order rather than advocating drastic changes.

Although Samuel Gompers, himself, had been a socialist originally, he early decided that labor should work for immediate improvements instead of wasting resources in futile efforts to create a revolution. Commons knew Gompers very well and counted himself as his follower. In the obituary which he wrote for Gompers Commons might well have been describing his own views:

> No one understood better than Gompers the limits beyond which the organization of labor could not go. It could not lift itself as a body out of manual labor and become a body of business men or professional men. For this reason Gompers was always against "theorizers" and "intellectuals" in the organization of labor. They were "industrially impossible." Amid all the differences in America of religion, of race, of languages, of politics, there was only one direction toward which labor could unite—more wages, more leisure, more liberty. To go further than this was to be misled by theorists, idealists and well-meaning but "fool" friends of labor. Labor could have "moral power" only when it struggled for better homes, better living conditions, better citizenship, by its collective action.[45]

Commons like Gompers believed that the "intellectual" with theories of social revolution had no place within the labor move-

---

43 Curti, p. 611. Also see Goldman, p. vii.
44 Perlman, Selig, p. 280.
45 Commons, John R., *Current History,* Vol. XXI, p. 674.

ment. Revolutionary activity on the part of labor leaders led only to trouble and was not effective in changing the social order. Instead, labor should direct its efforts toward immediate gains and be content with slow but orderly progress.

The view Commons shared with Gompers grew out of both a skeptical view of intellectual systems and a belief in gradualism in reform. The latter view was reinforced not only by American traditions, but also by the trend of the times. During the nineteenth century technological changes, economic expansion, growth of communities, and other changes, held to be improvements, had been developing at an accelerated pace. In the intellectual field the frontiers of knowledge had been expanded. Even in the social field reforms such as the end of the slave trade, and then finally the end of slavery in this country and abroad, finally were accomplished. Debtors' prisons were abolished; mechanics' liens protected the workers' wages; manhood suffrage had extended democracy; and free popular education promised an ever more enlightened citizenry. To most observers it appeared that the world was getting better, and progress seemed to be the natural course of events. When the concept of evolution of man from lower forms to his present state was expounded, this belief in progress appeared even to have scientific verification.

To Social-Darwinists like Herbert Spencer and William Graham Sumner, progress was an automatic process that men could not purposely assist. Men who thought they could make the world over were absurd.[46] Progress could come only by a process of natural selection of individuals most fit to survive. Any reforms that would ameliorate the conditions of the unfit merely would retard progress.

In contrast to this view that dominated academic sociology during the 1880's and 1890's, Commons and other reformers believed that man, himself, was the instrument for social change. He agreed that the change should be slow, but not as slow as the operation of hereditary selection. Revolutions might unloose serious and unforeseen complications, but step-by-step steady improvement could proceed safely and surely toward an equitable and stable social order.

Commons had a strategy for social reform. It consisted of adaptations of economic institutions in our capitalistic system in

---

46 Sumner, William Graham, "The Absurd Effort To Make The World Over," *War and Other Essays*, (New Haven, Conn.: Yale University Press, 1911), pp. 195-210.

such a way that the businessmen and others would have economic incentives to improve the conditions of the working class. Furthermore, he believed that reforms could be organized in such a manner that they would benefit even the employers.

As an example of his method of campaigning for reforms, consider his efforts to sell "workmen's compensation" coupled with a safety program.[47] The first step consisted of finding a few enlightened employers who were convinced of the wisdom of safety programs. These were publicized as examples for others to follow, thereby demonstrating that compensation to injured workmen, regardless of legal obligations, paid dividends in improved morale of the workers. Commons then persuaded the enlightened employers to help him sell similar measures to other firms. As soon as he had political support, he persuaded employers to join with labor leaders on committees to help him draft a state law to require all employers to accept his principles. By giving both sides the impression that some type of law on the subject was inevitable, he induced them to compromise their differences. This joint product he perfected for submission to the legislature. At the legislative hearings on the proposed law he had both the "enlightened employers" and labor leaders testify on behalf of his proposals. Their testimony created the impression that a large group of employers and labor leaders were in favor of the bill.

Finally, after the legislature enacted his proposals into law, he used representatives of both employers and union leaders on advisory boards to aid in its administration. In doing this he recognized that the selling of the program was not over when it became a part of the law. He continued to educate both employers and workers as to the fairness of the program and the need for successful administration. Then with a record of success in one state (Wisconsin), he began a campaign to extend the program into other states.

In the case of workmen's compensation, the program not only provided the injured workmen with compensation, but it also relieved the employer of liability from potentially expensive lawsuits. The employer continued to pay insurance premiums, but the money went to take care of his employees instead of protecting himself from unpredictable liabilities. Along with the compensation program went an intensive safety program aimed at cutting the premiums for those employers who were successful in limiting

---

47 See chapter on "Commons and Social Legislation."

injuries to their employees. Consequently, the new workmen's compensation insurance could be provided at lower rates than the insurance against liability, benefiting both sides. The injured employee received predictable and certain payments without the necessity of suing his employer. At the same time the employer could benefit from the improved morale and from advantages accruing from reduced accident rates.

In all reforms Commons pushed, negotiations and persuasion played crucial roles. To him reform without the acceptance of all interested parties was unsatisfactory. Consequently, he stressed education of employers, workers, and the general public during all stages of his campaign. By giving the interested parties responsibility for the formulation and administration of the program, he sought to make it theirs. His role was to stand in the background prodding them, but giving them full credit for the actions.

When Commons finally evolved this method his troubles from reform activities were over. Instead of being branded as an agitator, he gained prestige from the success of his reforms. Furthermore, he found the method of operating which suited his capabilities, temperament, and outlook.

JRC | 3

COMMONS' WORKING ENVIRONMENT

WHEN COMMONS joined the University of Wisconsin's economics department in 1904 he arrived at a particularly favorable time, when the state government and the administration of the university were controlled by LaFollette's Progressives. In Wisconsin Commons found himself an insider whose talents were useful to those in power, where elsewhere he had been considered a dangerous radical. He could continue to engage in reform activities in Wisconsin, but he did so for the authorities instead of in spite of them.

Almost immediately he and Robert M. LaFollette formed an intimate friendship that profited both careers. It was LaFollette's habit to call on university professors to serve as experts to advise him on his program. During his governorship a close relationship developed between the state government and its university. The officials of the university, by providing time off for them, encouraged the professors to work for the state. Commons, as one of them, found numerous opportunities to serve the state during La-Follette's administration and for years afterwards. In the drafting of laws for social legislation he made his most significant contributions.

LaFollette

Without Robert M. LaFollette's leadership it is doubtful that the Progressive movement would have come to power in Wisconsin. He was a master politician who, in the face of extreme odds, organized a powerful machine.[1] At first he was a lone voice crying for reforms against corrupt politicians. By sheer persistence he fought his way into the governor's chair. Twice he was defeated, but on the third time circumstances favored him. When he sought the Republican nomination for governor in 1900 the party councils were divided by dissident elements. He chose his support wisely, and then quickly organized a bandwagon movement before other candidates gained enough strength to oppose him. Because the party had no other strong candidate he was accepted by political factions that had been hostile before and would be hostile again. But LaFollette quickly seized the opportunity to gain power, even if it meant making peace with his natural enemies.

Soon after his election to the governorship his determination to carry out his program antagonized many of his temporary friends.[2] When they discovered that his campaign promises were more than oratory they quickly deserted him. Once in power, however, LaFollette was able to build his own political machine. Although his party had a majority in both houses of the legislature during his first term, he could count on the support of only the Assembly. Consequently, he failed to obtain much of his program. During his second term he gained a slight majority in the Senate and retained control of the Assembly. Some of his program he then was able to push through, but most of it had to wait until his third term when he had solid support from both houses.

The Progressive movement was created largely through LaFollette's efforts. He was an indefatigable campaigner who visited every significant community in the state. Although by today's standards, his three-hour speeches were long, they were not dull. They were sufficiently interesting to attract people for miles.[3] Using emotional appeals blended with his logical arguments, he could make even a railroad timetable interesting.

LaFollette would have been a better politician if he had not been a zealot. Although he used some of the methods of his op-

---

1 Robert S. Maxwell, *Wisconsin*, p. 56.
2 Joseph W. Babcock, the leader of Wisconsin's congressional delegation, and Emanuel Phillip, who later became governor of Wisconsin, supported LaFollette during the 1900 election, but led the opposition soon afterwards. These Republicans who opposed LaFollette were called "Stalwarts."
3 Maxwell, p. 57.

ponents to gain power, he was fundamentally the foe of all political machines, including his own. During the early years of his governorship, he appointed numerous party workers to be oil inspectors, game wardens, etc. However, he later made them take civil service examinations, and a few lost their jobs when they received failing grades.

His strong feeling against political machines was developed early in his life. When he was a farm youth, he sympathized with the Grangers' struggles against entrenched interests.[4] These agrarian prejudices deepened into convictions when the machine politicians placed barriers in the way of his ambitions.[5] As a young man he ran for the office of district attorney of Dane County. Although the political boss of the county, Elisha W. Keys, opposed him, he won by the vigor of his campaign. Later, when he ran for Congress in 1884 he again won in spite of the opposition of professional politicians. Then in his victory, when he might have made his peace with them, he continued to fight his political battles fiercely and independently. By the time he sought the governorship he was committed to a crusade against machine corruption.

All politicians must deviate to some extent from their ideals, but that extent was not very far for LaFollette. Stubbornly he clung to a position, even though doing so grievously affected him. Furthermore, he expected his followers to share loyally the consequences of his righteous stands. In time, the list of his ex-supporters grew to be almost as extensive as that of the ones who continued to follow him.[6]

His inflexibility was not entirely a handicap.[7] His fierce honesty and devotion to his cause earned him loyalty no mere politician could command from his followers. Furthermore, the time was ripe for a crusade that required such a man as leader. For over a quarter of a century farmers had been frustrated in demands to regulate railroads. In the cities citizens were frustrated in their efforts to control public utility companies. Blocking both efforts were the machine politicians, whose behavior earned them the reputation for being corrupt.[8]

---

4 Robert M. LaFollette, p. 24.
5 Belle and Fola LaFollette, p. 119.
6 "The trail of 'Fighting Bob' LaFollette, in his climb to national fame and prestige, was strewn not only with his political opponents but also with many of the colleagues who helped him win his earlier political battles. Davidson, Stephenson, and McGovern, and later Irvine Lenroot, loyal supporters of the Progressive cause though they had been, were all read out of the party by the implacable senior senator." Maxwell, p. 194.
7 Frederic C. Howe, p. 7.
8 Lincoln Steffens, p. 94.

LaFollette meant to snatch power from the machines and give it back to the people. High on his list of reforms was the introduction of the direct primary for the state of Wisconsin.[9] After his experience with the convention system in which he was deprived of the nomination for governorship twice by what he considered fraudulent means, he was determined to change the system.[10] He reasoned that the direct primary could be used as a means of preventing political machines from frustrating the popular will.[11] In this reasoning he probably was overoptimistic, but the change could be used to weaken the machine existing at that time. At least the opposing politicians feared that LaFollette was right. Consequently, they fought the proposal and prevented its adoption during his first two terms. Pressure from the people stirred up by LaFollette's constant urging, finally forced the legislature during the second term to submit the proposal to a referendum vote. The measure then was adopted by the voters of Wisconsin at the same time they voted a third term for LaFollette.

In creating the direct primary system the state of Wisconsin made an innovation copied by the majority of the states in the union. Although it is not without its faults, the direct primary is at least an improvement over the convention and caucus system where candidates emerged mysteriously from discussions in "smoke-filled" rooms. Political organizations, or machines, as La-Follette would have called them, remain important mechanisms. However, they must operate more in the open than under the former system. To LaFollette must go the credit, or blame, for this important change in our political system.

To bring political influences out into the open, LaFollette in his third term pushed an antilobbying act through the legislature. He had urged its passage in messages to three legislatures. Finally, in 1905, the law was enacted.[12] It required that all lobbyists or representatives should register with the secretary of state. They were to state the character of their employment and the names of their employers. Although they were to be given the widest opportunity to present publicly their messages to legislative committees or other officials, they were prohibited from conducting any private

---

9 Howe, p. 51.

10 LaFollette claimed that he had enough delegates to nominate him for governor in both the 1896 and the 1898 conventions, but last minute changes defeated him. Some of his supporters reported that they had been offered bribes to change to other candidates. LaFollette asserted that $8,300 was used "to handle delegates before the balloting began," for the 1898 convention. Robert M. LaFollette, pp. 192, 220.

11 Edward N. Doan, p. 29.

12 Howe, p. 27.

communications with members of the legislature on any subject of legislation.

To prevent any future political machine from using the spoils system to gain political power, LaFollette created a civil service system for the state of Wisconsin. In this undertaking he turned to John R. Commons to draft the legislation. He asked Commons to study all similar laws in the country and then draw up a proposed law that would be the best in the nation. All employees of the state, except department heads and elected officials, were to take civil service examinations to determine whether they were competent. This included his own appointees as well as those who would be hired in the future. When Commons explained that all other civil service reforms had "blanketed in" existing employees, La-Follette replied firmly that no exception would be made.[13]

Besides attempting to trim the power of political machines, LaFollette also aimed at making tax burdens more equitable in Wisconsin.[14] In 1903 the legislature created an inheritance tax law with rates from one and one-half to fifteen percent, depending on the closeness of the relationship of the heirs and the size of the estate. Because the personal property tax had not been successful, it was partially replaced by an income tax. The rates varied from one percent on the first $1,000 of taxable income up to six percent on taxable incomes over $12,000. Of the revenue from this tax, ninety percent was remitted to the county, cities, and villages in which it was collected. Because it was collected by state rather than local officials, its administration was an improvement over that of the personal property tax.

To complete his revision of the tax system, LaFollette then proposed to change the method by which railroads were taxed. Up to this time railroads had been paying a percentage of their gross income in taxes instead of paying property taxes as did other business firms. According to the tax commission, which had been set up under a previous governor, railroad property yielded half as much in taxes as did the property of similar value belonging to private persons.[15] These estimates proved to be exaggerated, but after adoption of the new type of tax, the revenues increased sharply.[16]

---

13 Commons, *Myself*, p. 103.
14 Howe, p. 139.
15 Robert M. LaFollette, p. 243.
16 Howe, p. 135. Revenues rose from $1,948,340 under the system for 1903 to $2,494,-282 for 1904, the first year under the new system. The increases for the first three years of operations were: $551,642, $671,381, and $645,790.

After the legislature, in 1903, voted the new tax on railroads, LaFollette turned his attention to getting railroad regulation. Ever since the repeal of the Granger-inspired Potter Law, some agitation had kept the idea of regulation alive. Not only did the railroads fail to satisfy the farmers' demands, but they used strong political influence to prevent any re-enactment of a similar law. In doing so they aligned themselves with those opposing LaFollette. Consequently, when LaFollette's political power grew to sufficient proportions, their day of reckoning arrived. Finally in his third term, he managed to push through the legislature a bill regulating railway companies.

The Wisconsin Railroad Regulation Law of 1905 was so carefully drafted that it became a model for those in other states.[17] By creating the first truly modern administrative commission it provided effective means of regulation. More about this commission and others will be given in later chapters.

Although LaFollette was a zealot, his program was not unreasonable. Nor was he a true radical, in spite of his reputation among his contemporaries. None of his proposals were aimed at destroying legitimate business interests. They were aimed at providing protection for consumers, investors, voters, and workers. Although he at times could be vindictive towards his political opponents, his reforms were moderate. Like his friend, Commons, he believed that conflicting interests could be resolved. His method entailed the use of the best available experts who could devise reasonable compromises. All of his proposals were framed carefully and the legislation for them was drafted carefully. As a consequence, his enlightened reforms became models for numerous other states to follow. What was even more important, they were successful.

The key to LaFollette's success in formulating his program was in finding a sufficient supply of experts. At a time when governments and businesses used few such persons, not many were available. LaFollette found his supply among the professors of the University of Wisconsin. He created what during the New Deal days would have been called a "brain trust." It enabled him to frame his program along reasonable and workable lines, and it had the important byproduct of providing rich experiences for professors such as Commons.

---

17 Eliot Jones, p. 202.

The University of Wisconsin

LaFollette was fortunate to have among his resources the many scholars of the University of Wisconsin. At the time he took office as governor, the university had an excellent reputation. When the distinguished Mosely Education Commission came from England to study education in America, it ranked the University of Wisconsin high among the best universities of the nation.[18] In addition to its prestige, the university had very practical assets which the state could use. Its faculty contained a corps of experts who were to play leading roles in formulating the program of the Progressive movement.

LaFollette was the first Wisconsin governor to graduate from the state university; he entered in 1875 and graduated in 1879.[19] During his student days the university was an intimate institution with an enrollment of only 400 students.[20] The influence of its president, John Bascom, pervaded the entire university.[21] The students, including LaFollette, respected and honored him. LaFollette, at least, adopted some of his high moral purpose and his views on the obligations of citizens.

Bascom was the last of the old style presidents at the university.[22] Being an extremely broad scholar, he held the concept that a cultured man should be at home in all fields of learning. His own writings included contributions in philosophy, psychology, religion, economics, art, literature, and social reform. Although he desired to strengthen its scholarship, he believed the primary function of the university was to educate and cultivate undergraduates. Consequently, any graduate study existing there was incidental.

In 1887 Bascom was succeeded by an entirely different type of educator, Thomas Crowder Chamberlin.[23] Instead of neglecting graduate studies, Chamberlin worked to make such a program possible. To attract high caliber graduate students, he established a number of fellowships. To strengthen the faculty, he recruited a number of men eminent in their various fields. He insisted that promotion for the younger faculty members be made conditional upon their acquiring Ph.D.'s. To allow time for supervision of graduate students he reduced the teaching load of his professors.

---

18 Curti and Carstensen, Vol. II, p. 107.
19 Belle and Fola LaFollette, p. 27.
20 *Ibid.*, p. 37.
21 *Ibid.*
22 Curti and Carstensen, Vol. I, pp. 246-295.
23 *Ibid.*, Vol. I, pp. 534-560.

He planned a new library to make research possible for both faculty members and graduate students. Above all, he encouraged faculty members to engage in research. In short, he aimed at the creation of a modern university.

Although Chamberlin was a geologist, he did not favor the sciences over other studies. He attempted to strengthen all departments, but he was most successful in the social sciences. A key figure in this development was the distinguished historian, Frederick Jackson Turner. Chamberlin made it clear that Turner must earn a Ph.D. if he expected a career at the University of Wisconsin. Consequently, Turner took a leave of absence in 1888 to study at Johns Hopkins University. There he met Richard T. Ely, who already had gained an outstanding reputation as an economist. When Turner learned that Ely was not happy at Hopkins, he persuaded Chamberlin to hire him.[24]

Wisconsin got Ely in 1892 but only after offering him considerable inducements, including a salary higher than it had paid any other professor. Ely wanted more than money; he wanted to establish a new School of Economics, Political Science, and History, which would "do for civil life what West Point did for military life."[25] Not only would it advance knowledge in the social sciences, but it also would offer training for public careers. The regents of the university agreed to the establishment of the school, provided some fellowships, added to the faculty, and provided $5,000 for books.

Ely was a difficult man to satisfy, and so was his colleague, Turner. After returning to Wisconsin with his Ph.D., Turner attracted nationwide attention for his work on the significance of the frontier in America. When various other presidents continually urged him to accept calls to their respective universities, Wisconsin had the serious problem of holding him. Although it could not match some of the offers financially, it did offer him other inducements. Because Turner's demands coincided with what would enhance the study of American history, the university profited by acceding to his demands.

The unusually rapid growth of scholarships in the social sciences at Wisconsin resulted primarily from the demands of Turner and Ely. They demanded that distinguished colleagues be added to

24 *Ibid.*, Vol. I, p. 618.
25 *Ibid.*, Vol. I, p. 632.

the staff. To strengthen their fields further, they insisted on increased funds for books, fellowships, and facilities for publishing research findings. Because they got what they wanted, Wisconsin became a leading center for scholarship in the social sciences.

Although he created a modern university out of a small college, President Chamberlin remained in office for only a short time. After five years he resigned to become a professor at the new University of Chicago. But the foundation he laid was so solid that his successor, Charles Kendall Adams, could complete the job.[26]

President Adams possessed both the desire and the ability to complete the program of transforming Wisconsin into a leading modern university. His natural abilities and his experience as the president of Cornell University fitted him for his job. Being something of a politician as well as an able administrator, he persuaded the legislature to provide funds for the ambitious building program begun under his predecessor. He continued the process of strengthening the faculty and encouraging research. By the time of his retirement because of ill health in 1902, the University of Wisconsin was approaching the goal sought by Chamberlin and Adams.

During Adams' administration an event involving Ely demonstrated some of the growing pains of a university. In 1894 Oliver E. Wells, the state superintendent of public administration and a member of the Board of Regents of the university, wrote a letter to the editor of *The Nation*.[27] He charged Ely with believing in strikes, boycotts, and in radical doctrines. As a consequence, Ely had to defend himself in a public hearing before a committee of the Board of Regents.[28] After hearing the evidence, the committee decided that Ely was actually conservative.[29] Although academic freedom was not an issue in the investigation, the committee decided to issue a statement on the subject. A portion of their statement became Wisconsin's "Magna Carta"[30] and was inscribed afterwards on a prominently displayed bronze plaque.

---

26 *Ibid.*, Vol. I, p. 561-579 .
27 Wells, p. 27.
28 Ely, *Ground Under Our Feet*, pp. 218-233.
29 Curti and Carstensen, Vol. II, p. 526.
30 *Ibid.*, Vol. II, p. 525. ". . . We cannot, however, be unmindful of the fact that many of the universally accepted principles of today were but a short time ago denounced as visionary, impracticable, and pernicious. As Regents of a University with over one hundred instructors supported by nearly two millions of people who hold a vast diversity of views regarding the great questions which at present agitate the human mind, we could not for a moment think of recommending the dismissal or even criticism of a teacher even if some of his opinions should, in some quarters, be regarded as visionary. Such a course would be equivalent to saying that no professor should teach anything which is not accepted by everybody as true. This would cut our curriculum down to very small proportions. We cannot for a moment believe that knowledge has reached its final goal, or that

Although the Ely "trial" did not decide the issue of academic freedom for all time, it did create a presumption that Wisconsin was a university where such matters were important. From then on, any interference with a scholar's freedom would be in violation of the supposed policy. The incident dramatized the fact that the university had taken an important step in the transition from a small college to a modern university. Unlike the universities that dismissed Commons, it became known for its ideal of academic freedom.

The development of the university that took place before La-Follette became governor did not cease. Its development was further aided by the regent's choice in 1903 of a successor to President Adams. After considerable search for a suitable candidate, the board finally selected one of its own professors, Charles Van Hise.[31] He became the first graduate of Wisconsin to become its president.

Van Hise and LaFollette were close friends and classmates. While their relationship might have been expected to increase the unity between the university and the state, the closeness was remarkable. Van Hise could depend on the support of the state government during all of the years the Progressives were in power, and the government could depend on the university for a supply of experts to formulate its program.

Although the university vigorously continued to emphasize research, Van Hise encouraged professors also to contribute their services to the state. He gave them liberal amounts of time and leaves of absence to do such work. By 1908 forty-one members of the university's faculty were serving on one or more commissions.[32] Setting an example for the members of his faculty, Van Hise served on five different commissions. Although such service was not unknown in other states, the extent to which it was offered

the present condition of society is perfect. We must therefore welcome from our teachers such discussions as shall suggest the means and prepare the way by which knowledge may be extended, present evils . . . removed and others prevented.

We feel that we would be unworthy [of] the position we hold if we did not believe in progress in all departments of knowledge. In all lines of academic investigation it is of the utmost importance that the investigator should be absolutely free to follow the indications of truth wherever they may lead.

Whatever may be the limitations which trammel inquiry elsewhere we believe the great state University of Wisconsin should ever encourage that continual and fearless sifting and winnowing by which alone the truth can be found."

31 *Ibid.*, Vol. II, pp. 3-122.
32 *Ibid.*, Vol. II, p. 88.

during Van Hise's administration was unprecedented. The Van Hise-LaFollette friendship created a state and university partnership.

Wisconsin and the use of the expert

Although the use of the expert in framing legislation did not originate there, the state of Wisconsin certainly was an important leader in this field.[33] But this leadership did not arise until LaFollette became governor. Being a man with a program, he did not wait for the legislature to submit bills for his approval. Instead he made detailed proposals to the legislature and backed them as fully as he could.

Before he submitted any proposal he had detailed studies made by experts on the subject. Such studies provided him with information as to whether such proposals had been tried elsewhere, and whether they were successful. Based on the best knowledge available, they were a safeguard against mistakes that might lead to costly failures. To avoid legal difficulties and the possibility that the legislation might be declared unconstitutional, experts carefully drafted each bill. As a result, the Progressive's program was so successful that very little of it was discarded when the opposition gained power.

LaFollette explained that many of his experts were from the university:

> . . . While I was governor, I sought the constant advice and service of the trained men of the institution in meeting the difficult problems which confronted the state. Many times when harassed by conditions which confronted me, I have called in for conference President Van Hise, Dr. Ely, Professor Commons, Dr. Reinsch and others.[34]
> . . . During the last session of the legislature a Saturday lunch club was organized, at which the governor, and some of the state officers and legislators regularly meet with the university professors— Van Hise, Ross, Reinsch, Commons, Scott, Meyer, McCarthy and others—to discuss the problems of the state.[35]

This Saturday Club of which he spoke was formed when LaFollette no longer was governor. Yet it does symbolize the close relationship between the state and the university. LaFollette initiated the relationship while some of his successors continued to foster it.

33 Howe, p. 38.
34 LaFollette, Robert M., p. 30.
35 *Ibid.*, p. 32.

Frederic C. Howe in his *Wisconsin, An Experiment in Democracy,* described the relationship:

> The close union of the university with politics prevented any serious reaction during the years which followed the election of LaFollette to the Senate. University graduates occupied many of the important state offices, whether elective or appointive. In 1901 there were thirty-five professors and instructors giving part of their time to the public service. President Van Hise and Dean E. A. Birge are members of the conservation commission, state park board, the forestry and fish commissions. John R. Commons, professor of political economy, and now a member of the newly created industrial commission has promoted much of the industrial, labor, and railway legislation of recent years. Thomas S. Adams, former professor of political economy, is now a member of the tax commission, while Dr. B. M. Rastall is director of the state board of public affairs. Dr. B. H. Meyer, now of the Interstate Commerce Commission at Washington, was a member of the railway commission and at the same time professor of transportation. Charles McCarthy, head of the legislative reference library, is lecturer in political science, and E. M. Griffith, the state forester, is instructor in forestry. C. F. Burgess, professor of mechanical engineering, is on the engineering staff of the railroad and tax commissions, while Richard Fischer, professor of chemistry, is the state chemist. Chauncey Juday, state biologist, is lecturer on zoology. J. G. D. Mack, W. D. Pence, C. G. Burritt, N. P. Curtis, Otto L. Kowalke, H. H. Thorkelson, and H. H. Voskuehler are all members of the engineering faculty and connected with the railway and tax commissions in the appraisal of property, the investigation of equipment, meters, and conditions of service of the local public utility corporations, and the working out of technical problems connected with the regulation of these industries. Professors in agriculture, in chemistry, in law, and in medicine are identified with other state activities and give a considerable part of their time to public affairs. Groups of students spend their vacations in all kinds of state work and are the most efficient of employees.[36]

The professors used their graduate students in studying state government problems. Some of them secured positions for their students to aid them in such work. Fellowships were set up for other students who worked on such problems. Many students participated in seminars devoted to the state's problems. Before Professor T. S. Adams and D. O. Kinsmen drafted the state income tax bill of 1911 students spent several years on the subject. Before the state considered initiative, referendum, and recall, graduate student seminars worked over the proposals. Commons' students aided him in most of his proposals.

---

[36] Howe, p. 40.

To a considerable extent this type of study was an extension of Ely's idea of creating a school to train persons for public service. Under this study the state became a laboratory where students could gain practical experience. As a result, Wisconsin became an early leader in the training of students for service in public administration.[37]

Perhaps Wisconsin's greatest contribution to the use of experts was the introduction of specialists in the drafting of legislation.[38] Although the use of such specialists was an innovation in America, it long had been a part of British practice. Because the powers of government are not divided in Britain as they are in America, there never were inhibitions against using experts from the executive branch in drafting bills to be presented to Parliament, and the Cabinet frequently would consult a specialist before submitting bills. Finally, in 1871, British law formalized the procedure by creating parliamentary counsels to insure proper and legal wording for all government bills.[39]

Specialists in bill drafting may prevent the inclusion of loose wording that might lead to confusion and much litigation. So-called "jokers," or loopholes, in laws may not be apparent even to a well-trained attorney. The history of legislation is filled with instances of laws that have been unenforceable or enforceable in ways quite unforeseen by their originators. Much of the invalidation of legislation on constitutional grounds has resulted from improper wording.

Slow though America was in turning to bill-drafting specialists, the need has been more acute in the U. S. than in Britain. The U. S. Constitution, subject to complex interpretations, has made the drafting of legislation hazardous. Battalions of corporation lawyers have been quick to find legal flaws that could be exploited for their own purposes.

Before the time when Congress or various state legislatures hired official bill draftsmen, individual members of these organizations had to depend on their own or unofficial aid. Many such members were lawyers, but their abilities to draft laws were limited.

---

37 Leonard White, p. 326.

38 Dr. Witte explained that there are two types of bill drafting. One, such as that done by Commons, is the developing the general concepts for a bill. The second involves the technical job of phrasing the provisions in legal language. This second type is done to ensure that the law will operate as intended and is not vulnerable to attack on constitutional grounds. E. E. Witte, Letter of February 9, 1960.

39 H. J. Leek, p. 46.

Some copied, without making adequate changes, laws of other states. Those who wished to further lighten the task submitted bills drafted by lobbyists of special interest groups. The honest but simple souls who labored over their own submissions often proposed what they never intended. In his *Legislative Reference Work: A Comparative Study,* J. H. Leek told of numerous examples of poorly drafted laws, some humorous and others merely expensive.[40] He cited both state and federal laws which led to troubles. In some cases, the legislation remained nugatory, and in some extreme cases governors had to call special sessions of their legislatures to correct the mistakes.

LaFollette preferred to use university professors as his draftsmen, among whom Commons was his favorite.[41] Yet Commons and his associates used an agency LaFollette might have used, had he so desired. This was the drafting service of the Legislative Reference Library of Wisconsin, under the direction of Charles McCarthy. Commons found the facilities of the library speeded him in his work.

While Commons and other professors developed the general concepts in proposed legislation, McCarthy and his experts phrased the provisions into legal language. Because this latter group was equipped to do more than this technical work, LaFollette's proposals usually were considered by two sets of experts before being submitted to the legislature.

At least part of the reason LaFollette did not use the service directly was that his habit of consulting professors antedated its establishment. Furthermore, the drafting service developed gradually and reached operating efficiency late in LaFollette's administration.

The year 1901 usually is given as the date of the founding of Wisconsin's Legislative Reference Library.[42] It was then McCarthy was hired as a document cataloger for a branch of the Wisconsin Free Library. He did this work in such a manner that materials could be assembled easily to provide background material for anyone interested in drafting legislation. Such materials included comparable laws and proposals in other states, the national government, and other nations.

40 *Ibid.*
41 Fitzpatrick, p. 112.
42 *Ibid.*, p. 41.

In the course of his work McCarthy began to aid individual legislators more and more. He invited them, individually and collectively, to use the library's facilities. In 1903 the legislature recognized the library by providing regular appropriations and suitable quarters. By 1905 McCarthy requested that the legislature authorize employment of a lawyer for drafting bills. Accepting his recommendation, the legislature in 1907 authorized him to add a bill-drafting service to his library.

Any member of the state legislature could go to the library for aid both in compiling materials for studying proposals and in the drafting of bills.[43] Furthermore, he could be sure the bill embodied his ideas and was free from defects. In one extreme case the library staff drafted a bill to abolish its own services. Although the bill did not pass (partly because of the humor it caused), it was indicative of how the service remained nonpartisan. Because members of the Democratic Party and both branches of the Republican Party used its services, the library even withstood the attacks of a later governor who opposed the Progressive movement.[44] Members did not want to return to the alternatives of paying high fees out of their own pockets to private lawyers or accepting the work of lobbyists. With the library staff even the most insignificant legislator could submit technically correct bills.

The success of the Wisconsin drafting service led to prompt imitation elsewhere.[45] During 1907 seven other states followed Wisconsin's example. During the next decade the majority of the states followed both with drafting services and legislative libraries. Many states kept the two institutions separate, but provided both functions.

Within a few years the national government also followed Wisconsin's example. LaFollette, as a senator, fought for extending the Wisconsin principles to the federal government. In 1915 his efforts were rewarded by the establishment of the Legislative Reference Service. Finally, in 1918, Congress established the Office of Legislative Counsel, which provided a bill-drafting service. Both services have grown over the years, indicating that the members of Congress have found them useful.

Wisconsin thus led in the introduction of experts in government. Because the Progressives were introducing extremely con-

---

43 McCarthy, p. 197.
44 Fitzpatrick, pp. 72-89.
45 Leek, p. 58.

troversial proposals, success could not come by the mere passing of laws. Those laws were challenged with all the means at the disposal of the opposition. If any defects could be found in the wording or in the constitutionality of them, the bills might be defeated. LaFollette and his Progressives faced these possibilities by taking extreme care in framing their proposals. They used the best minds available to search for reasonable solutions to the problems. They tried to be fair to all interests involved, without compromising their main objectives. Then when their proposals were well thought out and sold to the people, they introduced carefully worded legislation to implement their programs. In doing so, Wisconsin became a leader in both its progressive legislation and in its reasonable method of attaining it.

The LaFollette-Commons friendship

In contrast to those at other universities, the situation at Wisconsin favored Commons' reform activities. The administration of the university and that of the state combined in the encouragement of professors to participate in the formulation of reform programs. Both institutions were in the hands of liberals who were congenial to the ideas of Commons. Instead of condemning him for meddlesome reform activities, the authorities put him to work on important reforms.

Many of Commons' opportunities resulted from his friendship with LaFollette. The two men had met when Commons made a trip to Madison on a study for the National Civic Federation in 1902.[46] At that time, LaFollette, as governor, consulted Commons on a matter pertaining to the taxation of railroads. Previously, Commons had written a few articles on the subject and was then currently the secretary of the taxation department of the National Civic Federation. Apparently, LaFollette was pleased with Commons' help because for many years thereafter he turned to him for aid in drafting legislation. They became close friends and intimates of each others' households.

While LaFollette was governor Commons drafted the Civil Service Law of 1905. Shortly afterwards, although he had left Wisconsin to become a United States senator, he requested that Commons draft the 1907 law regulating public utilities. Commons did so and continued to draft laws in Wisconsin for many years.

---

46 Belle and Fola LaFollette, p. 157.

At times he even aided LaFollette with bills to be submitted before the United States Senate.

Although Commons was not a politician, he did aid LaFollette politically. During both the 1910 and 1912 campaigns he took time away from his numerous other activities to help LaFollette.[47] He spoke on his friend's behalf and helped with the raising of money for the 1910 senatorial campaign.[48] During the 1912 campaign he lived as a guest at the LaFollette home while preparing campaign materials and performing other duties at campaign headquarters.[49]

Early in 1912 it appeared that LaFollette was a serious contender for the Republican presidential nomination. For several years he had been gaining leadership of a growing number of his party's senators who were defying the Taft administration's leadership. Although Taft forces were in control of the party, the growing opposition seriously challenged that leadership.

Meanwhile, former President Theodore Roosevelt gave increasing encouragement to the revolt. Because he was either reluctant to run again for the presidency or because he wished to appear reluctant for strategic reasons, Roosevelt remained in the background. Although he refused to state that he definitely would not run, he fostered the impression that he was not a candidate. Without him, the obvious candidate to oppose Taft was LaFollette.

Yet LaFollette did not wish to run only to find that the more popular Roosevelt would dramatically step in at the last minute and take over all of his supporters.[50] He did not regard Roosevelt as a true Progressive he could support, but without the support of Roosevelt's friends, the Progressive movement would be a lost cause. Yet Roosevelt would not openly give him active support. Instead, he sent numerous emissaries to assure LaFollette that he would back him at the appropriate time and that he, himself, did not mean to run. Although LaFollette was not quite sure he could trust Roosevelt, who avoided making any *written* promises, he did have to act on the assumption that Roosevelt's relayed promises were in good faith. After being assured of support from most of

---

47 *Ibid.,* p. 299.

48 Although the Seventeenth Amendment to the United States Constitution did not come until 1913, Wisconsin in 1906 had enacted a law providing for direct primary elections for the office of United States Senator. Although such a choice was not binding, it was expected that the state legislature would choose the winning candidate.

49 Belle and Fola LaFollette, p. 381.

50 *Ibid.,* p. 329.

the Progressives and sufficient financial support, LaFollette announced his candidacy.

Even after he had begun his campaign, he was not completely convinced of Roosevelt's sincerity. Consequently, he sent Commons to visit him.[51] Commons had lunch with Roosevelt at the Alpine Club in New York. There, in response to his direct question, "Would he support LaFollette?" Roosevelt replied, "Yes, tell him to go ahead."[52] LaFollette did go ahead, and the Roosevelt supporters did back him, until at the strategic moment when they switched to Roosevelt.

Commons also helped in LaFollette's campaign by writing press releases, campaign material, and by working on his platform. During January, 1912, he spent two weeks in the LaFollette household preparing some biographical material on LaFollette. When finished, he sent it to the campaign headquarters where it eventually reached the hands of Medill McCormick, who was directing publicity. At this point, McCormick, who was a Roosevelt supporter, substituted a manuscript he had written himself. The substitute was so worded that it could be construed as committing LaFollette to support Roosevelt in case Roosevelt later chose to run.

McCormick then directed a clerk to send it to the printers to have 10,000 copies printed. To assure speed in the printing he offered the printer $200. If the substitute had been printed not enough funds would have been left to pay for printing the original manuscript.

Fortunately, the clerk took the manuscript to Congressman John M. Nelson, who was temporarily in charge of the headquarters, and explained the offer McCormick was making the printer. Immediately Nelson submitted the substitute manuscript to Mrs. LaFollette and Commons. They decided it should not be printed and that the original manuscript should be printed at once.[53]

By this time Roosevelt forces were beginning to equivocate, many of them looking for an excuse to desert LaFollette. Although Roosevelt had not yet announced his candidacy, some of his supporters began to campaign openly for him. Finally, LaFollette, himself, gave them the break for which they were waiting.

51 *Ibid.,* p. 345.
52 Commons, *Myself,* p. 187.
53 Belle and Fola LaFollette, p. 382.

At the Periodical Publishers' Association dinner at Philadelphia LaFollette made a disastrously poor speech.[54] Exhausted from his strenuous campaign and worried over the illness of his daughter, he was hardly at his best. Before he had departed for Philadelphia he had promised Commons he would not speak for more than thirty minutes.[55] However, under the strain of speaking before what soon was a hostile audience, he lost all sense of timing. For two hours he rambled on and on. His voice became strident and his words were inappropriate. When he was done, he was sick and exhausted.

At once reports were circulated that he had been drunk, had a mental collapse, or at least was broken in health. Seizing on the incident as an excuse, many of his former friends deserted him. By the end of the month, Roosevelt had "thrown his hat in the ring." Although LaFollette continued his campaign to the bitter end, his chances were killed that night in Philadelphia.

After the campaign, during which LaFollette limited himself to some attacks on Roosevelt and to support for some local Progressives, he managed to regain some of his leadership over the Progressive senators. At last, after many years, he had enough support to push through a law requiring "physical valuation" of the railways of the nation. At the time of the passage of the Hepburn Act, he had argued without success for an amendment for this purpose. He had declared that railroad rates could not be regulated effectively unless there were some objective criteria to determine what would be reasonable rates. In LaFollette's opinion the best method would be to relate the rates to a reasonable return on the value of capital invested. Yet he did not want to accept the figures of the companies involved regarding how much they had invested. Instead, he believed their properties should be appraised by engineers, accountants, and other experts to determine what would have been a reasonable investment.

In December of 1912 Representative Adamson introduced a bill in the House for "physical valuation" in virtually the same form that LaFollette had introduced seven years before as an amendment to the Hepburn Act. Early in 1913 the bill went to the Senate and was referred to the Interstate Commerce Committee, whose chairman appointed LaFollette as a chairman of a subcommittee to consider it.

---

54 *Ibid.,* pp. 398-414.
55 Commons, *Myself,* p. 186.

To improve the bill, LaFollette worked "night after night" with John R. Commons until one o'clock in the morning.[56] With them Professor Edward W. Bemis, a leading utility expert, also worked on the bill. Finally, shortly before March 4, when Congress was to adjourn automatically, the bill was reported out of committee and was passed unanimously by the Senate. Taft signed the law as one of the last acts of his administration.

Thus, this Physical Valuation Act, which Commons helped write, brought the Interstate Commerce Commission's power almost up to par with that which Wisconsin's commission had in its own state. However, this valuation on a national scale proved more difficult than in the state of Wisconsin. It was not completed until the 1930's.

In June of 1913 LaFollette's friendship brought Commons another opportunity for public service. LaFollette sent him a telegram stating that President Wilson offered him the position of chairman of the new Industrial Relations Commission.[57] Unfortunately, Commons felt compelled to decline because to accept would have necessitated a three-year leave of absence from the University of Wisconsin. He had just completed a two-year leave while serving as a commissioner on Wisconsin's Industrial Commission.

Yet Commons did become a member of the President's commission. Although he could not accept the chairmanship, he did agree to serve as a public member on condition that he would be available only during vacations from the university. The story of his service will be told in a later chapter.

Commons' friendship with LaFollette faced a crisis during World War I. After his son had enlisted, Commons caught the war spirit and began to see Germany as a threat to national existence of the U. S.[58] He feared that if the French and British lost the war, Germany, after gaining the world's largest navy, might threaten this continent.

Some time after America had entered the war, Commons made a business trip to Washington. While there he called on his friend, Senator LaFollette, in his office. The two men became involved in a heated discussion on the declaration of war.[59] Finally,

---

56 Belle and Fola LaFollette, p. 455.
57 Commons, *Myself*, p. 165.
58 *Ibid.*, p. 183 .
59 *Ibid.*, p. 185.

when nothing more could be said, they parted. Commons described their parting:

> On our walk from his office toward the Union Station, neither of us could say a word. I saw then his unconquerable will with his jaw shut tight. Never before had I come against it in my own person. I determined that, when I should get back to Wisconsin, I would do what I could to elect opponents of LaFollette.[60]

Their friendship was at an end. With both of them passionately believing the other wrong, there could be no reconciliation. Commons, in the height of the war patriotic fever, turned against his friend. To LaFollette this was desertion and disloyalty during his own critical time.

LaFollette had been for strict neutrality from the time Europe first was plunged into war. Fearing war would set back the progress of democracy a generation, he was determined that the United States should remain out of the war. Such a war, he reasoned, would provide the reactionaries with the chance to undo all of the hard-won reforms.

When Congress voted for war, he accepted the majority decision, but with no enthusiasm. His opposition to the majority then changed to an attempt to retain as much democracy during wartime as possible. At times his proposals were interpreted as obstructing the war effort. Such condemnation reached climactic proportions when his speech in St. Paul was misquoted by a national news service. The account of the speech quoted him as saying that, "We had no grievances against Germany."[61] Actually he had said that we did have serious grievances. He had even added that although he had not been in favor of the war, it was necessary to fight it once we were in.

When the people of the nation thought that LaFollette believed we had no grievances they were ready to call him a traitor. In the Senate an attempt was made to expel him. At home he was fired from the Madison Club. The Wisconsin legislature passed a resolution condemning him. President Van Hise conducted a meeting of professors who circulated a petition asking for his expulsion from the Senate. Even John R. Commons signed this petition.

In time the truth of the St. Paul speech became known. Eventually, with the end of the war, the storm raging around LaFollette

---

60 *Ibid.*
61 Belle and Fola LaFollette, p. 769.

subsided. Many who had turned against him were ashamed of their action. In 1922 voters in Wisconsin vindicated him by re-electing him, by an unprecedented majority, to the Senate.

Commons lost a good friend when he condemned LaFollette. Yet he never lost his respect for him. In his autobiography, *Myself,* he described LaFollette with almost hero-worship. As to losing his friendship, Commons wrote:

> . . . It was grief to me that, during the years following 1917, when I was often in Washington, I could not get up the courage to visit him at his home. I was afraid of his family. I received no invitation. I met him and his son Robert on public affairs at his office in the Senate Building. They were the same to me as ever.[62]

Fola LaFollette described her father's reaction at the first meeting of the two men after their parting:

> . . . That same day, after an Interstate Commerce Committee hearing on the railroad issue, he saw John R. Commons for the first time since Commons signed a petition calling for Bob's expulsion from the Senate. The two men, who had been so intimate for many years, talked briefly of family matters. Bob wrote his family that Commons "shook hands with me" and said he would call and see me, but he has not been around. He looked old and thinner than ever.[63]

The two men never did have a reconciliation. Commons supported LaFollette in his third-party presidential campaign in 1924. Furthermore, he wrote articles supporting his candidacy. Yet the contact between these two men remained "official." The old intimacy never could be restored.

The LaFollette-Commons friendship combined two forces that were trying to cope with the problems arising from the growth of big business in America. LaFollette represented the agrarian interests, resenting the shift of power from rural to metropolitan interests. These rural interests watched with fear the growth of huge economic enterprises. If they could have done so they would have prevented such a growth. Faute de mieux, they fought a defensive battle to prevent the more flagrant abuses of power by corporations. They pushed through antitrust laws only to find them ineffective. In only a few cases, where the public interest was clearly apparent, were they successful. Such cases included the need to regulate railroads and public utility firms.

Because of the strong political opposition from business, much of the battle by the agrarians centered on measures to suppress

---

62 Commons, *Myself,* pp. 187-188.
63 Belle and Fola LaFollette, p. 934.

corruption. They fought for direct primaries; civil service systems; corrupt practice laws; direct election of United States senators; and initiative, recall, and referendum elections. Their theory was that business interests might corrupt the caucuses, legislatures, and the Congress, but that the electorate itself is relatively incorruptible.

Perhaps their reforms were not adequate insurance against corruption, but these changes were good tactical moves in achieving their objectives. Selling the people on the need to safeguard against corruption aided the reformers in pushing old interests out of office. In many states the reforms, and for a time the reformers, were successful. Although the reforms did not completely succeed in ending corruption, they have remained as a legacy from a brief period of reform.

JRC

4

COMMONS' CAREER AT THE
UNIVERSITY OF WISCONSIN

WHEN COMMONS joined the staff of the economics department of the University of Wisconsin in 1904 his career reached its turning point. His conflict with university authorities concerning his radicalism was over, as was his succession of short-term positions. In the congenial atmosphere of Wisconsin he was destined to remain.

As explained in the previous chapter, conditions were particularly favorable for him when he arrived at Wisconsin. The administration both of the university and of the state encouraged professors to engage in the very sort of activities that attracted him. Like those of any modern university, authorities urged faculty members to undertake research projects. What was unique about Wisconsin was that work for the state in the formulation of its legislative program counted as research. Hence, Commons was provided with the opportunity of combining the career of a reformer with that of a scholar.

The third element in his career was that of a teacher. At the time he was hired by Wisconsin his record showed little promise as a teacher. When he had attempted to substitute for Professor Ely at Johns Hopkins during his graduate days he could not cope with his students.[1] On his first teaching job, at Wesleyan Uni-

---

1 Commons, *Myself, op. cit.,* p. 44.

versity, he was fired after one year because he was a poor teacher.[2] Although his difficulty in holding positions supposedly was caused by his radicalism, his deficiencies in the formal techniques of teaching may have had some influence on the authorities. He never did become a good or systematic lecturer, but he became a great teacher in spite of superficial difficulties. But to anyone hiring him in 1904 his teaching ability was not an attraction. Fortunately for him, Wisconsin had evolved sufficiently toward becoming a modern university that its officials tended to value research more than teaching.

He was hired by Ely, who knew exactly what to expect of him. By this time he had acquired considerable experience of the kind respected by Ely. His study and work involving labor unions provided him with qualification for what Ely had in mind. Ever since publishing the book, *The Labor Movement in America,* Ely had been nursing the idea of writing an extensive and complete history of labor in the United States.[3] This project he turned over to Commons, who with the help of his students, finally published two long works on the subject. The first, *A Documentary History of American Industrial Society,*[4] contained a compilation of source material in labor history, while *The History of Labor in the United States*[5] became the classic work on the labor movement. The first he published in 1910 and the second, to the extent of its first two volumes, in 1918. Finally, in 1935, Commons' students finished the last two volumes of the labor history. More on this history will be included in a later chapter.

Ely contributed more than materials for Commons' work on labor history. He solicited $30,000 for the expenses involved.[6] Among the contributors were V. Everit Macy, whom Commons knew from his National Civic Federation days; William English Walling, who previously had employed Commons on research projects; Stanley McCormick, a friend of Walling; F. Fulton Cutting, a New York lawyer; State Senator W. H. Hatton of Wisconsin, with whom Commons later worked on labor legislation; Captain Ellison A. Smyth, a textile manufacturer about whose labor relations Ely had written; and Charles R. Crane, who was a backer of LaFollette and later of Woodrow Wilson. Later,

---

2 *Ibid.,* p. 45.
3 Ely, *The Labor Movement in America.*
4 Commons and Associates, *A Documentary History of American Industrial Society.*
5 Commons and Associates, *The History of Labor in the United States.*
6 Commons, *Myself,* p. 136.

Professor H. W. Farnham of Yale University furnished another $25,000, in addition to creating the Board of Research Associates in American History, an organization which furnished further funds. Even the University of Wisconsin provided money for the projects.

Because of his own contacts, Commons, before long, solicited funds for his projects. The history project provided him with a method of operating, beneficial to both him and his students. Operating before the days when the great foundations provided numerous large grants of money, Commons turned to his wealthy friends when he needed to raise funds. From them he obtained money for travel expenses for himself and his students. Always he used clerical and research assistants, paid with the money he raised.

Rather than try to do all of the writing, he parceled out work to his students, to whom he gave generous credit. He reserved the role of editor and co-ordinator for himself. Such a technique had disadvantages, but it did permit him to accomplish far more than he could have done alone. When the *Documentary History* was published, and later when the first two volumes of the *History* were completed, the critics heaped praise upon them.[7] In sharp contrast to his failure with *The Distribution of Wealth,* this success in the labor field established him as a leading labor economist.

However, he became involved in many more activities than writing a labor history and teaching at the University of Wisconsin. As was explained in the previous chapter, his friendship with LaFollette started him on a series of projects for government. In addition, LaFollette helped him make useful contacts for his other work. Some of LaFollette's friends, because they tended to be liberal, were interested in Commons' activities. Those with money, like Charles Crane, helped finance a number of his projects. Many of them aided him in securing contacts necessary to get government financing for some of his projects. With this money, plus what was available from the comparatively new foundations, he was able to carry on projects requiring the aid of a number of researchers.

Commons' outside activities

While at the University of Wisconsin Commons engaged in so many activities in addition to his teaching that it is almost im-

---

7 See the chapter, "Commons, Student of the Labor Movement."

possible to account for all of them. Individual chapters will be devoted to some of the more important ones, but many others can be mentioned only briefly.

Soon after he arrived in Wisconsin he drafted the Civil Service Law of 1905 for Governor LaFollette. Shortly afterwards, in 1906, he participated in the National Civic Federation study of some thirty-five municipally and privately owned gas, electric light and power, and street railroad companies in the United States and England. As part of the study, he made a five-month trip to the British Isles. After his return he undertook the supervision of the labor portion of the Pittsburgh Survey, which was financed by the Russell Sage Foundation. This study was made by a number of investigators and some social workers who later published the magazine *Survey*. Commons' part of this survey of social conditions in Pittsburgh included a study of the problems of the wage earners. To aid him in his share of the work he took along several of his students.

His experiences in these two studies, the one on public utilities and the second on working conditions, provided him with background for drafting two important Wisconsin laws. In 1907 he drafted the Public Utility Act, which became the model for many others throughout the nation. His observance during the Pittsburgh Survey of the need for improving safety conditions and compensating injured workers contributed to the study he made preparatory to drafting the law creating Wisconsin's Industrial Commission. This law placed the formulation and enforcement of industrial safety regulations under an administrative commission. It also provided compensation for workers injured on their jobs. Before drafting each of these laws he used a number of his students to aid him in compiling information needed both for devising proposals and for influencing the legislature to accept him.

Not only did Commons write bills for submission to Wisconsin's legislature, but he also participated in campaigns to sell the public on the need to adopt the reforms he advocated. He enlisted the aid of organizations in which he was very active. In 1907 he was elected secretary of the newly formed American Association for Labor Legislation. This association, composed of state and federal officials dealing with labor problems, and of professors and social workers, continually developed plans for labor legislation. After Commons' plan for labor administration by commissions was adopted by Wisconsin, this organization helped spread it to numerous other states. To make the organization more effective it soon elected a full-time executive secretary, John B. Andrews, who was a Commons' student. Also, in 1910, it moved its headquarters to New York City to be nearer important industrial centers.

Commons continued to be active in this and in another organization also interested in labor legislation. This second organization, the National Consumers' League, operated on the basis of persuading consumers not to buy goods produced by companies whose employees worked under unsafe or unsanitary conditions. They attempted to shock consumers by showing them exhibits of such conditions. Commons' role in the organization in 1911 included the drafting of a model bill for a minimum wage law for women. Later, in 1923, he became the president of the organization, succeeding Newton D. Baker.

After drafting the Industrial Commission Law, he served as one of the first members of Wisconsin's Industrial Commission. When his two-year term of office ended in 1913 he declined a six-year reappointment at an annual salary of $5,000. This refusal, he said, attracted attention because he went back to the university for $3,500.[8] However, his friend, Charles Crane, gave him the difference each year, until after World War I, when his salary was raised to $6,000.

Just before and after being a commissioner he did other government work. In 1910 he began eighteen months' work for the city of Milwaukee. He and his students made an exhaustive study, resulting in a number of money-saving suggestions for the Socialist administration then in power. They streamlined city organizations, devised cost-accounting systems, and installed modern filing systems. Afterwards, Commons influenced Governor McGovern to create the Wisconsin Board of Public Affairs, which was to do the same work for the state. In this undertaking, unlike in the Milwaukee survey, he did little beyond starting the project.

Shortly after the expiration of his term as a member of the Industrial Commission, he became a member of the United States Commission on Industrial Relations. Again, as in both the Pittsburgh and Milwaukee surveys, he confined his participation to weekends, holidays, examination and vacation periods. He was offered the chairmanship but refused as he did not feel he could spend the necessary three years away from the university.

---

8 Commons, *Myself,* p. 164.

At the conclusion of his work with the United States Commission he suffered from a nervous collapse, the first in ten years. From shortly before examination time in the spring of 1916 until the second semester in the following year he did nothing but rest.

When he returned to the university in February of 1917 he limited his activities to those of scholarship and the classroom. Many of the reform organizations to which he belonged were inactive during the period. He was elected president of the American Economic Association for 1918, at its December, 1917, meeting. This office provided him with his chief nonacademic activity. Although many economists worked for the government during the war, Commons remained at the university. By then the Progressives were out of power in Wisconsin and the conservatives did not request his services. Because he had quarreled with his friend, LaFollette, over the issue of the war, his other main entree to government service was gone. As for military service, he was too old. His son, Jack, enlisted shortly after the United States became involved. Consequently, Commons' interest in the war was that of a father of a soldier.

Although up to this time he had engaged in numerous other activities, he had managed to pile up impressive contributions to economic literature, especially on the subject of labor. Many of his contributions were short articles, but some were in the form of books. The books which he wrote by himself included: *The Distribution of Wealth* (1893), *Social Reform and the Church* (1894), and *Races and Immigrants in America* (1907).[9] In addition to these, he edited *Trade Unionism and Labor Problems* (1905),[10] *The Documentary History of American Industrial Society* (1910), and *The History of American Labor* (1918). These last two established him as a leading authority on the history of labor. In 1916 he and his student, John B. Andrews, published the first edition of their *Principles of Labor Legislation*,[11] which was the first of its field published in the English language.[12] Through four editions, the last in 1936, it maintained its place as the standard treatise on the subject.

During the war Commons continued his study of labor problems with an investigation of industrial relations. In 1919 he published *Industrial Goodwill*, which summarized his ideas on scientific

9 John R. Commons, *Races and Immigrants in America.*
10 John R. Commons, ed., *Trade Unionism and Labor Problems.*
11 Commons and Andrews.
12 Barnett, "Review: *Principles of Labor Legislation* by John R. Commons and John B. Andrews."

management, employee morale, and the responsibility of the public toward the worker.[13] It explored some of the shortcomings of scientific management while at the same time proposing methods of obtaining the willing co-operation of workers in increasing their productivity.

During the summer of 1919 he made a study of some thirty factories that had reputations for good labor relations. Financed by some leading paper manufacturers in Wisconsin, he took a number of his students on a tour of factories from Wisconsin to Maine. After their return he edited a number of their reports into the book, *Industrial Government*.[14] Although there was less lasting interest in this book than in his others, the research for it and its writing provided excellent experience for his graduate students.

While studying labor conditions for this book he observed effects of the 1919 inflation and the subsequent depression on workers. His appetite for reform was awakened so much that for more than the next decade he concentrated on plans to dampen the operations of the business cycle.

In 1920 he and Wesley Mitchell joined with Malcolm C. Rorty[15] to found the National Bureau of Economic Research, the organization that pioneered in the study of business cycles. The staff included Mitchell as research director, two of Mitchell's students, Frederick R. Macaulay and Oswald W. Knauth, and one of Common's students, Willford I. King.[16] Commons served as director until 1928.

Commons saw the solution to cyclical unemployment in terms of monetary policy. Serving as president in 1922 of the National Monetary Association, he carried on a campaign to spread the knowledge of monetary controls among both economists and laymen.[17] He pursued this interest further in 1927 and 1928 by aiding Congressman Strong of Kansas in the framing of a bill instructing the Federal Reserve System to stabilize prices. Financed by a private donor, he spent five months with the congressman work-

---

13 Commons, *Industrial Goodwill.*
14 Commons, *Industrial Government.*
15 Malcolm Rorty was chief statistician for the American Telephone and Telegraph Company.
16 Dorfman, *Economic Mind in America,* Vol. IV, p. 365, also Wesley C. Mitchell, *The National Bureau's First Quarter Century.*
17 Members of the Research Council of the organization included: W. F. Foster, David Friday, E. W. Kemmerer, W. C. Mitchell, W. M. Persons, John E. Rovensky, Carl Snyder, H. Parker Willis, and Allyn A. Young.

ing on the bill.[18] Although members of the House Banking and Currency Committee complimented him on his testimony during hearing, the bill failed to pass.

Because he realized that monetary policy cannot cure all unemployment, he drafted in 1920 for submission to the Wisconsin legislature a bill providing for unemployment compensation. It was rejected by the legislature in 1921 and other versions of the proposal were defeated at each subsequent session for the next decade. Finally, in 1932, Wisconsin enacted a law drafted by him, which created the first unemployment compensation system for any American state. From the time Commons began his campaign until well after its success in Wisconsin he organized pressure groups and wrote and spoke extensively on the subject. In 1924 he even served as an administrator for a voluntary unemployment compensation program of the Amalgamated Clothing Workers in Chicago.

Although the problems of depression and unemployment dominated his activities, they did not prevent him from following a number of other interests. He, William Z. Ripley, and Frank Fetter, in 1923, served as experts for the Associated States Opposing Pittsburgh-Plus (Illinois, Wisconsin, Minnesota, and Iowa).[19] They provided economic arguments that were used in hearings before the Federal Trade Commission. When the commission ruled against the Pittsburgh-Plus basing plan, the steel companies abandoned it rather than appeal to the courts.

Commons was also a guiding light for a significant project on workers' education, which was under the direction of one of his students, Don Lescohier.[20] Commons sold the university officials on the idea, served as an adviser to the project, and later was a member of its governing committee. To this day, the University of Wisconsin has carried on this educational project by providing special classes for workers.[21]

During the twenties, despite his many other activities, Commons managed to continue with the usual activities of professors. In addition to teaching, he made numerous contributions to economic literature. Many of the articles involved proposed reforms,

---

18 Norman Lombard of the Stable Money League (the reorganized National Monetary Association) raised $2,500 for the expenses of Commons and his statistical assistant, Myrtle Starr. Commons was on a leave of absence with pay from the university. Commons, *Myself*, p. 191.

19 "Hearings," *Congressional Record*, 69th Congress, pp. 3834-3848.

20 Commons, *American Economic Review*, Vol. XIV, pp. 505-519.

21 Schwarztrauber, p. vii.

but not all. He demonstrated his ability to keep up with economic literature by writing numerous reviews of other economists' works. In 1924 he published his *Legal Foundations of Capitalism,* the first of his mature theoretical works.[22] In 1934 he followed with his *Institutional Economics.* Although each of these brought him a certain amount of respect from many of his fellow economists, they failed to present his ideas in a usable form. Consequently, he wrote a third book, *The Economics of Collective Action,* which was to clarify the first two.[23] This last book finally was published after his death. Like the other two, it has had a limited impact on American thinking. Commons' recognized contributions remain those of a reformer and a teacher of graduate students.

Commons as a teacher

Commons' qualities shaped the direction of his success both as a teacher and as a reformer in Wisconsin. Not being a brilliant and systematic lecturer, his success came from a more individual approach. Using his enthusiasm on individuals and small groups, he accomplished more than those who held large audiences spellbound. He did lecture and he often gave talks to large groups, but his success came from his marshalling of facts and from his enthusiasm for what he was advocating.

His student, Edwin Witte, explained:

> Professor Commons was not a brilliant lecturer. His courses never were well organized. But he inspired his students to devote their lives to the improvement of our democratic way of life and our economy of free enterprise, for which he developed in them not only profound admiration, but also an appreciation that the American idea is one of continuous progress.
>
> As is common with young people, many of Commons' students were dissatisfied with things as they are. But they emerged from his classes, indeed, as men who wanted to improve what they thought was wrong, but without destroying our political, economic, and social structure. Commons taught them to see that they must thoroughly know the facts and offer workable proposals for improvements. He told them not only to study all that was written about a given subject and to reason logically about it, but to make their own observations, and to think in terms of remedies, rather than criticisms, and to learn from the people directly interested.
>
> Beyond this teaching, which was done far more by way of example than of preaching, Professor Commons possessed those qualities which endeared him to them as "John R." He was generous in his praise for conscientious effort and credited his stu-

---

22 Commons, *Legal Foundations of Capitalism.*
23 Commons, *The Economics of Collective Action.*

dents with ideas they got from him, or which he inspired. To many of us he was a second father, unselfishly interested in our welfare, in and out of the classroom. Nor did his interest cease when they left the university. He kept in touch with everything they were doing and gave them counsel and assistance whenever they sought his help, as they were constantly doing.[24]

Commons' warm personality added to his effectiveness with graduate students. By frequent demonstrations of his personal interest in their work he stimulated their enthusiasm. His encouragement nurtured their confidence and kept them at conscientious effort. Generously, he gave them credit and recognition for whatever they accomplished.

His method of using students to work on his various projects also increased his effectiveness as a teacher of graduate students. His reforms appealed to his students, who as youths tended to be idealistic. Instead of working on the usual projects, which are often destined to dusty shelves, they worked on reforms that in many cases became laws. It was easy for them to feel the importance of what they were doing. Consequently, their work took on an urgency that drew from them considerably more effort than they otherwise might have given.

Working with Commons, who moved about with prominent persons while working on his projects, heightened the glamour of their work. Besides meeting with influential people, they often traveled to interesting places. In the meantime they were treated by Commons as important colleagues making significant contributions. Furthermore, those who worked closely with him on his projects benefited from the extra attention they derived from their intimate relationships with him.

Especially when the project involved governmental functions the work often prepared the students for specific positions. By being in on the creation of a new agency, the student often found opportunities for further employment when his work at the university was completed. By actually participating on a project involving such work he gained an advantage over other potential applicants.

Commons was not the only professor at the University of Wisconsin who worked on governmental projects. Not only did LaFollette and the Progressives call in numerous professors as

24 Edwin E. Witte, "John R. Commons, Teacher, Economist, and Public Servant" (Remarks at the John R. Commons' Birthday Dinner, October 10, 1950).

expert consultants, but university officials encouraged faculty members to accept such invitations. Howe, in his *Wisconsin, an Experiment in Democracy,* called the university the fourth department of the state, along with judicial, executive, and legislative branches.[25] He described how state officials turned to professors who would use problems in the state as projects to train their graduate students. As a result of such training, numerous students found their way into governmental service for Wisconsin, other states, and the federal government.

Yet the methods which Commons and his colleagues at Wisconsin used were not without drawbacks. Although a student might gain general knowledge of economics from his other courses while at the university, the extent of his training from the projects under Commons might be too narrow. Interesting and important as the project might be to the student, its training value might be slight. If the student concentrated too much of the time studying a specific case, he might fail to develop an understanding of broad principles. Studying such a case might not develop his ability even for general analysis.

Although Commons did not completely neglect economic theory in the training of his students, he certainly did not make sure that they gained a command of the conventional tools of economic analysis. When he was concentrating on his reforms he left the teaching of analytical techniques to others. But even when he was developing his own economic theory students could not learn from him much of the corpus of economic theory. He used his seminars as sounding boards for his own ideas; unfortunately many of his students later confessed privately that they did not understand what he was trying to do. Even Commons was aware of this fact and confessed that he had difficulties in making his students understand his theories.[26] Some of his students, especially those who taught in universities, did learn modern economic analysis, but not from him.

Although somewhat handicapped by a lack of economic theory, a great number of Commons' students rose to prominence. By adopting Commons' focus on the solution of practical economic problems they found many opportunities for constructive work both in and out of government. Many of them found good government positions and a large number found their way to the eco-

---

25 Howe, p. 39.
26 Commons, *Institutional Economics*, p. 1.

nomic departments of many important colleges and universities. Witte said of his fellow students:

> Commons' students went everywhere and many of them made great contributions as scholars, public officials, or men of practical affairs. Even a listing of the students who carried on the work of Commons—as all of them always said they were doing—is impossible on this occasion. But I may be pardoned in mentioning a few, although I omit others of equal merit. I mention among University teachers: Harry Millis, Ira Cross, Theresa McMahon, William Haber, Ellison Chalmers, Selig Perlman, Don Lescohier, Elizabeth Brandeis, Kenneth Parsons, and Harold Groves—most of whom, significantly, have not been merely scholars but men and women who have made real contributions of a practical nature to human betterment. Among men and women whose careers were mainly in the public service, I enumerate: Arthur Altmeyer, William Leiserson, Katherine Lenroot, Ewan Clague—and, on the state level, Paul Rauschenbush, Maud Swett, and Meredith Givens. Quite a few of his students came from abroad and returned to their native lands to make distinguished records, among them Mark Somerhausen, the Chief Justice of Belgium,[27] Hilary Marquand, the British Minister of Pensions, and Andre Philip, French professor and journalist and a Minister in several Cabinets. All these, and many others, have said that John R. Commons was the greatest influence in their lives. Commons, moreover, had much the same effect upon many people who came into close contact with him in his many endeavors outside of the classroom.[28]

Because Dr. Witte was speaking in Madison, his list naturally included more of the students who had remained close by. He might have extended his list to include John B. Andrews, who, as executive secretary for the American Association for Labor Legislation for years, spearheaded many of the reforms in labor legislation. Those prominent in university teaching whom he might have added are: Alvin Hansen and Sumner Slichter of Harvard, Theodore Schultz of the University of Chicago, Francis Bird of the University of Cincinnati, Frank T. Carlton of Case Institute, Holbrook Working and John Troxell of Stanford University, Calvin B. Hoover of Duke University, Harold McCracken of Louisiana State University, Bruce Knight of Dartmouth, and Martin Glaeser of the University of Wisconsin. Other students he might have named include: Emerson Schmidt of the United States Chamber of Commerce, Roy Blough, Wilbur Cohen, Paul H. Nystrom, Florence Peterson, Willard I. King, and Senator Wayne Morse. Then, of course, Dr. Witte neglected to include his own name. In addition to heading the University of Wisconsin

---

[27] Dr. Witte later corrected this to read "justice of the high Administrative Court." Letter, February 9, 1960.
[28] Witte, *op. cit.*

department of economics, Dr. Witte served as executive director for President Roosevelt's Committee on Economic Security, which drafted the Social Security Act of 1936. Even if Dr. Witte had included the above names, the list would be only illustrative.[29]

Of course Commons' students were subject to many other influences besides his, but so many of them have been active in reforms and social welfare activities that there is no doubt of the impact of Commons' personality on them. When talking about Commons these students reveal an affectionate remembrance verging on hero worship. They proudly tell of his accomplishments and are fond of describing his personality. Above all, they emphasize his greatness, especially as a teacher. One of them, Selig Perlman, said:

> As a teacher and inspirer of graduate and undergraduate students, Professor Commons ranks with America's greatest. In Commons' presence the student was aware of greatness, yet never felt dwarfed.[30]

Dr. Witte also called him a great teacher, but added he was "the most lovable man I have ever known."[31] Undoubtedly, the devotion of his students stemmed from his unselfish interest in their welfare. Although he had sufficient prestige to command considerable respect, he remained human in his relationships with them. Each Friday night a group of his students, seniors, and graduates met informally at the Commons' home for a lap supper and two hours of talk. They were free to bring their wives, husbands, and friends. Sometimes, according to Perlman, the group numbered sixty.[32] At some of the meetings prominent economists or public men of the world presented their observations. At other times these "Friday Niters," as they called themselves, were asked to discuss what they were doing in addition to their studies. Introducing themselves to the group, they recited their own biographies. In these informal meetings they became acquainted with Commons and each other. Often they became close friends, and according to Commons, would help one another whenever they could.

---

29 When his students were preparing for a birthday party for him on his seventieth birthday, Ernestine Wilke, writing for Meredith Givens, gave W. Ellison Chalmers a partial list of Commons' students. The list containing 140 names with addresses disclosed a wide distribution of positions in universities, research foundations, governmental organizations, and welfare organizations. (Letter of September 21, 1932.)

30 Selig Perlman, "John Rogers Commons," in Commons, *The Economics of Collective Action.*

31 Witte, *op. cit.*

32 *Milwaukee Journal,* May 18, 1924.

Commons' influence did not cease when his students received their degrees. He continued to follow their progress after they had left the university. If he knew of any positions for which they would be interested or qualified he got in touch with them. At times he was almost a one-man employment bureau. At least some of the success of his many students can be attributed to his aid in getting them suitable positions.

At one point his students thought they had a job for him. When President E. A. Birge announced his plans for retirement in 1924, rumors spread that John R. Commons was being considered along with a few others as the next president of the university. Although he was a little old (sixty-two) to be considered seriously for such a post, his prestige and the affection of his students undoubtedly contributed to the starting of the rumor.[33]

Commons continued his teaching at the University of Wisconsin until he retired in 1932. Although the Board of Regents gave him special permission to continue even though he reached the age of seventy in that year,[34] his desire to finish his *Institutional Economics* influenced his decision to retire. Furthermore, by then his health was too poor for him to remain very active. He decided in favor of his book, which he published in 1934.

On his seventieth birthday his students prepared a party for him. *Survey* magazine reported on this party in a short tribute:

> Men and women in all parts of the United States who owe their training and inspiration to John R. Commons of the University of Wisconsin joined with students and friends in Madison in celebrating the seventieth birthday of their professor on November 18. From Syracuse University, where Professor Commons' chair was abolished because his teachings were not in favor there a quarter of a century ago, came a message signed by thirty-three students saying that they wished the celebration might have been on their campus. Prof. Thomas S. Adams of Yale wrote that he knew the guest of honor would not go to heaven because he would be happy only where there are problems to solve and evils to fight. Dr. E. A. Birge, former president of Wisconsin, rose up as a biologist to take issue with Adams. He was sure that Commons would be in heaven to reform the transportation system there, about which the biologists, who don't see how wings can be set on shoulder-blades, have so long complained. President Frank, who was unavoidably out of town sent a message to the teacher who had achieved immortality in the affections of his students; and this

---

[33] The thirty-eight year old Glen Frank was given the position.
[34] *Wisconsin State Journal* (Madison, Wisc.), October 15, 1932.

seemed to express the feelings of the audience better than any other words. An employer and two union leaders testified to the gratitude of capital and labor for the services Professor Commons had rendered them. Governor LaFollette spoke of those to the government and the people of the state. Students presented a check for $1,500 to be used for a trip abroad to afford a much needed rest. Students also announced that a John R. Commons Library had been presented to the University consisting of a complete set of Commons' works and copies of all the books that his students had written. Before the dinner broke up Professor Commons charmed his audience with glimpses of the personal side of his life, about which he rarely speaks.[35]

Commons' later years

When Commons retired in 1932 at the age of seventy his health was too poor for him to take the trip abroad that his students wished for him. By then he had had a lifetime filled with an unbelievable amount of work. His wife, Nell, who had been a considerable source of strength as well as affection for him, was dead. Together they had planned to tour Europe in 1928, but on January 1 of that year she failed to survive a surgical operation. Rather than make the trip alone, Commons cancelled it and then worked harder than ever. Soon the combination of grief, overwork, and his lifetime propensity to break down at intervals, resulted in a nervous collapse.

He recovered only to receive another blow. His son, Jack, apparently suffering from his war experiences, developed a persecution mania and suddenly disappeared in 1930. Leaving his wife and child, he drove off in the family car. For the next fourteen years nothing was heard from him. Heartbroken, Commons made every effort to locate him both through friends and through the American Legion. From time to time the father received reports of his whereabouts, but invariably they turned out to be false. Finally, in 1944, Jack was found driving a milk wagon in Hartford, Connecticut. What he did during those fourteen years is not clear, but Dr. Witte was under the impression he spent much of that time in mental hospitals.[36]

Shortly after Jack disappeared Commons suffered yet another blow. His other child, Rachel, died mysteriously shortly after her marriage. There were strong reasons to suspect suicide.[37]

---

35 *The Survey*, LXVIII, p. 674.
36 E. E. Witte, letter of February 9, 1960.
37 *Ibid.*

Despite his personal tragedies and poor health, Commons continued to work. Although he could write for short periods only, he continued to work on his *Institutional Economics*. At the urging of his students he wrote his autobiography, *Myself*. Although somewhat disconnected, it is one of his most interesting books. Many of his friends feared he would not have sufficient strength to finish either book, but finally in 1934 he published both of them; and, as it turned out, he had another decade of life before him.

In his home overlooking Lake Mendota he had been living with his sister Anna. They were comfortable and his incomes from his emeritus pay and a Carnegie pension were adequate for their expenses. Unfortunately while he was driving down a highway his car was struck from the rear. His sister died as a result of this accident. After this tragedy in 1934 he sold his home, bought a trailer, and set out for Florida with his niece, Bertha Best. There he recovered his health and worked on for another decade.[38]

When his niece died in 1941 he was left alone again. For a while one of his graduate students, Chester Meske, stayed and worked with him on his last work, *The Economics of Collective Action*. Finally, in 1942, when the old man no longer could stand the discomforts of life in a trailer, Mr. and Mrs. A. B. Carpenter took him into their home and cared for him. He remained under their protection until 1945 when he went to North Carolina to join his one surviving sister and his son, Jack. After Jack was found, Commons, his sister, and Jack decided to live together in Chapel Hill.

In 1943 Commons had written his student, Kenneth Parsons, asking him to come to work with him for "a month or two."[39] He feared that without help, he might not finish his book before his strength ebbed away. Because Parsons had published an essay explaining Commons' point of view, Commons thought of him as the logical one to help. Parsons spent five weeks with him in the summer of 1944. After returning to Madison, Parsons checked the references, smoothed the wording in a few places, and then sent a retyped copy back to Commons. After making a few suggestions for modifications, Commons returned the manuscript late in April of 1945.

---

38 Kenneth Parsons, "Editor's Preface," in Commons' *Economics of Collective Action*, p. v.
   39 *Ibid.*, p. vi.

Although the work was not done, Commons left for North Carolina. Parsons described this journey in these words:

> He spent a few delightful days in North Carolina, visiting President Frank Graham and Professor Howard Odum of the University of North Carolina at Chapel Hill, and with Professor C. Bruce Hoover of nearby Duke University. As he reveled in the university atmosphere, he was young again for a few days; and then the little canter at the end of the race was over and he died rather suddenly in May, 1945, at Raleigh, North Carolina, with his son and sister at his side.[40]

Five years after Commons' death, his *Economics of Collective Action* was published by the University of Wisconsin Press, financed by funds made available when Commons assigned his right to royalties from the *Documentary History* and *The History of Labor in the United States* to the University of Wisconsin as a revolving publishing fund. According to Dr. Witte:

> *Economics in Action* was contemplated by him as a last publication and was many years in preparation. He made much of this theoretical writing unintelligible to present day economists and so invited his student, Kenneth Parsons, to come to Florida to live with him to work over the draft of what he had written for this book. Parsons did so and revised the first half of *Economics of Collective Action* but did not have time to touch the later chapters. When Commons died the manuscript of this, his last book, was in the shape indicated. It was clear that no one (not even Kenneth Parsons, who probably understood Common's theoretical views better than any one else) could probably revise what Commons, himself, had written. There was money, however, in the fund the University of Wisconsin had for the publication of worthwhile books in economics which came from the royalties that John R. Commons had assigned on his two greatest books for this purpose. So it came to pass that the University of Wisconsin Press published *Economics of Collective Action* as the first book financed from this fund. In all, *Economics of Collective Action* is as Commons wrote it, the earlier chapters as revised with Parson's help, the later chapters as written by Commons, but not revised as he hoped they would be.[41]

Also in 1950, former students held a party celebrating the anniversary of his birthday. Numerous speakers summed up his contributions. Their remarks were recorded in a pamphlet published by the State Historical Society of Wisconsin. Among the

---

40 *Ibid.*, p. viii. C. Bruce Hoover is Calvin B. Hoover.
41 Witte, letter of February 9, 1960.

remarks in his tribute Edwin Witte revealed the affection typical of Commons' students, by stating:

> John R. Commons was a great teacher, if judgment is to be based upon the students he influenced. His public services rank among the most valuable given by any academic man in the history of the state and nation. His contributions to the advancement of economics, while not appreciated by many of the present day economic theorizers, are likely to endure and further enhance his fame. But I shall ever remember him as "John R.," the most lovable man I have ever known.[42]

---

[42] Witte, Commons' Birthday Dinner, *op. cit.,* October 10, 1950.

PART II | WORK
WITH THE
COMMISSIONS

JRC

5

COMMONS AND SOCIAL LEGISLATION

JOHN R. COMMONS sponsored three Wisconsin reform programs which proved to be unusually significant. The first placed the regulation of public utilities in the hands of an administrative commission. The second created the Wisconsin Industrial Commission and gave it power to make safety regulations and installed a compensation program for injured workmen. The third provided Wisconsin with the first unemployment compensation in the country.

Each of these programs was highly controversial at the time of its enactment. Many persons doubted whether such laws were consistent with the U. S. economic system, form of government, or the federal Constitution.

At the turn of the century, when Commons drafted the public utility law, laissez-faire was not quite an absolute principle of government. Legislatures, the Congress, and the courts had by then admitted that some businesses such as railroads might be regulated in the interest of the public. Intervention to prevent the growth of monopolies was conceded to be a legitimate prerogative of government. Even some social legislation, such as laws to limit the hours of work in such unhealthy places as mines, had been declared legal by the courts. Laws to require safety devices in factories also were accepted. However, these were exceptions. In general, business men, lawyers, economists, and even government officials agreed that government intervention in business should be limited to a bare minimum.

The prevailing concept of the role of government might be compared to that of a referee of a game as contrasted to that of director of a play. The government provided a legal system under which individuals were free to determine their own roles. They could do this by exercising their freedom to make contracts. They were free to make contracts to sell their own or to purchase someone else's services, and to acquire and dispose of property. The government aided in the enforcement of contracts but did little in the way of interfering with the making of them.

Because freedom of contract was held to be a "sacred" tenet of the economic and legal system, much in the way of social legislation was blocked during the early years of the twentieth century. Laws to regulate hours of work, minimum wages, and conditions of work were said to be abridgments of a fundamental freedom.

A corollary to freedom to contract was the individual's responsibility for his own welfare. The legal system might protect him from fraud or robbery, but not from the consequences of his own stupidity. Furthermore, each individual was expected to save to provide for his own security or suffer the consequences if misfortune should overtake him. Private charity might aid him in case of extreme adversity, but he usually could expect no help from the government.

Local governments provided aid for the indigent poor but not for the able-bodied unemployed. Those receiving such aid were unable to make a living and had no relatives to support them. Hence, they were exceptions to the principle of individual responsibility.

Any legislation providing aid to the able-bodied poor with money derived from taxes was held to be class legislation. Taxpayers whose money went for such purposes were said to have been deprived of their property without due process of law.

Because governments did little regulating of economic activities at the turn of the century, their structures could be comparatively simple. The time-honored three-part division of powers had remained substantially as it was in the early days of the republic. The legislative branch passed laws determining public policy while the executive branch carried them out. The legality of the actions of both the legislative and executive branches was reviewed by the third branch, the judiciary. Each branch had its own powers and functions. There was little overlapping. However, as governments came to deal with the complex problems involved in economic regulation, the simple division of powers and functions had to go. The administrative commission upset the old concept of tri-partite division of government. At the turn of the century these commissions were new and their fate uncertain, but by the time of the New Deal they were numerous and powerful. The successful operation of the two commissions created in the laws drafted by John R. Commons aided immeasurably in the spread of this form of government machinery.

Three laws sponsored by Commons were milestones along the road from the Progressive era to the New Deal. The public utility law plus the slightly earlier legislation regulating railroads in Wisconsin were the Progressives' important laws to regulate industry. To be sure, they were designed to provide regulation only where it was not being done adequately by competition, but nevertheless they ruptured the principle of laissez-faire. The law creating the Industrial Commission went even further. It brought all employers under the regulations of the Industrial Commission. It also interfered with freedom of contract by eliminating the subjects of safety conditions and compensation for accidents from contracts between employers and employees. Even more important, it provided compensation for injured workmen regardless of who was to blame for industrial accidents. As such, it was the opening wedge by which government regulations would in many areas replace private contract. The third law was the one creating unemployment compensation.

The Public Utility Law

Commons patterned the Public Utility Law of 1907 after the Wisconsin Railroad Rate Commission Law of 1905. The earlier law was as important in bringing railroads under effective regulations as the new law was in extending the regulation to public utility companies. Up to the time of the Wisconsin law of 1905, neither the national nor the state governments had been effective in controlling railroads. The laws under which they operated were either poorly written or failed to provide the regulatory bodies with adequate powers.

In contrast to the earlier laws, the 1905 Wisconsin law gave its commission power considerably beyond that of the Interstate Commerce Commission at the time. In Wisconsin's law the legislature required every railroad to charge reasonable rates for hauling passengers and property between points within the state. Anyone believing rates to be unreasonable could appeal to the Railroad Commission which the act created. If the commission found any rates unreasonable it could substitute rates that were reasonable on the theory that "reasonable rates" could be ascertained. The commission did not set maximum rates; it specified actual rates. To determine what reasonable rates were, the commission was given considerable power of investigation and the help of highly trained staff. It could determine with the aid of its staff accountants and engineers the value of the properties used by the railroads. To assure fairness, it was required to conduct hearings at which the railroads could present evidence to be considered by the commission before it rendered decisions. Railroads disagreeing with the commission's decisions could appeal to the courts, but the burden of proof that the rulings were unreasonable was on them. Furthermore, all evidence first had to be presented in hearings before the commission before being presented in court. Thus, the evidence as verified by transcripts of the commission's hearings was to be considered prima facie. To avoid lengthy litigation, cases involving the commission were to be expedited through the state's courts.[1] Thus, Wisconsin created the first truly modern-type regulatory administrative commission with power to do the work intended.

Soon after the creation of the Railroad Commission in the state of Wisconsin attention shifted to the need for regulation of public utility companies. By this time it was recognized that regulation by competition had not been satisfactory. The nature of public utility operations made duplication of plants undesirable. Yet potential and sometimes real abuses indicated that some kind of public control was necessary. One alternative had been municipal ownership of the public utilities. Unfortunately, this controversial alternative was not without its serious problems. Mismanagement in the municipally owned gas works of Philadelphia attracted considerable attention throughout the country. As a result, an investigation of the situation was made by the National Civic Federation,

---

1 *Wisconsin Laws of 1905,* Chapter 360.

which also discovered other examples of corruption and mismanagement of publicly owned utilities. These findings cast doubt on the proposition that public ownership was the proper alternative to inadequately regulated private companies.

Up to this time, public utilities had been regulated through the granting of charters with all conditions of operations specified in advance. Rates, quality of service, and obligations of the company had been spelled out in the franchise, as well as its rights and priviledges. Franchises were considered contracts between cities and the companies. Some cities bargained carefully for contracts protecting their residents thoroughly, but others were less exacting. Some franchises were for long periods, even into perpetuity, while others were for comparatively short periods.

When franchises were for long periods, changes in conditions often worked hardships on either the companies or their customers. In periods of rising prices companies faced rising costs without any possibility of raising prices. Unless some adjustments were made, companies lost money until they were forced to curtail or suspend services. On the other hand, during periods of falling costs, the customers were at a disadvantage if rates remained constant.

When franchises were of short duration, investors had to bear great uncertainty. If all capital improvements had to be amortized over the remaining life of a short-lived franchise, rates would have to be high. If rates were not high enough to cover amortization, improvements needed for satisfactory service would not be made. Furthermore, as each franchise neared its expiration date, negotiations between the company and the city became urgent. Such urgency provided incentives for the company to employ all the political pressure it could. Such pressure often accompanied corruption. Consequently, short term franchises were not satisfactory either.

In 1906 the citizens of Wisconsin knew that the regulation of public utilities would be a leading problem before the 1907 legislature.[2] Residents of both Madison and Milwaukee were disgruntled with the treatment they were receiving from public utility companies. The city of Madison sued the Madison Gas and Electric Company to get it to charge reasonable rates and to provide service of good quality. When the city tried to get an injunction to this effect the Wisconsin Supreme Court dismissed the case on the

---

2 Staten.

grounds that it had no authority to fix rates for the future. Such a function, the court declared, belonged to the state legislature.

The gas company even succeeded in preventing the city from seeing its books. Such a refusal to divulge facts created suspicion that there was something to hide. A Wisconsin university professor, Dr. Victor Lenher, in an article in the *Wisconsin State Journal,* claimed that the amount of nonburnable gases in gas delivered by the Madison company was excessive and that the quality of the gas was much below standard.[3]

Sentiment in Milwaukee was aroused against the local electric company, which had brought legal action against the city when it tried to use money from the water fund for the purpose of constructing a municipal street lighting system. The company's suit increased the antipublic utility agitation throughout the state.

At the Republican convention at Watertown, Governor Davidson, in his keynote address, attacked the public utility companies.[4] He maintained that the rates for heating and lighting gas in Wisconsin cities were higher than in sixteen other leading cities in America. Other abuses, he claimed, included the watering of stock. As a result of both the governor's interest and popular demand, the Wisconsin Republican Party included in its state platform a promise to pass a law regulating public utilities. Senator Robert M. La-Follette and Herman L. Elkern, speaker of the Assembly of the state legislature, asked Commons to draft a law extending the jurisdiction of the railroad commission to include all public utilities in the state of Wisconsin.

Immediately prior to this Commons had been part of the aforementioned investigation by the National Civic Federation. This investigation had covered the operations of public utility companies both in the United States and England. Though Commons' part in the investigation centered on labor problems, with other members of the staff he had visited many public utility operations in this country and Great Britain, and had acquired both interest and knowledge in the public utility field.

Commons worked on the proposed law with Charles McCarthy and his staff of the Legislative Reference Library of Wisconsin. McCarthy assigned M. S. Dudgeon of the legal staff to work closely with him, but Commons also sought help from anyone who could give him useful suggestions. He frequently consulted with

3 *Ibid.*
4 *Ibid.*

the public utility companies, and especially with their legal representative, C. B. Winslow. He also got the advice of the members of the Railroad Commission, who would be called upon to administer the law. Several members of the legislature, notably Senators A. W. Sanborn and W. H. Hatton, aided in establishing contact between the various parties interested in the legislation.

Commons went beyond the state for ideas on a public utility law. Francis Staten, in his dissertation for the University of Wisconsin wrote:

> While several bills were introduced early in the 1907 session, the serious business of drafting a public utility law was left to the Joint Committee on Transportation. This committee had the aid of Professor John R. Commons of the University of Wisconsin, of Charles McCarthy of the Legislative Reference Library, and M. S. Dudgeon. Months of time were spent in preparing the bill. Typewritten copies were prepared and sent to informed people throughout the United States to receive their comment and criticism. Letters were received by Mr. McCarthy and Dr. Commons from such men as Newton D. Baker of Cleveland; Frederick B. DeBerard, statistician of the Merchants' Association of New York; M. R. Ingalls, chairman of the Cleveland, Cincinnati, Chicago, and St. Louis Railways; and Professor Charles Merriam of Chicago University. The work was done deliberately, and carefully, and the draughtsmen continually invited criticism and suggestion.
>
> The bill as drafted was introduced simultaneously in the Senate and in the Assembly and extended hearings were held before the Joint Committee on Transportation of which Senator Hudrall was chairman. The utility men were well represented at the hearings, and a comparison of the bill as originally introduced and as passed indicates clearly their objections and suggestions were of considerable influence.[5]

With his usual modesty, Commons denied that he introduced anything new into the law. He said he adopted as a starting place most of the recommendations of the National Civic Federation's investigation commission. In fact, he claimed he got everything from others and described himself as a "sieve for funneling ideas from everywhere into legislative enactment."[6]

Here we see an early example of his genius as a reformer. Not only did he keep his own personality discreetly in the background, but he also constantly endeavored to spread the credit and the responsibility for whatever was done. By doing so, he won the support of persons he needed to succeed in his undertaking. But in point of fact, he really did serve as a "funnel" for ideas.

---

5 *Ibid.,* pp. 12, 13.
6 Commons, *Myself,* p. 120.

Commons did not think of reforms as something to be rammed down the throats of those needing to be reformed. Rather he thought of them as institutional adjustments that could make the economic system more workable. He was most enthusiastic when he believed problems could be resolved in such a way that all parties concerned could benefit.

Consequently, when Commons drafted the law to control public utility companies he had no intention of injuring them. Such regulations as he proposed were intended to be beneficial to them as well as to the public. To formulate a law that would be fair to them, the utility companies co-operated in the framing of the legislation. In view of the conflicts in Madison and Milwaukee, it is interesting to note that when Commons was the man drafting the law he received co-operation. Perhaps the companies were only yielding gracefully to the inevitable, but Commons in other situations displayed the same ability to resolve conflicting interests.

The public utility law extended the authority of the Railroad Commission to the regulation of public utility companies. The three-man commission created in 1905 broadened its scope to include the regulation of any corporation or municipality owning or operating any plant or equipment in the state, for the purpose of providing telephone, electrical, gas, heat, power, or water services for the public.

The law required that all rates set by public utility companies be reasonable. If the members of the Railroad Commission believed any company was charging unreasonable rates they could investigate to determine reasonable rates. When any twenty-five persons complained that rates were unreasonable the commission was required to make an investigation. In deciding on reasonable rates the commission was to determine the value of the property used by a public utility company, so rates could be set to ensure the company a fair rate of return on its investment, but no more. No order setting rates was to be issued by the commission unless it first conducted formal public hearings at which all parties concerned could state their cases and present evidence.

The law required that public utility companies publish schedules of their rates and all the rules and regulations concerning them. These schedules were to be available for inspection by the public at places where customers paid their bills, and also were to be submitted to the Railroad Commission. Any deviation from them for the purpose of discriminating in favor of, or against, any customer was prohibited, as was any other form of discrimination. Before any company could increase its rates it was required to obtain approval from the commission.

Not only could the commission regulate rates, but it also was empowered to set standards of service and determine standards on measures of quality. If a company was not providing adequate service the commission could order it to bring its services up to standard.

So the commission could have adequate knowledge of each public utility it regulated, it was given the power to prescribe a uniform system of accounts. Not only was each company required to adhere to the commission's system, but it was forbidden to keep any other books or records not approved by the commission. In setting rates, the commission was to provide for depreciation of each type of property used. At intervals, and in such force as it might direct, the commission could require the public utility firms to furnish reports covering their operations. This information, in addition to providing a basis for the commission's regulatory activity, was to be made available to the public. Hence, both the public utility companies and the commission which regulated them were to be operated under the light of public scrutiny.

The commission was given authority to inspect the books, accounts, papers, and any records of the companies it was to regulate. It could require the attendance of witnesses and the display of books and records at any of its hearings. No person was to be excused from testifying on the grounds that to do so would incriminate him, but if he did testify, he was not subject to any penalty for what he disclosed.

Perhaps the most significant feature of the law was the introduction of the indeterminate permit. This type of franchise had been used in a few cities, but Wisconsin was the first to introduce it on a statewide basis.[7] Unlike the usual franchise, which had a specific expiration date, the indeterminate permit was revocable only upon purchase of the property by a municipality for just compensation. Thus, the problem of whether a franchise should be for a long or short period was solved. It was to be for an indefinite period, during which the company's investment would be protected, while the public would be protected from unreasonable rates. If a

---

7 "In 1907 the indeterminate form was introduced into state public laws, largely because disinterested students of the subject like Milo R. Maltbie of New York and Professor John R. Commons of the University of Wisconsin advocated its adoption." Glaeser, p. 293.

municipality wished to buy its public utility company's property, the Railroad Commission determined the compensation. If the company was dissatisfied with the commission's decision it could appeal its case to the courts.

The law did not make the indeterminate permit compulsory for existing companies, but rather it permitted them to surrender their existing franchises to obtain such permits. To provide incentive for them to do this the law provided that when a company had an indeterminate permit no permit could be given to a second company unless it first obtained a certificate of public convenience and necessity from the commission. Apparently, it was assumed that the commission was not likely to issue such certificates. Consequently, a company with an indeterminate permit was assured it would have a monopoly. On the other hand, a company without it had no such protection. The municipalities could create competition by issuing additional franchises. Furthermore, they could refuse to renew expiring franchises. In most cases, companies found it advantageous to accept the indeterminate permit.

After July 11, 1907, all new franchises for public utility companies in Wisconsin were to be indeterminate permits. Following Wisconsin's example, a number of other states adopted this innovation. Among them were Indiana, Ohio, Minnesota, New York, Illinois, and California.

Most of the procedures for enforcing the Railroad Commission's orders under the new law were the same as under the 1905 law.[8] Orders were to take effect twenty days after being issued, unless the commission set some other date. If any public utility or other interested party were dissatisfied with an order it could bring action within ninety days in the Dane County circuit court. By confining jurisdiction to this court, the commission was assured that its decisions would be reviewed only by judges who were informed on public utility problems. Furthermore, reducing the number of reviewing judges provided greater uniformity of decisions.

As in the railroad law, cases involving the commission were to have precedence over other civil actions. Before any new evidence could be presented to the circuit court the commission was to be given time to enlarge its investigation by further hearings. On the basis of all evidence, old or new, the commission could then amend or rescind its order. Rates set by the commission were to be con-

---

8 See this chapter, p. 92.

sidered prima facie lawful. Any party opposing the commission's order was required to show by clear and satisfactory evidence that it was unlawful and unreasonable before the court could set it aside. The law placed the burden of proof with the parties opposing such an order. From a decision of the circuit court, appeal could be made to the state Supreme Court within sixty days. Thus, all the way along the line, all legal action was to be expedited to prevent hindrance by harassing litigation.

For violation of the act or orders of the commission, penalties were specified. Such penalties consisted of fines for departures from published schedules, acceptance or giving of rebates, refusal to supply the commission with information, or interfering with the apparatus or appliances of the commission. To ensure prompt compliance with the act, each day's violation was to be considered a separate offense. In all cases where a public utility company was guilty of a violation, any injured third party could sue the company for treble damages.

Thus, the law created a modern-type administrative commission with ample power to regulate the companies under its jurisdiction. It became a model for many other states when they enacted laws to regulate public utilities. John A. Kurtz of the Missouri Public Service Commission, in 1923, wrote:

> Not until the 20th century, however, was the jurisdiction of state commissions extended to the regulation of local public utilities. The idea was ushered in by the recreation in 1907 of the Wisconsin Commission giving it jurisdiction over railroads, telephones and telegraphs, water and electric companies. New York and other states followed soon thereafter, until at the present time practically every state in the Union has a public service commission, with full power to regulate not only practices, but also the rates and security issues of both statewide and local utilities. Nine states of the Union have established their commissions by constitutional provisions, and thereby placed these quasi-judicial bodies beyond the pale of legislative power to destroy.
>
> We are prone to forget the reasons for the change. It was apparent to those who carried on the affairs of the state at the time, that the practices and rates of these recently developed and powerful corporations could not be fairly and intelligently regulated by technically inexperienced bodies like legislatures or city boards of aldermen; that on principle at least it appeared necessary to create a body which would become expert in its knowledge of the subject and which would be in continuous session to act at any time that it appeared from investigation to be necessary to protect the rights of the public. These bodies were given wide powers and were authorized to employ the necessary engineers, accountants, rate ex-

perts, and other technical men to make investigations and ferret out the true facts. To these commissions, by statute or constitutional provisions as the case may be, had been delegated the legislative power to regulate.[9]

Eliot Jones also picks 1907 as the year that marked the beginning of effective public utility regulation by state commissions. Both New York and Wisconsin enacted regulatory laws in that year, but he chose the Wisconsin law as an example for his textbook on public utility economics. Furthermore, he declared that the law was so carefully drawn that very few subsequent changes were necessary. He said:

> . . . By our description, in some detail, of Wisconsin's Public utility acts we have indicated our belief in the importance of wise and comprehensive legislation as a fundamental basis for public utility regulation.[10]

The law in Wisconsin met his requirements.

Yet this Wisconsin law Commons drafted was more than just a milestone in public utility regulation. It demonstrated a technique for regulating private business that was adopted throughout the country. Although the administrative commission was slow to develop in the federal government, despite the early creation of the Interstate Commerce Commission (1887), it was fully developed in Wisconsin from the beginning. Both the railroad and public utility laws gave the Railroad Commission the full powers characteristic of the modern administrative commission. This technique of government spread to the other states and in time to the federal government.

The Wisconsin Industrial Commission

The second of the three important Wisconsin laws in which Commons had a leading role in formulating and enacting created the Industrial Commission. It came as the culmination of a nation-wide program to install a program for compensating injured workmen. Prominent as Commons was in this campaign, he shared the leadership with many others. What Commons did that was distinctive was to broaden the program into a comprehensive scheme of safety regulation combined with compensation. He drafted Wisconsin's "Safe Employment Statute," which created the Industrial Commission that administered all the state's labor laws.[11]

9 John A. Kurtz, "State Public Service Commissions," in Freund, pp. 141-142.
10 Jones and Bigham, p. 187.
11 Chapter 50 of the Laws of Wisconsin, 1911, created an Industrial Accident Board to administer workmen's compensation. The Industrial Commission created in the Commons-drafted Chapter 485, Laws of Wisconsin, 1911, superseded this board.

Industrial accidents had been taking a toll that was compared to war casualties.[12] The victims and their families, however, in the majority of cases, were unable to obtain adequate compensation. By 1911 powerful voices demanded that something be done to end such obvious injustice. For the previous third of a century various states had attempted through legislation to force employers to take safety precautions, but the laws had a serious common defect. Under the prevailing legal concepts each safety device, safety rule, and precaution had to be mentioned specifically in a law. An inspector observing a dangerous condition was powerless to force an employer to correct it unless the law specifically gave him power to do so. Because technology was changing rapidly, safety regulations could become out of date rapidly. While old regulations became obsolete, needed new ones had to wait for legislative action. Sometimes the wait was extensive, as the task of getting bills passed before a legislature is never speedy. In many cases the ability to judge need for specific devices and safety rules necessitated special technical knowledge legislators did not have. In other cases, pressure from employers fearing additional costs often delayed action.

If employers continued to violate safety statutes, factory inspectors were required to initiate legal proceedings. In court the inspectors were the prosecution's witnesses, and as such, had to pit their knowledge and credibility against defense attorneys and witnesses. Opposing witnesses might outnumber the inspectors and outmatch them in technical knowledge of manufacturing conditions. Such knowledge was crucial because the court decided not only if the laws were broken, but also if they were reasonable. Under such circumstances the enforcement of safety laws was both uncertain and clumsy.

Laws governing employers' liability in case of industrial accidents or illnesses were equally unsatisfactory. An injured workman or the family of a killed workman usually were unable to obtain any compensation, even though the injury caused destitution. And in the infrequent cases where compensation was obtained, the payment was either inadequate or received after considerable delay —often after a prolonged and uncertain court fight.

The basis of the liability laws was in the labor contract, under common law. In such a contract employers and employees agreed to certain explicit conditions, such as wages, hours, and work to be

---

12 Downey, p. 1.

performed. Other conditions were considered to be implied under common law. One of these was that the employer would provide a reasonably safe place to work. If the employer provided tools they were to be reasonably safe. He was also duty-bound to exercise reasonable care in hiring agents and employees to work for him. So that the work would be relatively safe, the employer was obligated to provide suitable and reasonable rules for the carrying on of work in his establishment. He must warn his employees of any dangers, and especially warn and instruct any youthful or inexperienced workers.

The word "reasonable" had a very special meaning. It implied the usual or general practice of the average prudent individual in an industry. If the prevailing safety practices were low, then the standard of reasonable practice also was low. For an injured employee to obtain a legal claim from his employer he had to prove that his employer was negligent in the performance of his duties and that he himself was not. In any accident the fault had to be determined. If the negligence of the employer directly led to the accident, the employer was liable. In any other case there was no responsibility.

The difficulty with the liability laws was that the majority of industrial accidents legally were not the fault of the employer. They were the result of inherent risks of the industry. As such, they were to be borne by the employee unless the employer gratuitously extended aid. However, the employee seldom was able to bear the burdens that accompanied injury. In most cases the possibility of receiving pay (before the accident) high enough to compensate for risks was a lawyer's "legal fiction." Men who could get no other jobs took the risky ones at pay seldom higher than for safer jobs.[13] Disabling injuries or death of a wage earner usually made his family destitute or dependent on others.

When cases were brought to court, juries often sided with the injured workman, regardless of the legal liability. Knowing this, a group of lawyers sprang up to handle such accident cases on a contingency basis. Although many of the jury awards ultimately were

---

13 "It is apparent that the majority of them (workmen engaged in dangerous occupations) are not earning enough to enable them adequately to insure against accident at high rates necessitated by the nature of their occupation. That wages are not adjusted 'to cover risk' in the actual industrial world of to-day is a matter of common knowledge.

"The testimony before the Commission (studying Employers' Liability in New York, (1909)) of those familiar with the condition of the working classes also brought out the fact that the risk of the industry is not considered in determining a man's wages." Eastman, pp. 282, 283.

set aside when appealed to higher courts, enough were sustained
to provide substantial fees.

Although odds were against the winning of a court award by
a workman, a few did collect comfortable sums. Consequently,
most employers preferred covering their risks through liability insurance, even though it was expensive.[14] Liability insurance had
other drawbacks in addition to expense. It removed the employer
from a position in which he might be able to help an injured employee. Any help on his part might prejudice the case, which the
insurance company might have to fight. Consequently, the workman had to bargain with an impersonal insurance company that
had no interest in him. If the workman did not settle for a modest
sum he often found it necessary to conduct a bitter court fight that
might last for years. In the meantime, he might be almost destitute.
If such an employee had been a deserving worker, many of the
other employees felt an injustice had been committed. Although the
employer might be able to relieve himself of legal liability through
insurance, he could not always prevent poor morale among his
workers.

Industrialization created a discrepancy between the logic of
the common law rules of employer's liability and the layman's idea
of justice. At first, those who would reform the law sought to modify the common law.[15] States began to pass laws modifying the liability of employers for workers' accidents. While this increased the
possibility that an injured employee might collect from his employer, it did not reconcile the two conflicting systems of logic. As
long as the fault had to be placed on the employer before he was
liable for damages, any considerable liberalization of the law for
the benefit of the injured workmen required a torturing of the
logic of the law.

What was needed was a new concept of liability. A new concept did develop—that the cost of accidents and compensation to
the injured should be considered a part of the costs of an industry.
It was advocated that an injured employee should be entitled to
compensation from his employer regardless of who was to blame.
Because it was believed that industry costs eventually are passed on
to the consumers, the employer, except in temporary or isolated
instances, actually would not be deprived of any property. Hence,

---

14 Only 28% of the money paid by employers for insurance actually reached the injured employees, Commons and Andrews, p. 362.
15 Downey, pp. 143-46.

the ideas of "due process" and "equal protection under the law" again could be reconciled with the laymen's sense of justice.

While reformers in America attempted to modify the employers' liability laws, a number of European countries enacted laws providing for compensation for injured workmen regardless of whose negligence caused the accident. Germany under Bismarck led with its law in 1884, Austria followed in 1887, Hungary in 1891, Norway in 1894, Finland in 1895, and Great Britain in 1897. "By 1910 practically every European country including Russia, had adopted some system of workmen's compensation."[16]

Maryland passed the first workman's compensation law in America in 1902, but two years later it was declared unconstitutional. Several states created commissions to study the liability laws in the years that followed. However, the first legislation came when Congress, under the urgings of President Theodore Roosevelt, passed a law in 1908 providing for compensation for federal employees.

In 1906 a number of reformers, consisting of academic economists, law professors, administrators of labor laws, union officials, employers, and social workers formed the American Association for Labor Legislation. Of this organization, Abraham Epstein declared:

> Of all the organizations active in this movement the American Association for Labor Legislation deserves special credit. This Association did the most to procure adequate compensation legislation and, in innumerable ways, has valiently fought for these laws for a quarter of a century.[17]

John R. Commons was one of the important leaders of the association and was described by E. E. Witte as, " . . . in a very real sense also its founder."[18] At the first annual meeting in 1907 the association elected him its secretary. For several years thereafter

---

16 Harry Weiss, "Employers' Liability and Workmen's Compensation," Lescohier and Brandeis, p. 570.

17 Epstein, p. 593.

18 Witte, *John B. Andrews Memorial Symposium*, p. 8.
Richard Martin Lyon writing on the Association disagrees with this position. "While it appears inaccurate to regard Professor Commons in a very real sense . . . its founder, as asserted by Dr. E. E. Witte at the Wisconsin Symposium, there is no question as to the goodwill which Commons' name created for the American Association. This is documented best in a letter from President Farnam to the Wisconsin scholar, dated February 18, 1909: 'Your idea of resigning and letting Mr. Andrews take your place does not strike me at all favorably. It would, I think, only create confusion in the public mind to have you disappear from the secretaryship, and we need your name very much. I am quite willing to give him the title executive secretary and think it would be much better to let him try what he can do under you for the rest of the year and then if you insist on withdrawing, let him take your place." p. 42.

he maintained the association's office in a corner of his own at the University of Wisconsin and installed his student, John B. Andrews, as executive secretary. In 1910 the association moved its headquarters to New York City so that its influence could be brought to bear more directly in the more industrial areas. However, Commons maintained close ties with the organization.

During its early years the association spent a considerable part of its efforts on workmen's compensation.[19] At the first two annual meetings a number of papers on the subject were presented. It devoted the third annual meeting to constitutional problems of labor law. Until such problems could be solved, no legislation could be sustained.

By 1909 the campaign for workmen's compensation reached the point where three important states appointed commissions to study the problem. The officers of the association then worked with the members of commissions. John B. Andrews, the executive secretary, reported:

> Three states, Minnesota, New York, and Wisconsin, had special legislative committees at work on the subject. Secretary Commons made a trip to Minnesota where he discussed plans in detail with members of that Commission; and the Executive Secretary, while on a trip through the East, urged upon several members of the New York Commission, the importance of uniformity of investigation. Fortunately both the President and Secretary of our New York State Branch were added to this commission by Governor Hughes, while in Wisconsin, frequent conferences at the headquarters of the Association aided still more in bringing about the desired result. In June, Secretary Commons wrote to Mr. Mercer of the Minnesota Commission, urging him to call an Interstate Conference on Workmen's Compensation. The call was issued on July 14th. Thus the way was paved for a meeting which took place at the end of July (29-31st) in Atlantic City. The results of this conference, which was attended by members of the Minnesota, Wisconsin, and New York Commissions, by officials of the State and National Governments, and by experts from various insurance corporations, were most satisfactory.[20]

In Atlantic City a permanent National Conference on Workmen's Compensation was organized. It met three times in 1910—in January in Washington, and in Chicago in June and November. By the last conference, commissions from ten states sent representatives. By joining together, these commissions were able to iron

---

19 Pierce.
20 *Proceedings, Third Annual Meeting of the American Association for Labor Legislation,* New York, 1909, p. 19.

out many of their difficulties and smooth the way for effective
action.

By 1910 a number of powerful groups joined the American
Association for Labor Legislation in its work for workmen's
compensation legislation. Labor, which at first had not been entirely sympathetic with the movement, committed itself to the program in 1909.[21] Even the National Association of Manufacturers
appointed a committee whose studies committed it to workmen's
compensation. The National Civic Federation created a special department on Compensation for Industrial Accidents, which actively helped to keep the program before the people. It also prepared a "model bill" to aid legislatures in preparing laws on the
subject. Important among the groups newly won to the movement
was the American Bar Association. Finally, the American Academy of Political and Social Science devoted its entire 1911 meeting
to the subject.[22] It secured numerous speakers, many of whom
were important backers of the movement.

The first success came in 1910 when New York enacted two
laws on workmen's compensation. One law was a compulsory act
covering eight dangerous occupations. The other strengthened employers' liability, but permitted employers and employees to agree
to accept a workmen's compensation system instead of employers' liability. The framers made the program compulsory only in
the dangerous trades so that the law would have a better chance of
being upheld as constitutional. Under the doctrine of the time, regulation of dangerous trades, they believed, would come under the
"police power" of the states.

The New York compulsory act had a short life. The New
York Court of Appeals (Ives versus South Buffalo Railway Company) decided "the liability sought to be imposed upon the employ-

---

21 Previously the labor leaders had preferred strengthening employers' liability laws.
The prospect of large legal settlements for injured workers appeared more attractive than
modest insurance payments. Furthermore the leadership suspected any state operated pro-
gram. By 1909 the failure of the employers' liability laws had become apparent to them
and the leaders of the A. F. of L. endorsed the principles of workmen's compensation.
Rubinow, *Social Insurance*, pp. 156-163.
Lorwin, pp. 408-9.
American Association for Labor Legislation, General Administrative Council Meeting
Chicago, April 10, 1909.
Labor deserves very little credit for any protective labor legislation or social security.
Elizabeth Brandeis wrote that in regard to protective labor legislation, "Most of this
legislation was the result of the efforts of middle class humanitarian reformers working
in small but remarkably effective organizations, especially the National Child Labor Com
mittee, the National Consumers League, and the American Association for Labor Legisla
tion." Elizabeth Brandeis, "Protective Legislation" in Derber and Young, p. 196.
22 "Risks in Modern Industry," *Annals of the American Academy of Political and
Social Science,,* pp. 23-278.

ers is a taking of property without due process of law, and the statute is therefore void."[23] It imputed fault to the employers when
there was none, and took away their property without their con-
sent. As to the voluntary workmen's compensation law in New
York, it became a dead letter when employers and employees
failed to elect to come under its provisions.

But the Ives case did not stop the workmen's compensation
movement. By 1911 ten states enacted compensation laws, and nine
more legislatures created commissions to study the problem that
year.[24]

In Wisconsin agitation for workmen's compensation had been
going on since 1905. In that year F. Brockhausen, secretary-
treasurer of the Wisconsin State Federation of Labor and a member of the legislature, introduced a bill to that effect.[25] During the
1907 and 1909 sessions of the legislature he again submitted similar bills.

In the meantime, Commons and his group in the American
Association for Labor Legislation pushed their campaign both in
Wisconsin and in other states. In January of 1909 at a "Smoker
on Industrial Insurance," sponsored by the Merchants' and Manufacturers' Association of Milwaukee, Commons outlined a tenta-
tive plan. He stressed the need for a special committee to represent
all groups in formulating the plans. Because of the constitutional
difficulties, he said, the system of workmen's compensation insurance should be voluntary. Release from liability laws was what he
offered as an inducement to the employers.

Speaking with Commons was J. D. Beck, the commissioner
of the Wisconsin Bureau of Labor and Industrial Statistics, Max
Otto Lorenz of the same bureau, and Professor W. W. Cook, a
law professor of the University of Wisconsin.[26] One of the jus-
tices of the Wisconsin Supreme Court, who was to be a speaker
but was unable to attend, sent word that he favored remedying the
employers' liability laws.

Soon after his election in 1910, Governor McGovern asked
Commons to draft laws for workmen's compensation insurance and

---

23 Ives vs. South Buffalo Railway Co., 201 N. Y. 271; 94 N. E., 431, on March 24,
1911.
24 States enacting laws: California, Illinois, Kansas, Massachusetts, Nevada, New
Hampshire, New Jersey, Ohio, Washington, Wisconsin. *American Labor Legislation Review*, Vol. I, October, 1911.
25 Altmeyer, p. 25.
26 The Merchants' and Manufacturers' Association of Milwaukee Bulletin No. 24,
January, 1909.

accident prevention. Commons and his student, Francis Bird, joined Charles McCarthy in the Legislative Reference Library to work on the proposed legislation. These three, while working closely with other members of the American Association for Labor Legislation in other states, brought together employers, union people, safety experts, and anyone else who would contribute to the final results.

Commons' innovation was to combine the workmen's compensation program with the safety legislation. Previously, safety regulations were forced upon the employers by factory inspectors. Commons believed that coercion should be replaced by giving the employers an inducement. The state or the insurance company should charge the employers in proportion to their employees losses in wages from accidents. Then, instead of "police officer" factory inspectors, the state should use the safety experts to help the employers save money. Education, always a vital part of any Commons' project, was to be a prominent feature.

To replace the piecemeal factory safety legislation, he proposed to make use of the same device he used with the public utility commission. An administrative commission would have the power to make and enforce safety rules. However, at this point, he and the other framers of the law faced a constitutional problem. They agreed that the legislature had the power to authorize a commission to determine what would be reasonable standards of safety. They also agreed that the legislature could give the commission the power to enforce such standards. But the problem arose over the necessity of including the word "reasonable." McCarthy informed them that the word "reasonable" meant customary or ordinary practices.[27] If the commission could order only customary practices, it would be powerless to raise the standards of safety. Yet, McCarthy pointed out to his colleagues, without the word "reasonable," the courts would declare the law unconstitutional as taking property without "due process of law."

Commons had his student, Bird, work on the problem. After much research in law encyclopedias and court cases, Bird, according to Commons, came out with what was a brilliant solution. His definition of "reasonableness" included ". . . the highest degree of safety, health, well-being of employees, etc., that the nature of the industry or employment would reasonably permit."[28] Such a

---

27 McCarthy and his aides in the Legislative Reference Library, as usual, provided the technical wording while Commons and his students developed the concepts.
28 Commons, *Myself, op. cit.,* p. 155.

lefinition promised to be, and turned out to be, the key to effective safety legislation.

While Commons was working on the safe employment statute, he legislative interim committee worked on the workmen's compensation act. The legislature in 1909 had appointed Senators A. W. Sanborn, E. T. Fairchild, J. J. Blaine and Assemblymen Wallace Ingalls, George Drew, Walter Eagan, and Clarence Culbertson as members of the committee.[29] For counsel, the committee retained Harry Butler, a Madison attorney.

After considerable work by all concerned, the Wisconsin legislature, on May 3, 1911, passed the law authorizing workmen's compensation insurance.[30] It was to be administered by an Industrial Accident Board of three members—Joseph D. Beck, who had headed the Wisconsin Bureau of Labor and Industrial Statistics; Charles H. Crownhart, a lawyer; and John R. Commons. In July his board was superseded by the Wisconsin Industrial Commission, which had the same membership but wider powers.[31] It was to administer all the labor laws of the state. In the beginning the two most important were those providing workmen's compensation and safety regulations.

Wisconsin chose the elective form of workmen's compensation because many people, including Commons, believed that a compulsory law would be unconstitutional. The Ives case in New York seemed to confirm the opinions he expressed in 1909 before the Merchants' and Manufacturers' Association of Milwaukee. Furthermore, all other states at that time, except Washington, adopted the elective form.

Employers could choose to come under the law to avoid their common law liabilities to employees who also accepted the law. If they failed to accept the law, they could be sued by injured employees. But their chances of winning their cases would be diminished because the law stripped them of their common law defenses if they had four or more employees.[32] On the other hand, by accepting the law their liabilities were limited and could be covered by insurance.

Under the law, an injured workman was entitled to compensation based upon a percentage of his previous average earn-

---

29 Altmeyer, p. 25.
30 Laws of Wisconsin, 1911, Chapter 50.
31 Laws of Wisconsin, 1911, Chapter 485.
32 This provision was in a separate bill so that if it were declared unconstitutional, the entire law would not be invalidated.

ings. The percentage varied with the seriousness of the injury and was determined by the Industrial Commission. The awards were subject to review by the circuit court of Dane County, but the law limited the discretion of the courts.

Employers were to insure themselves against liability in any form of approved insurance they desired. Large employers with strong enough financial resources to meet almost any claim without the help of insurance would be exempt from buying insurance. It was expected that rates would vary in proportion to the size of the insurance claims companies had to pay to injured employees. Employers with good safety records would find their insurance premiums less than those with poorer records.

Commons envisioned a safety campaign that would reduce the industrial accident rates in Wisconsin sufficiently to make the compensation insurance cheaper than the liability insurance. During the first two years after the passage of workmen's compensation legislation, the private insurance companies charged more for compensation insurance than for common law liability insurance.[3] However, on September 2, 1911, a mutual insurance company, the Employers' Mutual Liability Insurance of Wausau, Wisconsin, was founded. It charged forty percent less than the rates quoted by private insurance companies on compensation insurance. Also its rates on such insurance were less than those charged by private insurance companies on full common law liability insurance. After two years' experience and competition, the private companies settled on rates for compensation insurance at ten percent under those on common law liability.

To bring down the accident rate in Wisconsin, the Industrial Commission overhauled existing safety regulations. To aid in this process, it established advisory committees, including employers, union leaders, and experts. Commons had inserted in the law the provision that the commission could appoint advisers without compensation. As a member of the commission, Commons chose as his particular concern the organization of the advisory committees. For some time he had been harboring the idea that important labor reforms are best devised by compromises among the interested parties. He had followed the practice of consulting all in

33 "The 'Conference' stock companies did not promulgate rates for compensation insurance until September 1, 1911. Their rates were fixed in combination and averaged more than two and one-half times those for common-law liability. Inasmuch as they had previously doubled their common-law liability rates, . . . the rates were practically prohibitory." Altmeyer, pp. 77-78.

erested parties whenever he drafted any legislation. By making his final proposals joint products of those interested in the legislation, he maximized its chances of acceptance, both before and after passage.

During Commons' membership, the commission adopted the practice of referring all proposed safety regulations first to an advisory committee. If the committee could agree on the regulations, the commission would adopt them. Apparently, the procedure worked satisfactorily, because after twenty years of operation, A. J. Altmeyer, the secretary of the commission, claimed:

> Moreover, the commission invariably followed the recommendation of its advisory committees. With the exception of one or two orders, the members of the advisory committees have always been unanimous in their recommendations, all differences of opinion having been reconciled and a working solution reached in the committee meetings.[34]

After an advisory committee recommended a safety rule, the commission held public hearings to ferret out any possible objections. Then, if the committee was convinced the regulation was reasonable it would issue a general order effective at some future date. Until that time it would use publicity to bring the order to the attention of all who might be concerned.

If an employer objected to a safety regulation he could appeal to the commission for a modification. If, after hearings, he was denied the requested modification, he could take his case to the Dane County circuit court. Employees or employers objecting to compensation awards could follow the same procedure. In either case, the court accepted the commission's findings of fact as conclusive. A decision was set aside only if the commission had acted in excess of its powers, if any award was procured by fraud, or if the findings of fact did not support the award or need for a ruling. As a matter of practice, the courts almost never questioned the reasonableness of the commission's safety rulings.[35]

Commons believed that education was as important as the enforcement of the laws. Besides turning the factory inspectors into "safety experts" to help save the employers' money, he also launched a safety program. He induced the commission to hire C. W. Price of International Harvester to head the program. At first he was hired on a loan basis from the company, but finally he was persuaded to take a full-time position with the commission.

---

34 *Ibid.*, p. 125.
35 *Ibid.*, p. 149.

Commons said that Price ". . . knew how to get technicians to work for safety and welfare. He was a whirlwind of energy, sagacity, and persuasiveness."[36] All over the state he organized safety committees, and he organized a statewide Conference of Safety.

The combined effects of the safety campaigns, the new safety regulations, and the workmen's compensation paid off in reduced accidents. Price declared that accidental deaths in Wisconsin were cut down sixty-one percent during the five years he worked for the commission.[37] He said at least half the credit should go to the "stimulus which the compensation law gave to the whole safety movement."[38] After his service with the commission Price became the director of the National Safety Council, an organization he and Commons were instrumental in founding.

The Wisconsin law had a considerable impact on the national scene. In the field of workmen's compensation it was just another law backed by the American Association for Labor Legislation; but the use of an administrative commission as a technique in creating and enforcing safety regulations was an innovation of great importance. At the 1911 convention of the American Association for Labor Legislation Commons explained his new creation. The conference subject was "The Prevention and Reporting of Industrial Accidents." After the earlier speakers described the difficulties with the laws then existing, Commons climaxed the meeting by describing the Wisconsin Industrial Commission and its safety program.

The discussion following Commons' talk demonstrated the interest of the audience. Henry Seager, a Columbia University professor, declared:

> The Wisconsin plan, described by Professor Commons, must appeal to everyone who has learned by experience how impossible it is to embody in rigid statutes the regulations called for by the complex and everchanging industrial conditions of today.[39]

Professor Seager went on to say that in New York it was feared such a delegation of power by the legislature would be declared unconstitutional. Others at the meeting expressed the same fear. However, Commons then explained the difference between the way his law was constructed and the way the uncon-

---

36 Commons, *Myself,* p. 161.
37 Quoted in *American Labor Legislation Review,* Vol. XVL, p. 190.
38 *Ibid.*
39 *American Labor Legislation Review,* Vol. I, December, 1911, p. 102.

stitutional laws were worded. He argued that for a law to be constitutional the granting of discretionary powers had to be within
certain limits and that it had to have procedures safeguarding
constitutional rights.

After Commons had shown the way past the constitutional
barriers, other important states followed Wisconsin's lead. *The
American Labor Legislation Review* reported in 1913:

> Of special significance in the labor legislation of this year are
> the laws of five states, California, Massachusetts, New York, Ohio,
> and Pennsylvania, extending the commission form of factory legisla-
> tion as adopted in Wisconsin two years ago. In these states the
> legislatures have laid down the law in a broad way, and as rapidly
> as circumstances permit, the commissions or industrial boards may
> fill in the detail through administrative orders.[40]

Commons helped spread the idea of the Industrial Commission by publishing several articles about it. The first was his 1911
speech to the American Association for Labor Legislation, which
printed it in their *Review*.[41] Two years later, he further explained
the commission idea in an article in *The Survey*, entitled, "Constructive Investigation and the Wisconsin Industrial Commission."[42] When he published his book, *Labor and Administration,*
he included reprints of both papers.[43]

In addition to writing on the subject, he also appeared before
the legislatures, or legislative committees of Ohio, New York, and
Colorado. Each of these states, plus many others, adopted his plan
for administration of safety regulations. Governor Cox of Ohio,
who was interested in much of the progressive legislation in Wisconsin, invited him to Ohio to explain his program.[44] In most
states the officials charged with administering labor laws belonged
to the American Association for Labor Legislation and were thus
in contact with him and other leaders of the association. If anyone could be said to be the leader of the movement to create industrial commissions, it would be Commons.

Important though the administrative commission was in the
field of safety regulation, the compensation program for injured
workmen was even more significant. In this latter movement Commons was a leader but not the innovator. The significance of workmen's compensation was that it opened the door to further wel-

40 *Ibid.,* Vol. III, October, 1913, p. 301.
41 *American Labor Legislation Review,* Vol. I, December, 1911, p. 61.
42 Commons, *The Survey,* January 4, 1913, p. 440.
43 Commons, *Labor and Administration.*
44 Cox, pp. 137, 163.

fare legislation. If workmen could be compensated because they were injured in their work, why shouldn't they be paid if they were sick from other causes, or if they were unemployed? Certainly they would be equally unfortunate and equally blameless in many cases. Individual responsibility would decrease, while social responsibility grew to accept more welfare state concepts and legislation.

The Unemployment Compensation Law

The last of the three most significant Commons-sponsored laws of Wisconsin created in 1932 the first state unemployment compensation program.[45] Like the law creating the Industrial Commission, its impact reached far beyond the borders of Wisconsin. Today its principles are embedded in most of the unemployment compensation laws in the country. Commons' students and colleagues in the movement designed the national law in such a way that it preserved the Wisconsin law and encouraged other states to follow its example.

Acceptance of the principle of unemployment compensation implied accepting the idea that the principle of individual responsibility should not bar aid to the unfortunate. The individual states and local government had always had poor laws to care for the indigent, but they had never, except in emergencies, accepted responsibility for the able-bodied unemployed. Such responsibility was clearly beyond the recognized scope of the federal government.

By the time of the first unemployment compensation legislation in 1932, the principle of individual responsibility was under severe strain. Local governments, with their antiquated laws concerned with poverty, struggled to meet the crisis arising from mass unemployment. When they faltered, the states assumed the burden. Finally, the federal government under a reluctant President accepted the responsibility for providing money to the hard-pressed states.[46] Shortly afterwards, a new President led the nation into acceptance of the responsibility to provide relief for the unemployed and to use its powers to combat unemployment. Finally, a few years after the passage of the Wisconsin law, the national

---

45 Wisconsin Statutes, Chapter 108, (Chapter 20, Laws of Special Session 1931-32).

46 President Hoover, in a vain effort to balance the budget, vigorously resisted the assumption by the federal government of the responsibility for providing relief for the unemployed. However, when it was apparent that state and local agencies were reaching the end of their resources in trying to feed the unemployed, he agreed to loans to the states by the R.F.C., so that they could continue to carry this responsibility. Broadus Mitchell, pp. 82-120.

government passed a social security law that provided both unemployment compensation and old-age pensions. The U. S. did not quite have a "welfare state," but the old laissez-faire individualistic order was gone.

Commons had long favored complete protection for workers against economic hardship. In his *Distribution of Wealth,* written in 1893, he insisted that the right to employment was a fundamental right. He claimed that each person has the "right to security in the tenure of employment against arbitrary discharge, as long as one proves efficient and honest," and that the unemployed have the right to work furnished by the government.[47] In 1896 he advocated municipal public works to alleviate unemployment.[48] A few years later, in 1905, in his *Trade Unionism and Labor Problems,* he included an article by W. F. Willoughby of Princeton University on "Insurance Against Unemployment."[49]

His increasing interest in unemployment insurance is mirrored in the successive editions of his textbook, *Principles of Labor Legislation.*[50] This volume, which he wrote jointly with John Andrews, came out in four editions, 1916, 1920, 1927, and 1936. The treatment in the first edition covered just five and one-half pages; by 1936 the authors used twenty-three pages.[51]

In the first edition, they wrote:

> Finally, the destitution due to unemployment, until recently considered a matter of purely individual concern, or at best as an occasion for charitable activity, is now beginning to be recognized as an evil which must be met by the coordinated forethought of society as a whole. The demoralization of individuals and communities by prolonged and widespread deprivation of income due to involuntary idleness, it is now generally agreed, should no longer be allowed to continue unchecked.
> . . . Here again the collective method of insurance has demonstrated its superiority.[52]

Commons and Andrews were pointing to the European picture where unemployment compensation had been accepted for some time. They believed European experience demonstrated a superior method of preventing destitution from unemployment. They urged that it be extended to American industry.

---

47 Commons, *Distribution of Wealth,* p. 81.
48 Commons, *American Federationist.*
49 Commons, *Trade Unionism and Labor Problems,* 1905.
50 Commons and Andrews.
51 Total pages in the 1916 edition were 464; the 1936 edition contained 534.
52 Commons and Andrews, p. 49 .

Commons' experience in 1919 and 1920 increased his interest in the unemployment problem to the extent that he became a leader in the movement to solve it. From July to September, 1919, he visited thirty industrial establishments with seven of his students. Their purpose was to study what they called industrial government in America. But their study resulted in more than *Industrial Government,* a book on apparatus for formulating and implementing personnel policies. During this study Commons observed the effects of the postwar inflation and subsequent depression on labor relations.

He reacted to the depression in two ways. First, he began a study of the cure for unemployment. This led him to study the banking system and to write a series of articles on banking policy. He even became president of the National Monetary Association, which was organized in 1922 as the successor to Irving Fisher's Stable Money League.[53] Besides writing articles on monetary policy, he explained banking policy before the 1927 Strong Committee of the Congress, which employed him as staff expert.[54] His interest in the problem of business cycles also led to his participation as an associate director in the National Bureau of Economic Research between 1920 and 1928.

His views were not novel. He believed that monetary controls of the Federal Reserve System should be used to stabilize the price level. He thought our economy was inherently unstable and that price movements, once started, tend to move either to an inflationary boom or into a deflationary spiral. Like other economists of his time, he claimed that depressions might be prevented if the booms preceding them could be moderated.

His second reaction to the 1920 depression was the drafting of an unemployment compensation bill in that year, with the help of some of his students. In 1921 Senator Huber introduced this bill into the Wisconsin legislature. Although the bill failed to become law, it set the pattern for future bills offered before other state legislatures. When local organizations in Pennsylvania requested the American Association for Labor Legislation to draft a bill on the subject, it submitted one similar to the Wisconsin bill.[55]

---

53 Irving Fisher named Commons as one of the eighteen foremost world authorities on money. *Wisconsin State Journal,* Madison, Wisc., Dec. 26, 1933.
54 "Hearings," *Congressional Record,* 69th Congress, pp. 3834-3848.
55 "Growth of the Job Insurance Program," *American Labor Legislation Review,* Vol. XXIII, p. 146.

For the next decade Commons' bill was reintroduced with modifications at each session of the legislature in Wisconsin. Finally, in 1931, when Harold Groves, a Commons' student and a professor at the University of Wisconsin, as well as a member of the legislature, presented another modified version of it, it met with success. Governor Philip LaFollette signed the bill on January 15, 1932.

This first unemployment compensation law came only after a long campaign by Commons and his colleagues in the American Association for Labor Legislation. The association campaigned not only in Wisconsin, but everywhere it could win a response. Using Commons' bill as a model, it drafted bills which were introduced into the Pennsylvania and Massachusetts legislatures in 1922. The Minnesota legislature considered a similar bill in 1923, 1925, and 1927. Although none of these bills became law, they were part of the constant pressure of the association to sell the unemployment compensation program. In its publication, the *American Labor Legislation Review,* and in its meetings, it kept the idea alive in spite of prosperity and public apathy.

During the twenties what discussion continued centered on Wisconsin's Huber Bill. Allen B. Forsberg's debater's handbook, *Selected Articles on Unemployment Insurance,* demonstrated this focus of interest.[56] Wherever the writers in it discussed a particular program, they mentioned either the British system or the proposed Wisconsin bill. Over and over again writers on both sides of the argument specifically mentioned Commons as if equating unemployment compensation with his program. Articles in the *American Labor Relations Review* suggested this same identification.

During the twenties, Commons published a stream of literature on the subject.[57] I. M. Rubinow, another leader in the unem-

---

56 Forsberg. [Forsberg was a student of Commons.]

57 Commons, "Putting an End to Unemployment," *LaFollette's Magazine,* Vol. XIII, March, 1921, p. 38.

————. "Unemployment: Compensation and Prevention," *The Survey,* Vol. XIII, October 1, 1921, p. 5.

————. "Unemployment Insurance," *The Monitor* (official publication of Associated Industries of New York State), Vol. VIII, February, 1922, p. 2.

————. "Unemployment Preventions," *American Labor Legislation Review,* Vol. XII, March, 1922, p. 15.

———— ———. "Unemployment: Prevention and Insurance—Chapter IV," *The Stabilization of Business,* ed. Lionel T. Edie, (New York: MacMillan Co.. 1923), p. 164.

————. *The Limits of Unemployment Insurance,* (Toronto: The British Association for the Advancement of Science, 1924).

————. "The True Scope of Unemployment Insurance," *American Labor Legislation Review,* Vol. XV, March, 1925, p. 43.

————. "Unemployment Compensation," *American Labor Legislation Review,* Vol. XX, September, 1930, p. 249.

ployment compensation movement, said of him:

> In keeping the torch burning for the principle of unemployment insurance throughout the years of the hectic decade, Professor John R. Commons, of the University of Wisconsin—the veteran fighter for better relations between capital and labor and for better labor standards—has performed a unique service.[58]

In addition to writing articles and giving speeches on the subject of unemployment compensation, Commons joined with other writers in a book, *The Stabilization of Business,* edited by Lionel Edie in 1923.[59] The other contributors were Wesley Mitchell, Irving Fisher, Frank Haight Dixon, Lionel Edie, Edwin R. A. Seligman, John B. Andrews, Walter Dill Scott, and Harry D. Dennison. Herbert Hoover furnished the introduction. Commons' part, as might be expected, was "Unemployment: Prevention and Insurance." In it he warned of the dangers to our society from unemployment. Workers without security, he said, become radical, but when secure they forget their radicalism. He offered his unemployment compensation program as a protection to America.

In 1925, jointly with Sam Lewisohn, Ernest Draper, and Don Lescohier (one of his students), he published the book *Can Business Prevent Unemployment?*[60] Lewisohn, vice president and treasurer of the Miami Copper Company, and Draper, treasurer of Hills Brothers Company, were two leaders in the movement for regularizing employment. The tone of the book was what "we businessmen" could do to prevent unemployment. The efforts of individual firms at stabilizing employment were displayed prominently. The book presented the government's responsibility

---

58 Rubinaw, *The Quest for Security,* p. 430.
59 Edie.
60 Commons, Lewisohn, Draper, and Lescohier.
──────. "Unemployment Reserves and Unemployment Insurance," *American Labor Legislation Review,* Vol. XX, September, 1930, p. 266.
──────. "Permanent Preventives of Unemployment," an address delivered before the Conference on Permanent Preventives of Unemployment, at Washington, January 26, 1931.
──────. "Should America Adopt a System of Compulsory Unemployment Insurance," *Congressional Digest,* Vol. X, August-September, 1931, p. 214.
──────. Address delivered at the Initial Conference on Unemployment, Madison, Wisconsin, February 11, 1932.
──────. "The Groves Unemployment Reserves Law," *American Labor Legislation Review,* Vol. XXII, March, 1932, p. 8.
──────. "Unemployment Insurance," an address delivered over N.B.C. network on April 9, 1932, Economic Series Lecture No. 24, (Chicago, Ill.: University of Chicago Press, 1932).
──────. "What is the Difference Between Unemployment Insurance and Unemployment Reserves?," *State Government,* Vol. V, May, 1932, p. 3.

for employment as a program for planning public works. Commons' ideas on the need for unemployment compensation, as well as its history and mechanics, rated a chapter.

One of the ways in which he contributed to the unemployment compensation movement was by serving as chairman for a compensation fund for the 35,000 clothing workers of Chicago. In 1923 Leo Wolman, the economist for the Amalgamated Clothing Workers, offered him this position in behalf of the manufacturers and the union. They chose him as their first chairman because, in the words of Earl Dean Howard, the labor manager for Hart, Schaffner, and Marx, "He is [was] undoubtedly by study and experience the foremost authority on the subject in the country."[61]

The clothing workers' program was very similar to the one Commons had devised and had been pushing. The job proved to be mostly an administrative one. After the first month his work was routine for the rest of his eighteen months. The position provided him with both experience in unemployment compensation administration and greater standing as an authority on the subject.

When the depression of 1929 hit the nation, interest in unemployment compensation intensified among experts. However, there was much skepticism. The intense criticism of the operations of the British unemployment insurance plan indicated the need for caution. In England the prolonged depression made it necessary to extend benefits to persons whose compensation rights had expired. Because the income of the program was not increased proportionately, huge deficits developed that had to be covered by other government funds. In the resulting controversy, considerable confusion arose as to whether the program was a cause or result of the depression. Many Americans pointed to the fact that since the inception of the British insurance system, in 1911, there had been either unemployment or war. They then jumped to the non sequitur that the British system, or "dole," as they called it, demoralized the workers, handicapped employers, and caused the government to become bankrupt. America, they said, would be wise to avoid such a system.

Consequently, when the members of the American Association for Labor Legislation presented their plan in 1930, they called it the "American Plan," and went to great pains to show its dif-

---

61 Quoted from the *Chicago Sun,* in *American Labor Legislation Review,* Vol. XIV, March, 1924, p. 135.

ferences from the British system. They had formulated this plan
at a conference called to study unemployment compensation.[62]
Members of the conference studied both American experience with
voluntary plans and British experience with a governmental plan.
Sir William Beveridge, a co-author of the British plan, recounted
British experience. Morris Leeds of Northrup and Leeds, and
Ernest Draper of Hills Brothers explained their voluntary plans.
The situation in the clothing industry was given by Leo Wolman
and Sidney Hillman. To help with the legal phases of the problem there was Joseph P. Chamberlain, then president of the association, as well as being a director of the Columbia University Legislation Drafting Bureau. Francis Perkins, who had been a member
of the association for years, and was then the New York State Industrial Commissioner, was also one of the contributors; and naturally, Commons and Andrews were there with their proposals.

This group formulated a draft of "An American Plan for
Unemployment Reserves," which they published in the December,
1930, issue of the *American Labor Legislation Review*.[63] The
association also distributed 33,000 copies of the bill. Essentially,
the bill was similar to the Huber Bill, which Commons had been
pushing. The Huber Bill would have required employers to buy
unemployment insurance from mutual insurance companies. In
turn these companies were to pay benefits to the unemployed
according to a scale prescribed in the bill. Presumably, the insurance companies would charge employers according to the risks
they encountered.

The association's American Plan provided for a system of
self-insurance by employers to meet unemployment compensation
liabilities. Those employers who could not demonstrate financial
ability to meet such liabilities were to be required to pay a tax
of one and one-half percent of their payrolls into state funds.
A fund was to be set up for each industry or in some cases for
groups of industries. Boards administering funds would have the
power to pay dividends to employers who maintained good records
of maintaining employment. Under both the Huber Bill and the
association's bill employers would have had a ceiling on their
liability. Also, under each, the employer would have had an incentive to minimize unemployment.

Powerful support developed for the movement in the summer
of 1930 when Franklin Roosevelt, then governor of New York,

---

62 *American Labor Legislation Review*, Vol. XXIII, September, 1933, p. 349.
63 *American Labor Legislation Review*, Vol. XX, 1930, p. 349.

joined it. At the conference of governors meeting at Salt Lake City, on June 30, 1930, he said:

> Unemployment insurance we shall come to in this country just as certainly as we have come to workman's compensation for industrial injury, just as certainly as we are today in the midst of a national wave of insuring against old age want.[64]

Roosevelt further demonstrated his interest by calling for a conference of governors of seven industrial states, to be held in Albany in January, 1931. There the governors met with "experts" of the unemployment compensation movement. After this conference a continuing committee was formed for further study. The committee published its report in 1932, supporting an unemployment insurance program similar to that of the American Association for Labor Legislation.

Interest in unemployment compensation spread rapidly across the nation. Numerous committees to study the problem were appointed by various governors. The state legislatures were presented with numerous bills. Finally, even the labor movement endorsed the idea. At the 1932 convention the American Federation of Labor reversed its previous stand and threw its support behind the movement.

In the meantime, Commons was busy campaigning. In addition to his writings and his efforts with the American Association for Labor Legislation, he made a number of speeches on the subject.[65] Some of these were published. One of his addresses in 1930 was to the convention of the Wisconsin Federation of Labor. Another was to the Employers' Association of Eau Claire, Wisconsin. He made a third before the Conference on Permanent Preventives of Unemployment, held in Washington in January, 1931. His fourth was before the Initial Conference on Unemployment, held in Madison in February, 1932. Finally, in April of

---

64 Quoted in *American Labor Legislation Review*, Vol. XX, September, 1930, p. 254.

65 Commons, "Unemployment Compensation," an address delivered before the 1930 Convention of the Wisconsin Federation of Labor, *American Labor Legislation Review*, Vol. XX, September, 1930, pp. 249-253.

——————. "Unemployment," an address delivered before the Employers' Association of Eau Claire, Wisconsin, February 28, 1930.

——————. "Permanent Preventives of Unemployment," an address delivered before the Conference on Permanent Preventives of Unemployment, at Washington, January 26, 1931, *Bulletin* of Department of Debating and Public Discussion, University of Wisconsin Extension Division, (Madison, Wisconsin: 1931), under title "Favoring Unemployment Insurance."

——————. Address delivered at Initial Conference on Unemployment, at Madison, Wisconsin, February 11, 1932.

——————. "Unemployment Insurance," an address delivered over the N.B.C. network on April 9, 1932. Also in *Economic Series Lecture* No. 24, (Chicago, Ill.: University of Chicago Press, 1932).

1932, he carried his message to a nationwide radio audience, in an address over the National Broadcasting Company network.

By 1931 the campaign for unemployment compensation began to show results in Wisconsin. The depression of 1929 had brought widespread unemployment throughout the state. During the summer of 1930 Governor Kohler appointed Don Lescohier, a Commons' student, to serve as executive secretary of the State's Citizen Committee on Unemployment.[66] With the municipal governments straining to provide relief to the unemployed, the state stepped in with a $6,500,000 appropriation in March of 1931.[67] To pay for increased relief costs the Progressives advocated drastic increases in income taxes. At this period employers spent most of their efforts fighting the increased taxes. At the same time farmers began to look on unemployment compensation as a program under which employers, instead of the state, would pay for the care of the unemployed. Consequently, several farm organizations at their 1931 fall meetings endorsed unemployment compensation.[68] Their support, when added to that already given by the Wisconsin labor movement, began to tip the scales in favor of the program. The only problem was to work out a program that would draw a minimum of opposition from the employers.

Commons and his students went over their previous proposals to reshape them into an acceptable bill. Two of them, a husband and wife team, Paul Raushenbush and Elizabeth Brandeis, drafted a bill that was introduced in 1931 by Harold Groves, a third Commons' student.[69] At that time Groves was an assemblyman, Senator Huber was lieutenant governor, and Philip LaFollette was governor. The Progressives had a clear majority in the Assembly, but needed a few independent votes in the Senate to pass the bill. After a few compromises to make the bill more palatable to the employers it was passed and signed in January, 1932.

The Groves Act provided for a two percent payroll tax to be paid by the employers, unless they created individual programs that provided workers with comparable benefits. Although the employers' contributions would go into a central fund, each employer would have a separate account. When an employer had paid fifty-five dollars per employee his contribution would be reduced to one percent until the account reached seventy-five dol-

66 *American Labor Legislation Review*, Vol. XX, September, 1930, p. 230.
67 Raney, p. 494.
68 Lescohier and Brandeis, p. 618.
69 Witte, *Yale Law Review*, Vol. 55.

lars per employee. As long as the employer's account remained above seventy-five dollars he was to be excused from all further contributions. If the benefits lowered the level of an employer's account too much the scale of benefits was to be reduced and even eliminated if necessary. No provision was made for the state to contribute any money to the fund or to incur any liability. Consequently, no employer would pay more than seventy-five dollars per employee, or pay benefits to anyone other than his own employees.

Unemployed workers were to be subjected to a two-week waiting period. Then their weekly benefits were to be fifty percent of their weekly wages, up to a maximum of ten dollars per week. Minimum benefits were to be five dollars per week. Benefits were to be paid in the ratio of one week for every four weeks of work, with a maximum of ten weeks' benefits. If a worker had more than one employer in the last year, employee benefits were to be charged against the account of his last employer. Then after exhausting his rights under that employer or exhausting that employer's account, if he had remaining benefits due him, such benefits would be charged to the next to the last employer's account. The law placed the administration under the Industrial Commission. Because this agency had handled Wisconsin's social legislation since 1911, the law could be implemented with a minimum of new machinery.

Although all employers were to have the same liability they had their choice of entering the statewide plan or instituting plans of their own, which would follow state standards. If employers already had voluntary plans for unemployment compensation the law allowed considerable flexibility in fitting their plans to conditions of the law. To encourage employers to enter into voluntary plans and to appease opponents the act provided that the program would go into effect only if employers of less than 175,000 workers of the state failed to set up their own plans by June 1, 1933. Because of the depression, payments by employers were postponed later until July, 1934. Benefits to employees began in July, 1936.

Commons believed that this unemployment compensation program was more than a relief measure for the unemployed. Just as he had designed his workmen's compensation law to provide incentives for employers to promote safety, he intended to use the unemployment compensation program to induce them to reduce unemployment. Those completely successful in preventing unemployment among their employees would be relieved of further payments once their reserves reached the seventy-five dollar level. On the other hand, those with poor records would be compelled to pay the full two percent of their payrolls.

Although there had been variations in the various bills he drafted, they all had the principle of providing an incentive. The *American Labor Legislation Review* of March, 1921, quoted the sponsors of the earlier Huber Bill of Wisconsin as saying:

> The bill offers an inducement to scientific production, where workmen are employed steadily. Nonprofit making mutual insurance companies will be the main agencies which will endeavor to prevent unemployment. Its experts will be at the service of its members. They will devise methods for reducing unnecessary labor turnover. Spasmodic employment of workmen will be discouraged by a system of premium rates which will be based upon the stability of employment for each establishment. The establishment with the greatest number of "hirings" and "firings" will pay the largest premium rates. Hence good management will be rewarded by its efficiency in preventing unnecessary layoffs. There are many employers today who so reduce their labor turnover that men are never laid off on account of lack of work. This bill would not affect these employers materially—their premium rates would be practically nil.
> . . . And of crowning importance in the movement toward regularization of industry is the careful development of this form of insurance with its continuous pressure toward the prevention of unemployment.[70]

Commons did not rely on this program to prevent all unemployment. It must be remembered that he also stressed the role of monetary policy in preventing booms from becoming dangerous breeders of depression. He also believed in public works programs to relieve unemployment during bad times. But he did have considerable faith in the incentives created by the unemployment compensation program. Because business operated on such narrow margins, he believed that relief from even a two percent assessment on payrolls would be an effective inducement in a great many cases.

The Groves Act went further than the previous bills in limiting employers' liability. Each employer's contribution was kept in a separate account out of which payments would go only to his own workers. If payments exhausted an employer's account, payments to eligible workers ceased even though there was an abundance of funds in other accounts. Previous bills had called for pooling of

---

70 *American Labor Legislation Review,* Vol. XII, March, 1921, p. 59.

funds so that all eligible workers could be paid. In other respects these previous bills were similar to the Groves Act and provided similar incentives to employers to prevent layoffs.

The limiting of employer's liabilities kept the scale of benefits at a very modest level. As soon as other states began investigating the possibilities of adopting unemployment compensation some of the experts began to doubt the wisdom of such limitations. Paul Douglas, I. M. Rubinow, Abraham Epstein, and even some of Commons' students, such as William Leiserson, questioned the practicality of using the program in an attempt to prevent unemployment. They declared that the program should be for relief and not economic manipulation. Hence, they stressed the insurance principle instead of Wisconsin's prevention feature.

The first rival plan to break sharply with Wisconsin's plan was the Ohio Plan. By providing a pooling of funds the sponsors were able to place the level of benefits considerably higher—a maximum of fifteen dollars instead of ten dollars per week, and a maximum of sixteen instead of ten weeks. However, the backers found they had to yield to mass sentiment sufficiently to include a modified merit rating system under which employers with good records would pay reduced rates.[71] The public opinion which forced the Ohio planners to yield was the product of the campaign initiated and pushed by Commons and his colleagues. From the first they had pursued a strategy of declaring the welfare of the unemployed workers to be the responsibility of those who layed them off and not that of the state or other employers.

The unemployment compensation campaign was not exclusively one by nonemployers trying to force employers to accept their responsibilities. It was a campaign that included an ever-growing number of employers as well as reformers. Commons had sought out employers who already had accepted voluntary programs. He used them to sell more employers on the profitability of such attempts to smooth out production. Then he combined these employers with a sprinkling of those a little less enthusiastic and had them participate in formulating a statewide compulsory program. For this program planning Commons brought together employers, employees, union officials, economists, and state government officials. In the resulting bargaining each group found itself arguing over details and not over the decision as to whether there should be any such program.

---

71 Rubinow, *The Quest for Security,* p. 442.

Employers accepted the principle of limited liability seriously. They also believed that Commons' preventive principle actually did work. Many of them had been chosen precisely because they had been the most successful with the voluntary programs. They thought other employers could also prevent layoffs if they were given proper incentives. Because employers were such an important group within the unemployment compensation movement, their acceptance of Commons' reasoning affected the thinking of many others.

However, a growing number of experts kept alive the objections to the Wisconsin plan. When the American Association for Labor Legislation continued to back Commons' program under the name "The American Plan," the other experts formed a new organization, the American Association for Social Security. It was a successor to an earlier group, the American Association for Old Age Security. Although then the unemployment compensation movement was split, it was divided on only one important issue, insurance versus unemployment prevention.

The coming of the New Deal provided opportunity for extending unemployment compensation to the nation. The Democratic Party platform of 1932 had endorsed the idea. President Roosevelt was committed to it, and had chosen Frances Perkins, an active and longstanding member of the American Association for Labor Legislation, for his Secretary of Labor.

Several proposals were placed before Congress, but the first significant move came on June 8, 1934, when the President in a message to Congress urged the adoption of unemployment insurance and other forms of social security. He followed up his message by appointing the Committee on Economic Security to study the problems and to propose legislation for the January session of Congress. The committee consisted of Frances Perkins, Secretary of Labor; Henry Morgenthau, Jr., Secretary of the Treasury; Homer Cummings, Secretary of Commerce; Henry Wallace, Secretary of Agriculture; and Harry Hopkins, Federal Relief Administrator.

Because Wisconsin was the only state with an unemployment compensation law, it probably was natural that it had an unusual influence in the drafting of a national law. The cabinet committee chose E. E. Witte of the University of Wisconsin as its executive director. Dr. Witte, one of Commons' students, was well qualified.

His experience as secretary of Wisconsin's Industrial Commission acquainted him with problems of administration. Perhaps his most important qualification was that he had been chief of Wisconsin's Legislative Reference Library. In this capacity he had worked with Commons as the technical draftsman of the Wisconsin unemployment compensation bills.

The committee created a bewildering group of advisory committees to aid in the drafting of the law. The co-ordinating group was an Advisory Council consisting of twenty-three outstanding citizens representing the public, the employers, and the employees. Dr. Frank Graham, President of the University of North Carolina, headed this group. A. J. Altmeyer, the second assistant Secretary of Labor, headed an Interdepartmental Technical Board of twenty members, bringing together persons interested in social security from the various executive departments. Altmeyer, another of Commons' students, also had been secretary of the Wisconsin Industrial Commission. Then, in addition to these groups, six special committees of experts were formed, including a Medical Advisory Board, a Public Health Committee, a Hospital Committee, a Dental Work Committee, an Advisory Committee on Public Employment and Assistance, and a Child Welfare Committee.

Not only were these groups made up of a generous sprinkling of Commons' students, but they also heavily represented the American Association for Labor Legislation. The employers in particular were those who had worked extensively with Commons. By this time he was too old to take an active part in the work, but his influence was strong.

Two reasons explain why the U. S. unemployment compensation system has fifty state programs instead of one, nationally administered. One reason was that the sponsors feared the action of a conservative Supreme Court. Because the Constitution does not explicitly give Congress the power to legislate such a program into existence, the sponsors reasoned it would be safest to depend on state legislation. Hence, they created a national law designed to induce the states to adopt their own programs. Such a law ultimately might be declared unconstitutional but not before it had served its purpose. At least some of the state programs might survive such a contingency.

The second reason for avoiding a national program was that agreement on any one program was impossible. The ranks of experts on the subject were split over the insurance versus the prevention principle. Those employers who favored any program insisted that the Wisconsin system be permitted to continue so they might be rewarded if they prevented layoffs. Therefore, the decision as to the type of program was thrown back to the states.

The law imposed a three percent levy on all payrolls. In states where adequate programs were adopted all but ten percent of the tax would be remitted. Within a very short time all the states responded by adopting their own programs. While a few of them adopted a merit system under which employers with good records ployers' liability, almost all of the states, in recent years, have adopted a merit system under which employers with good records pay less than the others.[72]

Experience has not vindicated Commons' preventive principle, but the idea is by no means dead. When Walter Reuther declares that the guaranteed annual wage makes layoffs expensive enough for employers to prevent them, he is enunciating the same principle. Commons' preventive principle may be questionable, but the validity of it is not its importance. The real significance was its part in the strategy of getting any program adopted. Using it, he could sell a few employers, then a state, and finally a nation.

This is not the place to describe or to analyze the nation's social security law or the corresponding state laws, except as they relate to Commons. What is important is to point out that these laws represented unprecedented acceptance of social rather than individual responsibility for personal security. The laws may be broadened from time to time until the U. S. becomes what is known as a "welfare state." No single man was responsible in bringing it about, but if anyone could be called its father, he would be John R. Commons.

The changes in this country's society from the turn of the century until the New Deal were many and profound. Although the New Deal would seem to be a break with the past, it was in reality only the climax for movements of rather lengthy duration. The acceptance of social responsibility for the welfare of the indi-

---

[72] The only method by which the states could reduce the total unemployment taxes was by adopting a merit system. Employers could deduct their payment of taxes to the state (up to two and seven-tenths percent of their payrolls). Except under a merit system under which the law permitted them to deduce a full two and seven-tenths percent whether they paid it to the state or not, any reduction of state rates merely caused a corresponding increase in the amount required to be paid to the federal government.

vidual, the expansion of administrative machinery, and the imposition of economic controls began on local and state levels. Three Wisconsin laws registered the progress of this development. They also provided models for other states and for the federal government in drafting legislation. Commons is comparatively obscure in American history, but his leadership in the drafting and adoption of social legislation entitles him to more attention than he has so far received.

JRC

6

THE UNITED STATES COMMISSION
ON INDUSTRIAL RELATIONS

IN JUNE OF 1913 John R. Commons received a telegram from Senator LaFollette, stating that President Wilson offered him the position of chairman of a new Industrial Relations Commission.[1] Commons declined the offer because he had just completed a two-year leave of absence from the University of Wisconsin, serving as a member of the Wisconsin Industrial Commission. He did not feel he should spend any more time away from the university. Finally, he did agree to become a member of the commission on the condition that he would work only during his vacation periods for the commission, and that his duties would not interfere with his teaching at the university.

The demands for a commission

The Congress that created the commission directed it to find the causes of industrial unrest and report back its findings and recommendations.[2] Evidence of such unrest had attracted the attention of the nation and the Congress after disclosures of

---

1 Commons, *Myself, op. cit.*, pp. 165, 167.
2 Mark Perlman, *Labor Union Theories in America*, pp. 279-304

union responsibility for the *Los Angeles Times* explosion.[3] After a sensational trial during which union officers confessed to the crime, labor and its sympathizers found themselves in an awkward position. No longer able to deny that labor unions were sometimes violent, they only could offer explanations of why unions might be provoked to take such action. Labor had a group of friends who were willing to find extenuating circumstances that would explain, if not excuse, such action. These friends consisted of a group of liberals very similar in outlook to some of the New Dealers of a later day. By profession they were social workers, ministers, officials in state labor departments or industrial commissions, journalists, university professors (such as Commons), and even a sprinkling of businessmen. Although these liberals represented a great diversity of opinion, the desire for reforms to combat poverty united them. They reasoned that diseases, crimes, and industrial unrest all grew out of miserable conditions which had to be endured by the poor. Because they concerned themselves with the suffering of the poor, they tended to develop the attitude that the distribution of wealth and income in our society was unjust. Yet most of them did not advocate a radical redistribution of wealth or change in our social order. What they agreed on was that labor's bargaining power should be increased so workers could obtain a greater share of the nation's income. Consequently, in the struggle between the great corporations and labor unions, the liberals tended to sympathize with the underdogs, the unions. Hence, they were righteously indignant whenever they found abuses by business leaders, but they sought extenuating circumstances for the misdeeds of unions.

Complete identification of this group of liberals is impossible because they included both genuine radicals and comparative con-

3 On the morning of October 1, 1910, an explosion wrecked the building of the *Los Angeles Times,* killing 20 and injuring 17 persons. After an extensive investigation, W. J. Burns, a well-known detective, arrested Ortie McManigal, and the brothers J. B. and John J. McNamara. Because John J. McNamara was the secretary-treasurer of the International Association of Bridge and Structural Iron Workers, the case was sensational. Most of the prominent leaders of the labor movement, including the cautious Samuel Gompers, rose to the defense. And the famed defense lawyer, Clarence Darrow, was obtained to represent the accused. Unfortunately for labor and its sympathizers, the facts were not as they believed. Ortie McManigal confessed and there was sufficient corroborating evidence to make conviction likely. Consequently, Darrow bargained with the prosecution to save his clients' lives; they confessed and J. B. McNamara received a life sentence, his brother was sentenced for fifteen years, and McManigal went free soon after the trial. There were further trials before the federal courts in Indianapolis, where fifty-four members of the International Association of Bridge and Structural Iron Workers were indicted. Of these, forty were tried and thirty-eight convicted of conspiracy to transport dynamite illegally across state lines. Their terms ranged from one year up to seven for the president of the union, Frank Ryan. Perlman and Taft, pp. 318-325. Adamic, pp. 249-352.

servatives. However they shared a passion for charity, doubts as to the justice of the status quo, and a sympathy for labor unions. They were found in such reform organizations as The National Council of Charities and Correction, The American Association for Labor Legislation, The National Consumers' League, and The National Child Labor Committee. The literature of these organizations shows many of the same names contributing articles, taking part in conferences, and being praised for reform activities.

One of the liberals' important publications was *The Survey,* which described itself as a journal of constructive philanthropy. Although it was, and is yet, dedicated to social workers, its contributors have included many people of other professions, such as Commons, who was a departmental editor.[4] It grew out of a magazine called *Charities,* which had been founded in 1897 by Edward T. Devine, who remained as editor until it was reorganized in 1909.[5] After reorganizing the magazine as *The Survey,* Devine turned over the editorship to Paul U. Kellogg. Although he remained an associate editor and frequent contributor, his chief occupation thereafter was heading the New York School of Philanthropy.

Devine and his group of liberals were shocked by the disclosures growing out of the McNamara trial, and they tried to find reasons why such things could happen.[6] Their answer had to be consistent with their sympathies for labor. They contended that labor had been driven to the point where violation was the only outlet for its frustrations.[7] To support this contention they pointed to widespread cases of grinding poverty and economic insecurity. Yet when the workers tried to help themselves by collective action, their organizations were ruthlessly suppressed by legal or even illegal means. The law protected the employers, but did little to benefit the worker.

To prove and, even more important, to dramatize these contentions, the liberals proposed that the federal government appoint a commission to investigate the causes of industrial unrest.[8] The group held a meeting, under the chairmanship of Jane Addams, to organize to campaign for the creation of this commission.[9]

---

4 Commons served as Departmental Editor for labor legislation while he was secretary for the American Association for Labor Legislation. In 1910 his student, John B. Andrews, replaced him on both jobs.

5 *The Survey,* Vol. XXX, pp. 561-564.

6 *The Survey,* Vol. XXVII, pp. 1430-1431.

7 *Ibid.*

8 *Ibid.*

9 *The Survey,* Vol. XXX, pp. 571-578.

During this meeting they formed a committee of which Edward Devine was chairman. The first act of this committee was to send a petition to President Taft, urging the creation of the commission. Then it began to lobby for an enabling act by Congress.

Edward Devine and Paul Kellogg approached Samuel Gompers to gain labor's support for their project.[10] He agreed readily, but insisted labor should be represented on the commission. Furthermore, he said labor should choose its own representatives. Consequently, the commission was to become a tripartite body with representatives of employers, unions, and the public, instead of a group of experts studying labor conditions. As soon as Gompers joined the campaign, the labor sympathizers in Congress, such as Congressman Wilson (later Secretary of Labor), began to give the measure support. Finally, in August of 1912, President Taft signed the Hughes-Borah Act creating the commission.

The commission consisted of nine members, three representatives each for the employers, the unions, and the public. The commissioners were to spend $500,000 and three years to study the general conditions of labor and the underlying causes of dissatisfaction. They were to submit their findings and the recommendations to Congress.

The selection of the commissioners

It was not until December that the President announced his nominations. When he did the liberals were disappointed with his choices.[11] They felt that the membership was neither distinguished nor sufficiently representative of all interests. The labor representatives, two of whom had been chosen by the American Federation of Labor and the third by the railroad brotherhoods, were considered too conservative by these liberals. Paul Kellogg complained that the two A. F. of L. representatives were so unrepresentative that they had been voted out of office by their own international unions.[12] He agreed that the A. F. of L. was entitled to representation, but not to the exclusion of the industrial unions. At least someone on the commission should be sympathetic with such unions, even if no one represented them directly.

---

10 Gompers, *op. cit.*, Vol. I, p. 447.

11 Public members: Senator George Sutherland, from Utah; George B. Chandler; Charles Simon Barnett. Employer representatives: Frederick A. Delano, Adolph Lewisohn, Ferd C. Schwedtman. Union representatives: Austin B. Garretson, John B. Lennon, and James O'Connell. *The Survey*, Vol. XXIX, p. 381.

12 *The Survey*, Vol. XXIX, p. 386.

"How absurd," he declared, "that there should be no one on it who has the least sympathy with, or understanding of, the new industrial unionism which is the dynamic element of that unrest."[13]

Apparently, Kellogg and his group believed that fairness required that all shades of opinion be represented no matter how extreme or in how much disrepute. The important segment of industrial unionism of that time was the International Workers of the World.

The liberals objected to the nominations for employer representatives on the grounds that they were men who tended to deal with the structural rather than the human side of industry. Two were engineers while the third was a large investor and director, who did not deal with the "immediate personal equations of a manager."[14] One of them was a vice president of the anti-union National Association of Manufacturers. Although the liberals conceded that these were admirable men, their good qualities tended to duplicate each other. None was a conspicuous defender of "democracy in industry."[15]

The liberals were more greatly disappointed over the nominees who were to represent the public. The absence of any woman on the commission and the failure to include any well-known economist or social worker were particularly disappointing. Paul Kellogg complained, "Freund, Brandeis, Commons, there is no name that rings out like these on the list."[16]

After the President's announcement, the New York members of the committee to sponsor the commission met to express their dissatisfaction. They read telegrams from the out-of-town members and then prepared a statement for the press, summarizing their views.[17] They hoped the President would either reconsider his nominations or that the Senate would fail to confirm them.

When the Senate refused to confirm Taft's nominees, the job of making the new nominations fell to President Wilson. The various groups began to exert pressure on the new administration to influence the President in his choices. Samuel Gompers met

---

13 *Ibid.*
14 *Ibid.*
15 *Ibid.*
16 *Ibid.*
17 Signed by John B. Andrews, Frank Oliver Hall, John Haynes Holmes, J. W. Jenks, Arthur Kellogg, Paul U. Kellogg, Paul Kennaday, John A. Kingsbury, Samuel McCune Lindsay, Owen R. Lovejoy, A. J. McKelway, Henry Morgenthau, Henry Moskowitz, James P. Reynolds, William Jay Schlieffelin, Stephen S. Wise, Edward T. Devine, Lillian D. Wald. *The Survey*, Vol. XXIX, p. 382.

with the President to discuss the nominations and had further access to the administration through Secretary of Labor Wilson.[18] The liberal group of charity and social reform workers also conferred with the President to get their point of view represented.[19] They urged the President to appoint Edward T. Devine as chairman and a public representative. For a woman as a public representative, they backed Florence Kelly. As to the third public representative, they suggested John R. Commons.

When Ralph Easley, secretary of the National Civic Federation, heard that the liberals had met with the President, he became alarmed.[20] He described them as "radical but superficial social reformers," and "sentimental and theoretical."[21] They were entitled to express their opinions, he said, "but when they put themselves on record in favor of a Red Flag revolutionary socialist to represent the women of the country," they were going too far.[22]

In place of Florence Kelly, Easley advocated substituting Mrs. J. Borden Harriman.[23] In addition to being an active member in the National Civic Federation, she also had qualified herself politically by being president of the women's organization for the Democratic campaign for 1912. Besides being an able person, sympathetic to labor, she was, in Easley's opinion, skilled in organization. She would help the commission achieve harmony rather than stir up continual rows, as would Florence Kelly. For the other two public members, Easley suggested Louis Brandeis and John R. Commons.[24]

On June 26, 1913, President Wilson announced his nominations.[25] The list included the same labor members as had President Taft's. He substituted Harris Weinstock and S. Thurston Ballard for two of the employers chosen by Taft, but he retained Frederic A. Delano from the previous list of nominees. Frank P.

---

18 Gompers, Vol. I, p. 544.
19 Green, p. 348.
20 *Ibid.*
21 *Ibid.*, pp. 345, 348.
22 *Ibid.*, p. 348. Mrs. Kelly had voted for Debs in the last election.
23 *Ibid.*, p. 349.
24 Marguarite Green quotes a portion of Easley's letter to an unnamed official high in the administration: "Mr. Commons would meet the expectations of the saner elements among what are termed radicals and, at the same time, would be very pleasing to Senator LaFollette and all his friends. He is an able man." *Ibid.*, p. 350. Easley's enthusiasm for Brandeis cooled upon learning he had been urging I. W. W. representation on the commission. *Ibid.*, p. 349.
25 Public members: Frank Walsh, John R. Commons, Mrs. J. Borden Harriman. Employer representatives: Frederick A. Delano, Harris Weinstock, S. Thurston Ballard. Union members: Austin B. Garretson, John B. Lennon, James O'Connell. On March 17, 1915 Richard H. Aishton was appointed to serve the unexpired term of Frederick A. Delano, who resigned.

Walsh, Mrs. J. Borden Harriman, and John R. Commons were named as the representatives of the public.

Frank P. Walsh, the chairman, was the third choice for his post after both Commons and Louis Brandeis had turned it down.[26] His appointment probably stemmed from the fact that he, a prominent liberal attorney from Kansas City, had thrown his support to the Democrats in the 1912 election. For the rest of his life he remained a member of the Democratic Party and held a number of high offices.[27]

The Wilson nominees seemed to please the major groups interested in the commission. Easley was pleased that no socialist, or member of the I. W. W. had been chosen.[28] He was particularly pleased that eight of the nine members, including Commons, belonged to the National Civic Federation. Labor had reason to be satisfied with the choices, because their slate of representatives had been chosen. Even the group of liberals found the new list substantially superior to the old. They were happy that no member of an anti-union organization had been chosen. *The Survey,* in an editorial, explained why Wilson's choices made a better impression than Taft's:

> An especial reason for this impression they find in the appointment of Professor Commons, the one man in America who, as economist and investigator, has thought out industrial reforms, as statesman has drafted them into laws which would give them effect and as administrator has practically enforced those laws with unexampled co-operation of employers and employee.[29]

After the nominations had been made public but before the Senate had confirmed them, *The Survey* published a symposium on what the commission ought to accomplish.[30] As befitted their liberal approach, they printed opinions from such diverse sources as W. D. Haywood of the Industrial Workers of the World and Ferdinand C. Schwedtman of the National Association of Manufacturers. They also included an article by John R. Commons that had been written before he knew he was going to be on the commission.[31] Not much agreement was apparent as to the goals of the commission, but the symposium did help arouse interest.

---

26 Harriman, p. 133.

27 Walsh later became co-chairman (with Taft) of War Labor Conference Board, and a representative of the people on the War Labor Board of 1918. In 1929 he was appointed by Governor Roosevelt as a member of New York Commission on Revision of Public Utility Laws. He became chairman of the Power Authority of the State of New York in 1931.

28 Green, pp. 349, 350.

29 *The Survey,* Vol. XXX, pp. 452, 453.

30 *The Survey,* Vol. XXX, pp. 571-578.

31 He stressed the need for better organization of agencies administering labor laws.

The commission's organization and work

On September 10, 1913, the Senate confirmed the President's nominees. One month later $100,000 for the first year's work was made available, and on October 23, 1913, the commission began its work at last. By then only twenty-two months remained in which to make investigations and prepare reports.

After a certain amount of discussion the commissioners decided on a two-part investigation. Part of the work was to be carried on in the form of public hearings where facts and viewpoints could be gained from numerous witnesses. For the second part of the investigations the commission hired a group of scholars to make reports on a number of topics. These reports were to be submitted to the commission for approval, and to be incorporated into the report to Congress.

Walsh, being a lawyer, was more interested in the hearings than in reports by scholars. He was a skilled interrogator who could perform well during the hearings. On the other hand, Commons, the scholar, was more interested in research. Before accepting the position he had made an arrangement with Walsh that he would concentrate his efforts on the staff reports.[32] They agreed that he would hire most of the experts on the staff and would give them a certain amount of supervision.

Not being able to devote full time to the work, Commons left the immediate supervision to W. Jett Lauck, who had been the chief examiner for the tariff board. When the progress of the work lagged, Commons persuaded the commission to hire Charles McCarthy, of the Wisconsin Legislative Reference Library, to be in charge of the staff investigations. As soon as McCarthy joined the staff, in the summer of 1914, the work proceeded more vigorously. Fitch reported, "To a singular degree Dr. McCarthy has promoted an *esprit de corps,* giving promise of results."[33] McCarthy divided the work into nine divisions, each with a chief and a staff. A system of submitting regular reports kept him informed as to their progress. If any member of the staff needed help he was ready with many fertile suggestions. It appeared that McCarthy would insure the success of this joint scholarly effort.

In the meantime, the commissioners conducted a series of public hearings around the country. Although the commissioners interviewed witnesses representing both employers and workers,

---

32 Commons, *Myself.*
33 Fitch, *The Survey,* Vol. XXXIII, p. 578.

the latter had more spectacular stories. When the commissioners heard lurid accounts of incidents such as the "Ludlow Massacre," their investigations became a study of employer abuses.[34] Before long the entire purpose of the commission seemed to shift. Instead of attempting to discover the underlying causes of industrial unrest, they changed to an attempt to prove that the blame rested almost entirely with the employers. Walsh, in particular, became abusive when he had such persons as John D. Rockefeller, Jr. on the stand.[35]

Rockefeller was drawn into the hearings because he and his father were principal stockholders in the Colorado Fuel and Iron Company, the company whose striking employees suffered in the Ludlow tragedy. Although the testimony did not support such conclusions, Walsh tried to prove that Rockefeller was personally responsible for the unfortunate conditions and events in Colorado. What the testimony and correspondence produced for the commission showed was that Rockefeller had given the company officials a free hand. He did this on the basis of misinformation which they had supplied him. Finally, when he became aware of the nature of the situation, he hired MacKenzie King to conduct an independent investigation on the causes of industrial unrest, including that in Colorado.[36] He made this a project of the Rockefeller Foundation.

Walsh, believing the King investigation to be a sinister propaganda move, attacked the Rockefeller Foundation as well as Rockefeller personally. He then extended his attack to all large foundations because he considered them potential menaces to democracy. During these hearings on foundations, Walsh strayed far away from the path of objectivity. Not only was he vindicative, but at times he abused his witnesses.[37] Furthermore, the relation between foundations and industrial unrest was tenuous at best.

The hearings of the commission produced much material useful for the students of labor relations. Almost every point of view,

---

34 Members of the Colorado National Guard fired into a tent city inhabited by evicted strikers. In the course of a pitched battle the camp burned, resulting in the killing of two women and eleven children. *Final Report and Testimony Submitted to Congress by the Commission on Industrial Relations,* Vol. 7, pp. 6346-6356.

35 *Ibid.,* Vol. 8, pp. 7763-7895.

36 MacKenzie King drafted and administered the Canadian Disputes Act. Later he became Prime Minister of Canada.

37 *The Nation,* Vol. C, p. 161. Mrs. Harriman also testified that "Frank Walsh was perfectly frightful; he was rude, dictatorial, and kept witnesses waiting unnecessarily. He was nice to labor people, but awful to Rockefeller." Personal interview on September 9, 1958, at the home of Mrs. Harriman's granddaughter, Mrs. Robert Fulton of Ross, California.

from those of arch reactionaries to those of extreme radicals, was expressed before the commission. Yet the overall picture the chairman, Walsh, tried to bring out was that the employers were responsible for industrial unrest. He succeeded in winning the labor representatives over to his point of view, but the others could not agree with him. Naturally, the employer representatives resented what they felt was an unfair approach. Commons and Mrs. Harriman, although both extremely sympathetic to labor, could not go along with Walsh's one-sided approach.[38] Hence, the commission divided on a five to four basis.

The commission ran into trouble

The hearings brought the commission more disagreements than those arising from the treatment of witnesses and testimony. Because the hearings consumed so much time and money, they began to crowd the other parts of the investigation. While hearings were going on, Commons' experts were making their own investigations to prepare their reports. This work required a considerable amount of money though not as much as for the conducting of hearings. Trouble came when it became apparent that the money appropriated by the Congress would not cover both types of activities.

Early in its life the commission had voted to give Walsh the power to control finances.[39] Thus, when the shortage of money became apparent, he was in a strategic position to decide which type of activity should have the priority. It is not surprising that he decided that money should go to the hearings, even if the staff investigations had to be abandoned.

It was some time before the commissioners became aware of the shortage of money. The shortage was due partly to bad management by Walsh and partly because of the way Congress appropriated the money. In the enabling act Congress had stated that the commission should spend $500,000, but it appropriated the money on an annual basis. Finally, the full amount was spent, but Congress doled it out in installments and then reluctantly under pressure. At times Walsh had to drop his work to go to Washington to plead for money. Congress appropriated only $100,000 for the first year, but finally was induced to supplement it with a deficiency appropriation of $50,000. For the fiscal year 1914-1915 Congress appropriated $200,000. By February of 1915 this last

---

38 Commons, *Myself*, p. 177.
39 *Ibid.*

appropriation was running out, and Walsh had to plead for $100,000 to complete the year and $40,000 for the work after July 1 until August 23, 1915, when the commission's term was to expire.

At the time of the last grant, money was needed both to complete the hearings and to edit and publish the staff reports, the commission reports, and the testimony. John Fitch of *The Survey* quoted an unnamed commissioner as saying that "$90,000 at least will be used for editing and investigations and $50,000 for public hearings."[40] This commissioner was inaccurate for two reasons: (1) the figure for the staff investigations was grossly insufficient to cover the cost of publishing the reports; and (2) any money that Walsh could obtain would go for the hearings.

When Walsh went to Washington to plead for this last appropriation, he met with great opposition. Congressman J. Hampton Moore of Philadelphia told the House that:

> . . . if some of the reported utterances of the chairman of this commission are correct, it would appear that the general disposition is to spend the money in the propogation of ideas and theories based very largely upon what is known as modern socialism.[41]

Moore was particularly disturbed about Walsh's lack of intentions to use any of the money to pay for the printing of the results of the investigation. He quoted Walsh as telling the Committee on Appropriations:

> My idea was this, that if you wanted anything printed there was some way of having it ordered printed in Congress so that we did not have to take cognizance of it in our appropriations.[42]

Although Congressman Henry Allen Cooper of Racine, Wisconsin, defended the commission,[43] Congress showed its disapproval by limiting the appropriation to $100,000. It specified that this appropriation was to cover printing costs. Having spent $350,000 already, Congress hesitated to kill the commission altogether, but by limiting its funds it nearly did so anyway.

The limitation of funds immediately made the Walsh-Commons compromise as to the conduct of the commission impossible. Not enough money was left to complete the staff investigations and also pay for completion of hearings, which already had been announced. Walsh had planned to take the commission to

---

40 *The Survey*, Vol. XXXIII, p. 582.
41 *Congressional Record*, 1915, p. 582.
42 *Ibid.*
43 *Ibid.*

Chicago; Houghton, Michigan; Atlanta; Boston; Pittsburgh; and Washington. And Walsh held the purse strings.

By early March the lack of money resulted in a controversy between Walsh and the chief of the staff investigations, Charles McCarthy. Without consulting the other commissioners, Walsh suddenly dismissed McCarthy.[44] Apparently friction had existed between the two men for some time. McCarthy had insisted that Walsh should draw up some sort of a budget for his guidance.[45] Instead of doing so, Walsh put him off, telling him not to worry about the money. Finally, when the financial plight of the commission became known, trouble was inevitable, as Walsh was ready to sacrifice the staff investigations, if necessary.

Though McCarthy was willing to work without pay to wind up the investigations, a bitter quarrel developed from which there was no compromise.[46] Although the budget problem probably was at the root, the avowed issue was McCarthy's friendship with John D. Rockefeller, Jr.[47] This friendship was of many years' standing, beginning in their college days at Brown University. Before Rockefeller had announced that Mackenzie King would conduct an investigation into industrial unrest for the Rockefeller Foundation, McCarthy had advised his friend on how to organize it.

The upshot of the dispute was that Walsh fired McCarthy.[48] The firing prompted resignations of a number of investigators Commons had hired.[49] Walsh then fired some of the others. Commons tried to undo Walsh's decisions by introducing resolutions before the commission to take back the power of the purse from Walsh. When these proposals were defeated by a tie vote, Walsh

---

[44] Harriman, p. 172.

[45] Fitzpatrick, p. 195.

[46] *Ibid.*

[47] At first, Walsh expressed no objections to McCarthy's relationship with Rockefeller; later after the quarrel over the budget had developed, he made it a major issue. *Ibid.,* p. 197.

[48] Blame for the dispute is not easily allocated; neither man was easy to get along with. Commons described them as "two Killarney Irishmen, who could never agree." Commons, *Myself,* p. 176. Walsh often became embroiled in futile controversies, such as that with Paul Kellogg, editor of *The Survey,* over the King investigations. As to McCarthy, the case is not so clear; many times in his career as Director of Wisconsin's Legislative Reference Library he had to restrain his feelings. However, he admitted that he could never get along with Robert M. LaFollette. (He was not unique in this respect.) Quoted in Fitzpatrick, p. 114. However, the conflict between the two types of investigation and the lack of adequate funds could well provoke a quarrel between men of very even temper.

Also see *The Survey,* Vol. XXXIII, November 14, 1914, pp. 175-181.

"Charles McCarthy On Why He Is Out of Federal Inquiry," *The Survey,* Vol. XXXIV, April 10, 1915, p. 40.

[49] Commons, *Myself,* p. 176.

was free to conduct the affairs of the commission as he saw fit.[50] Thus, the work of the staff of experts was almost entirely abandoned while the hearings were continued until almost the end of the commission's term.

Even if the expert staff members had been permitted to finish their work, it is doubtful the commission would have had time to consider their reports. Originally Commons had planned that these reports be submitted to the commission for approval or revision. Although the staff would compile information, draft proposed laws, and do all the work of a technical nature, the decisions would be left up to the commission. Its report would then be a consensus of opinion as to causes and possible cures for industrial unrest in America.

To aid in the reaching of such a consensus Commons organized outside of the commission a group of employers, union men, and some of his students to go over the staff reports.[51] Apparently, he thought of this group as having relations with the commission similar to that which the advisory committees in Wisconsin had with the State Industrial Commission. However, before this group had made more than a good start Walsh brought its activities to an end when he cut off all funds for Commons' staff. Furthermore, even if money had been available, it is unlikely there would have been time enough to complete such a project.

Because the reports of the experts never were submitted to the commission, Commons did not recognize them as part of its findings or recommendations. He believed they should be published as findings of individual scholars. Some of the investigators did publish their works, but most of the reports never were printed.

After McCarthy was dismissed, he was replaced by Basil Manly, who had been in charge of the staff for conducting the public hearings. Manly used the record of the testimony and reports that had been finished by the experts to write a report for the commission. Chairman Walsh and the three labor representatives signed this report. Each of these four made supplemental reports on details.

Commons, Mrs. Harriman, and the employer representatives rejected the Manly report. They submitted a report which Com-

---

50 *Ibid.*
51 *Ibid.*, p. 175.

mons wrote.[52] Thus, the majority signed Commons' dissenting report, but the employers registered additional dissents on certain points. All in all, there were two major reports and six supplemental reports. (Some of the commissioners signed more than one supplemental report.)

Exactly which report was to be the report of the commission never was made clear. In the printed volume the Manly report appeared first. It presented the findings and recommendations as those of the commission, even though only a minority agreed with them. In effect, this report by a minority was the "majority report" while the dissenting report was signed by the majority. Together these two major reports with their supplemental ones, demonstrated the chaotic disunity of the commission.

Although Congress had specified that the commission should bear the expense of printing all reports, Walsh ordered only the one-volume report to be printed.[53] The rest of the material, including transcripts of testimony, exhibits, and staff reports, was delivered in typewritten form in wooden drygoods cases to Congress. Several congressmen sharply criticized such a procedure,[54] and there was debate on whether to have the material printed. Because the chief value of the entire commission was in the record of testimony, Congress finally accepted the fact that it had no alternative but to print all of it if it wanted to salvage anything from its previous expenditures on the commission. As to the staff reports, Congress followed Walsh's recommendations not to print them. Even so, the printing expense, according to the estimate of the Senate Committee on Printing, was over $92,000.[55] Thus, the $50,000 Congress previously had withheld from the commission was more than replaced.

The Manly report

The Manly report placed the blame for industrial unrest with the employers and with the wealthy class.[56] It contained four main contentions which it documented with evidence from the testimony

52 Commons wrote the report with the help of Mrs. Harriman. During the last days of the commission's term they were together almost daily. They even worked on the report while taking a train trip to California where Mrs. Harriman was meeting her daughter to go to the Exposition. She and Commons corresponded for years afterwards. The last time Mrs. Harriman heard from Commons was when he wrote to her after hearing of her escape from Norway where she had been Ambassadress during World War II. She remembers him as a "dear sweet man." He was humble and retiring, slow to anger, but the cleverest man on the commission. Harriman, Personal Interview, *op. cit.*

53 *Congressional Record*, House Vol. 53, Part 1, 1915, p. 409.

54 *Ibid.*

55 *Congressional Record*, Senate Vol. 53, Part 5, 1916, p. 42761.

56 *Final Report and Testimony*, Vol. 1, pp. 17-152.

and also material from the unpublished reports of the expert staff. The report began with a description of the unjust and unequal distribution of wealth and income in the nation. It cited numerous statistics to demonstrate this inequality and went on to show the existence of widespread poverty as contrasted with the wealth of a few.

The second contention was a claim that the poor suffered considerable unemployment and were denied opportunities for earning their living. The unemployment, Manly asserted, was caused by the unequal distribution of income and the monopolization of land and natural resources. Workers did not receive sufficient income to purchase the products they produced, while the wealthy few had such large incomes that they could spend it only by investing in machinery for production or for further monopolization of land and natural resources. The result, the report claimed, was that productive capacity was twenty-five percent in excess of needs during normal years. Yet each industrial enterprise was supplied with workers who would be employed for only part of the year. A second cause of unemployment resulted from the withholding of land and natural resources for development. While the owners eventually might enjoy the fruits of an unearned increment, the withholding of such resources deprived many workers of opportunities for employment.

The third contention consisted of an indictment of the country's legal system. The report pointed to the great difficulty in passing any legislation protecting working people. When such legislation finally was passed in spite of unfair lobbying of employers, it often was invalidated by the courts. The courts had perverted the fourteenth amendment, the purpose of which was to protect human rights. By citing this amendment they had declared most social legislation unconstitutional. Yet the courts by unwarranted extension of their own powers had issued injunctions that suppressed the rights of the workers. In many cases the procedure had been evasion of the constitutional guarantees for persons accused of illegal acts. Instead of trying persons in criminal courts with juries for such activity as violence during strikes, authorities would cite defendents for contempt of court for violating injunctions. Such persons accused of such violations then were tried by the judges who had issued the injunctions. Not only did such a procedure deprive the accused of their rights, but it was an effective means to combatting unions.

In addition to alleging that one-sided justice was dispensed by the courts, it was argued that powerful employers often controlled governments by the use of political machines. Not only could such control insure employers of favorable legislation, but by controlling the governors, a powerful weapon would be at their disposal. During a strike the governor could declare martial law and send troops to the scene. While such troops would protect strikebreakers, anyone opposing these efforts could be subject to military law. Answerable only to the governor, the military authorities could exercise wide discretion in jailing those involved in a strike. Under martial law civil liberties could be suppressed. The Manly report cited a number of cases where such actions had occurred.

All in all, the report asserted there were two types of justice; one for the employer and another for the worker. The courts protected the property rights of the employer but were ineffective in protecting the rights of workers. The injured workman, or the workman who was unable to collect his salary, or one who had some other grievance, found the courts expensive and justice uncertain. Although the courts were quick to work against the poor, they tended to be indifferent in protecting them.

The fourth contention of the report was that the employers denied the employees the right to form effective organizations. Wherever the right to belong to unions had been denied, "Freedom does not exist either politically, industrially, or socially, and that the fiber of manhood will inevitably be destroyed by the continuance of the existing situation."[57] Methods used by corporations to stamp out unions had led to the supression of freedom not only of the workers involved, but also of others in the community. Furthermore, denial of the right to form unions prevented workers from seeking relief from the first three causes of industrial unrest.

To provide remedies for industrial unrest in the nation, the Manly report recommended a number of radical reforms. To reverse the trend toward concentration of wealth and income it advocated a graduated tax on inheritances with rates equaling one hundred percent on estates over $1,000,000. Taxes on unused land and natural resources were to be high enough to insure their use. A constitutional amendment was recommended to withdraw from the courts the power to declare legislative acts unconstitutional. The telephone and telegraph industry would be nationalized if the report's recommendation were followed. Other recommenda-

---

[57] *Ibid.*, p. 65.

tions included the creation of a labor mediation system, the prohibition of the transporting of company guards across interstate boundaries, prohibiting employers from refusing to deal with unions, law guaranteeing workers the right to belong to unions, government insurance against sickness for the workers, special protection for people living in isolated company towns, and an end to the use of the doctrine of conspiracy in suppressing union activity. Recommendations were many and detailed. Some seem reasonable today but all were radical for 1915.

The Commons Report

Commons, along with Mrs. Harriman, submitted a dissenting report.[58] Except on a few points the employer members (Harris Weinstock, S. Thurston Ballard, and Richard H. Aishton[59]) concurred with this report. These five rejected the findings and recommendations of the Manly report. They asserted that the Manly report contained "few or no practicable suggestions for legislation that would be enforceable, or because they are directed to making a few individuals scapegoats where what is needed is serious attention to the system that produced the demand for scapegoats, and, with it, the breakdown of labor legislation in the country."[60]

The real trouble was that "our statute books are encumbered by laws that are conflicting, ambiguous, and unenforceable, or partly enforced." Consequently, "as soon as people lose confidence in the making of laws by the legislature, in their interpretation by the courts and in their administration by officials, they take the law into their own hands."[61] The problem, therefore, was how to reorganize the law so it would fit existing conditions and be enforceable.

To be effective any proposals had to recognize that a permanent struggle existed between capital and labor. Yet the proposals also should take advantage of the fact that there were certain points where the interests were harmonious or could be made harmonious. This field of no actual conflict was wider than many realized.

The heart of the Commons report was a recommendation that industrial commissions, modeled on the one in Wisconsin, be set up in the various states and that a similar one be created for the

---

58 *Ibid.*, pp. 171-230.
59 Appointed commissioner March 17, 1915, to serve the unexpired term of F. A. Delano who resigned.
60 *Final Report and Testimony*, p. 11.
61 *Ibid.*

national government. All bureaus and divisions of the states or federal government dealing with conditions of labor, such as industrial safety or sanitation, workmen's compensation, employment offices, child labor, industrial education, statistics, immigration, and so on, would be placed under the direction of the commissions. The commissioners were to be appointed by the governors for the states and by the President for the federal commission. Their terms should be for six years, staggered in such a way that two expire each two years.

To aid the commissions in their work, advisory councils such as used by the Wisconsin commission should be created representing employers, unions, and the public. Two of the members representing the public on the federal advisory council would be the Secretary of Commerce and the Secretary of Labor. Although the President, in the case of federal advisory councils, and the governors for those in the states, would appoint the representatives, appointment of employer or union representatives should be from lists submitted by organized groups of employers and labor. These councils would have no power to vote on any issues but would make recommendations to the various industrial commissions. They would advise on all appointments, investigations, publications, and rules and regulations which should be decided by the commissions. Such recommendations would be published with both majority and minority opinions. Although the commissioners would not be bound by the advisory councils' recommendations, they could use them to strengthen their own decisions.

Exactly what the powers of the various commissions were to be, the report did not make precisely clear. Presumably, the state commissions were to be patterned after that of Wisconsin's Industrial Commission. But the dividing line between the powers of the state and federal commissions was left indefinite in the report. Apparently the report was not an attempt to outline a complete labor legislation program, but just an attempt to suggest some procedures for formulating and then administering any program.

Perhaps in recognition of the fact that it was not complete, the report stressed the role of investigation by the various commissions. The commissions were to make and publish investigations and recommendations on all subjects whose administration was entrusted to them. Any other investigations were to be made only at the request of the legislatures, Congress, or the courts.

Such investigations might include basic information for drafting laws by the legislatures and for formulating rules by which the commissions would enforce labor laws. More routine investigations would include the assembling of data on wages, hours, industrial disputes, and other labor matters.

The report also spelled out how labor laws would be enforced, a procedure similar to that used by Wisconsin's commission. In the case of safety laws, the various legislatures would set down the broad requirement that all factories should be as safe as they could reasonably be made. Then the commissions would determine the exact standards that would meet the legislative directive. In setting such standards they would utilize the services of the advisory councils to reach a reasonable basis on which employers, labor leaders, and experts in the field could agree. After public hearings at which all interested parties would have opportunities to raise objections, the commissions would promulgate their rules. If then there were objections, recourse could be had to the courts. Yet the burden of proof that the rules or regulations of the commissions were unreasonable would be on the party contesting them. In all these recommendations as to procedure the report was following those prescribed for the Wisconsin Industrial Commission.

To aid in settling industrial disputes the report recommended that each commission (state and federal) appoint a chief mediator and several assistants. Such mediators would have no powers to compel testimony and would be prohibited from arbitrating any dispute. Also they were prohibited from disclosing any information they might obtain from any parties to an industrial dispute. If a mediator was unable to obtain agreement between the disputing parties he might recommend arbitration and aid the parties in selecting a board of arbitration. Such a board would have the power to compel testimony. However, in no case would arbitration be compulsory. If the disputing parties did not want intervention the mediators would be barred even from making investigations of the situation.

Any approach towards compulsory arbitration, or even compulsory investigation would plunge labor disputes into politics. Each side would try to capture the power to appoint arbitrators partial to its cause. Such widening of the area of conflict between capital and labor was considered unwise. Collective bargaining, it stated, should be the means of resolving industrial disputes.

While the recommendations of the report placed its chief reliance on collective bargaining in the determination of industrial conditions, Commons went even further. He insisted there should be no interference with the coercive weapons of strikes, lockouts, boycotting, or blacklists. He reasoned that because it is impossible to prevent blacklisting, it is unfair to take away labor's comparable weapon, the boycott. He even would permit secondary boycotts on the ground that any damage to third parties is minor and can be avoided by such parties if they comply with the primary boycott. The real victim is the boycotted employer who is involved in a dispute with a labor union. Because such an employer is free to use a blacklist against labor, Commons argued that he does not deserve protection against boycotts, whether primary or secondary.

The employer members of the United States Commission on Industrial Relations dissented from this "no holds barred" point of view. They condemned both the blacklist and the secondary boycott. The latter they believed was illegal, but the former they merely condemned. But on the whole affected employers agreed with Commons' position. The only other major point of disagreement was the employers' belief that the commissions should have the power to make investigations and to publicize the facts when an unsettled dispute seriously affected the public interests. They cited as examples disputes affecting necessary public utilities.

In addition to setting up commissions and providing them with mediation services, the Commons report also had a few suggestions for labor laws. It recommended legislatures or Congress to enact laws requiring companies that operate their plants on a twenty-four hour basis to divide their operations into three shifts. Such companies should require their employees to work only one shift a day for a six-day week.

Congress or legislatures also should enact laws similar to the British Trades Disputes Act of 1906. The purpose of such laws would be to relieve employers' associations and labor unions of liability from criminal or damage suits and injunctions arising from a combination or conspiracy connected with a labor dispute. Any act that would be legal for an individual to perform ought to be legal when done by a union or employers' association.

The commissions were to have the authority to regulate detective agencies and the hiring of armed guards to be used in industrial disputes. The War Department, after consulting with the federal commission and its advisory council, should draw up rules for preventing improper use of state militias during strikes.

Miscellaneous proposals of the report included placing the enforcement of immigration laws under the federal commission. Also, the report contained the suggestion that some sort of land reform be instituted to prevent absentee ownership over farm lands. Other proposals endorsed minimum wage laws for women and children and a system of national and state employment offices.

To finance any program for social welfare that might be adopted by Congress and legislatures the report recommended levying a federal inheritance tax on all estates over $25,000, beginning at one percent on the excess above $25,000, and rising to fifteen percent on the excess above $1,000,000 for the class of direct heirs, such as wives, children, and parents. For more remote relatives and strangers, the report recommended higher rates, but did not specify what they should be. Such taxes were to be super-taxes added upon existing states taxes. However, any state that would repeal its inheritance taxes would qualify to receive fifty cents per capita of its population from the federal government each year. The remaining money would be used to cover the expenses of the federal commission for subsidies to the state commissions to aid in their part in the social welfare program. Such money would be granted on condition states maintained certain minimum conditions.

Of what this welfare program actually would consist, and how the roles of the various state commissions would differ from that of the federal commission was not made clear. Formulation of such a program could be made by the federal commission after appropriate study and consultation with its advisory council.

Finally, the report ended with the suggestion of reforms to prevent corporations from controlling government. It suggested that protection of the secret ballot, limitation of expenditures and the number of paid electioneers in elections, direct primaries, proportional representation, initiative and recall (except for Supreme Court judges or members of legislatures) should be provided to prevent corrupt practices.

On the whole, the Commons report aimed at providing machinery by which capital-labor issues could be resolved. While the main reliance remained on collective bargaining for specific disputes, the report, recommended the creation of commissions, advisory councils, and mediation machinery to resolve disputed issues. Although a few specific recommendations were made as to desirable labor laws, the report did not provide any detailed description of a labor program. Instead it suggested means by which investigations could be made, as well as compromises by capital and labor in the formulation of such a program of labor and social legislation. Clearly, it was patterned after what Commons had learned in the creation and administration of the Wisconsin Industrial Commission.

The aftermath

When the United States Commission on Industrial Relations submitted its several reports on August 23, 1915, other more dramatic news held the public's attention. News from the various fronts of World War I competed for newspaper space and headlines. Russia on the Eastern Front and the allies on the Western Front and at Gallipoli furnished reams of copy demanding attention. At sea the submarine campaign was highlighted by the sinking of the Arabic. Stories of the sinking and testimony of the survivors crowded much of the other news from the front pages.

The final press release from the commission did make the front pages of most important newspapers of the country, but only for one day. Then, after a day or two, each newspaper provided editorial comment on the commission's work. The magazines soon followed with their comments. By and large, the commission ended its career with a minimum of notice from the press.

Except in the labor press most editorial comment was extremely critical. Much of the criticism was of Chairman Walsh. For example, the *New York Times* made a fairly typical estimate of him:

> Unfortunately, the Chairman of the commission, one of the three public members appointed to represent the public, has displayed from the first a heat and violence of bias and a passion of intemperant speech that have disgusted some of his colleagues, destroyed confidence and deadened interest in the commission, made it plainly a fantastic futility.[62]

Commenting on the proposal to levy a 100 percent tax on all inheritances over $1,000,000, the *Times* suggested that a new verb

---

[62] "The Walsh Commission," *New York Times,* August 23, 1915, p. 8.

"to walsh" might enrich the language and be used to describe such a confiscation. Echoing this sentiment, *The New York World* sarcastically suggested there was no reason why such confiscation should begin at the $1,000,000 mark.[63] As to the *World's* general impression of the commission's work, it called such a performance "barren."[64] It displayed a cartoon showing Uncle Sam throwing the *Report of Federal Commission on Industrial Relations* into a wastepaper basket. Under the cartoon the caption read, "And it costs only $500,000."

The magazines tended to agree with the newspapers. They too centered their fire on Chairman Walsh. The *Nation* called the performance of the commission a "fiasco."[65] Commenting on the demise of the commission (its term expiring August 23, 1915), the *Outlook* declared that it would have few mourners.[66] Dismissing the work of the commission as "agitation," *Harper's Weekly* predicted that ". . . all the reports, aggregating some two hundred thousand words, will be neglected by the public and the Congress."[67]

Some of the editorial comment made a distinction between the Manly and the Commons reports. The *Nation* predicted:

> The Commons-Harriman portion of the Industrial Relations Commission will receive discussion where Walsh's maunderings will be thrown aside.[68]

Yet the *Nation* expressed doubts as to whether the proposed commissions could function harmoniously. It feared that deadlocks and quarrels might mar its performance. The fiasco of the Walsh commission had spotlighted such dangers. The *New York Times* characterized the proposed commissions as "another addition to bureaucracy."[69] *Outlook* tended to look with favor on the use of commissions but thought the work could come under the Federal Trade Commission.[70] The country, it declared, was not ready for the creation of the proposed commissions. Such a contention was probably correct after the example provided by the Walsh commission.

---

63 "Why $1,000,000?" *The New York World*, August 24, 1915, p. 8.
64 "A Barren Performance," *The New York World*, August 23, 1915, p. 8.
65 "'The Fiasco of the Industrial Commission," *The Nation*, Vol. CI, p. 251.
66 "Industrial Relations Committee Report," *Outlook*, Vol. CXI, pp. 7, 8.
67 "Agitation," *Harper's Weekly*, Vol. LXI, p. 342.
68 "The Week," *The Nation*, Vol. CI, p. 277.
69 *New York Times, op. cit.*
70 *Outlook, op. cit.*

More than any other periodical, the *Survey* contrasted the Manly report with that of Commons:

> What the Manly report most obviously lacks is, first a philosophy and second, a constructive plan of action. Both of these the Commons report has. Evidence of the first appears in those fundamental conceptions which are discussed in our summary of the report. Where the Manly report has no explanation of the conflict between capital and labor unless it be the wickedness of capital, and no plan except to get the capitalists on the run, the Commons report sees in the struggle between capital and labor two factors of permanent opposition and progressive co-operation which can both be employed as forces for advance. Where the Manly report presents merely a partisan demand that labor be freed of all restraints and be permitted to organize at will to further its own interests, the Commons report holds that organization is essential in the interest of fundamental justice to all classes of society . . .
>
> The time will come, however, when it will be recognized that in the conscientiously thoughtful proposals of Professor Commons we have a program that is broad and constructive, the product of clear-sighted statesmanship.[71]

The writer of the above words, John A. Fitch, was a student of Commons. As the correspondent of *The Survey*, he attended most of the hearings and reported on them.[72] He knew most of the investigators Commons had hired. Perhaps no one else not connected with the commission was as familiar with its work. Although he might be expected to be sympathetic with Commons, his reactions were typical of the others in the group of liberals who contributed to *The Survey*. On the editorial page, *The Survey* echoed Fitch's view as to Commons' contribution.[73]

These liberals tended to accept Commons' proposed commission because it had been on the basis of his experience with the successful Wisconsin Industrial Commission that they had backed his nomination to the United States Commission on Industrial Relations. In his contribution to their symposium printed before the commission began its work, Commons stressed the need for "better organization and co-operation of all state and federal agencies that deal with labor problems."[74] Consequently, his recommendations were in line with what they might have anticipated. The same group of liberals rejected the Manly report as a partisan document. Although they tended to sympathize with labor when

71 Fitch, *The Survey*, Vol. XXXV, pp. 401, 402.
72 Fitch, "Probing the Causes of Unrest," *The Survey*, Vol. XXXII, Vol. XXXIII, Vol. XXXIV, Vol. XXXV.
73 *The Survey*, Vol. XXXV, pp. 406, 407.
74 Commons, *The Survey*, Vol. XXX, p. 578.

it was forced to play the role of the underdog, they could not condone the lack of objectivity in the report.

On the other hand, the labor papers praised Walsh and the Manly report.[75] They pictured Walsh as a fearless fighter who dared expose the misdeeds of the employers. Newspaper criticisms of him they construed as the reaction of the capitalistic press which was bent upon suppressing the facts. To prevent such suppression, the labor leaders warned their readers that they should urge their congressmen to authorize the printing of the commission's findings.

Although their praise of Walsh and his findings were enthusiastic, the labor editors said very little concerning any of the recommendations of the commission. This is not surprising. They had had more time to digest and react to what happened during the hearings than they had had to analyze the numerous proposals contained in the various reports. For months they had been following the course of the hearings, but if they wished their comments to be timely, they needed to express their opinions on the commission's report as soon as possible after its release. Furthermore, it is doubtful that labor editors (or their union leaders) could have agreed in any numbers on the numerous and complex proposals in either the Manly or Commons report. However, it was easy for them to react enthusiastically to the partisan support on their behalf by Walsh. They could even rejoice that Commons, Mrs. Harriman, and the employers supported the principle of collective bargaining.

Gomper's editorial was typical. He wrote, "The spirit of the report . . . is representative of the fearless, direct investigations the commission made into industrial evils and injustices."[76] He quoted the Manly report on the subject of low wages and inequality of income. While he enumerated some of the proposals for redistribution of wealth and income, he did not comment on them. Instead, he quoted passages indicating that the commission supported the principle of collective bargaining. On this subject he quoted the Commons as well as the Manly report. Because the spirit of the report interested him more than the recommenda-

---

75 Gompers, "Industrial Relations Commission's Report," *American Federationist*, Vol. XXII, pp. 861, 862.
   The Bricklayer, Mason, and Plasterer, Vol. XVIII, p. 200.
   Machinists Monthly Journal, Vol. XXVII, p. 682.
   The Painter and Decorator, Vol. XXIX ,p. 457.
   The Typographical Journal, Vol. XXXXVII, p. 441.
   "Report of the Industrial Relations Commission," *United Mine Workers' Journal*, Vol. XXV, pp. 4,5.
76 Gompers, *American Federationist*.

tions, most of his comments centered on the Manly report. He promised to comment later on the details of the recommendations, but he never did. Even in his autobiography, he mentioned the "educational effect" of the commission's work while ignoring the recommendations.[77] Obviously, he did not agree with many of them, but he was grateful for the commission's partisan support.

The United Mine Workers, some of whose members had been killed in the Ludlow Massacre (which the commission investigated) sided with the Manly report.[78] While they praised Walsh and his recommendations, they criticized Commons. They feared that his advisory councils would smother the attempts of the workers for self help. Conceding that the Commons report was made in good faith, they asserted that because the authors were not of the working class, they could not be expected to understand the problems of the workers.

The miners were not content merely to praise the Manly report. According to Mrs. Harriman, they attempted to pressure her into signing it.[79] "Mother" Jones, the fiery defender of the miners, pleaded with her by the hour. Commons, himself, found it distasteful to oppose the report backed by labor members.[80] Two of the labor members, he said, did not take his dissent personally, but the third, A. B. Garretson, displayed his continuing dislike of Commons later by snubbing him whenever they met.

Some labor leaders also gave their support to a committee formed for the purpose of furthering the recommendations of the Manly report.[81] The committee hired Basil Manly to conduct a campaign in Washington to sell his report to influential people. Whatever influence he and his committee may have had, they failed to make much of an impression on Congress.

Except for a wrangle over whether the reports and the record of testimony should be printed, Congress paid little attention to

77 Gompers, *Seventy Years of Life and Labor*, Vol. I, p. 448.
78 *United Mine Worker's Journal, loc. cit.*
79 Harriman, p. 173.
80 Commons, *Myself*, p. 168.
81 "A Follow-up Committee on Industrial Relations," *The Survey*, Vol. XXXV, pp. 155, 156. In addition to the three labor commissioners, Lennon, O'Connell, and Garretson, a number of prominent labor officials joined the committee. Among them were John P. White, president of the United Mine Workers, and John Fitzpatrick, president of the Chicago Federation of Labor. With them was Helen Marot of the Women's Trade Union League of New York and Agnes Nestor of the Woman's Trade Union League of Chicago. Members of the committee not identified with the labor movement included Frank P. Walsh, Amos Pinchot, Frederick C. Howe, commissioner of immigration at New York, Bishop Williams of Michigan, and Dante Barton of Kansas City.

either the findings or the recommendations of its commission. It ignored equally the Manly and the Commons reports.

For its twenty-two months of work, the United States Commission on Industrial Relations had nothing to show except its rejected reports and eleven volumes of reports, exhibits, and record of testimony. It could not agree on the basic underlying causes of industrial unrest. During its hearings, it uncovered and publicized evidence of unrest. Yet when the commission's term expired, its reports did not bring the problems into focus. Because of the disagreements, these reports were written at the last possible minute and in considerable haste. The public was given the impression that there were as many reports as there were commissioners (if all the supplemental statements were counted). Furthermore, most of the staff reports were abandoned even though considerable sums had been spent on their preparations. All in all, the confusion in which it expired at the end of its term, merely underlined the fact that the commission was a failure.

The effect on Commons

The miserable failure by the commission did not alter Commons' faith in his method of resolving conflicts through negotiation and compromise. His success with the Wisconsin Industrial Commission prevented such a disillusionment. But he did recognize that one ingredient of his former success was lacking in this second experience.[82] In Wisconsin he had convinced both sides that their respective welfare depended on accepting some one of the alternatives he offered them. He had managed to create the impression among those responsible for the negotiations that the reforms he proposed ultimately would be adopted with or without their co-operation. Consequently, they should concentrate their energies in trying to reach an acceptable compromise. If their opposition destroyed the basis for such a compromise, they would be narrowing the possibilities to two; one totally acceptable and one completely unacceptable. Because he made the latter appear the most probable to whichever side was hesitating, Commons succeeded in effecting compromises.

Yet Commons' method could not work on the Commission on Industrial Relations except to a limited extent.[83] Commons did not

---

82 Commons, *Myself,* p. 179.
83 The extent to which it succeeded was shown by the employer representatives' acceptance of most of Commons' proposals, even though they were radical for their day. When faced with a choice between the flagrantly radical Manly report and Commons' slightly less radical one, they signed the one least objectionable to them.

have the same control over the situation. Instead of being the leading figure (as a chairman might be), he was merely one of the commissioners. Instead of spending all of his time on the job, he had to divide it between his university teaching and the commission work.

Perhaps the most important difference between Commons' Wisconsin experience and the one on the federal commission was in the political situation. In Wisconsin he had strong political influences behind him, pushing toward reform legislation. The urgency of the situation almost compelled the various conflicting interests to work through him to achieve compromises.

In contrast, the United States Commission on Industrial Relations had almost no real political support behind it. Few expected that Congress would adopt any legislation because of it. Its role was the vague one of seeking the causes of unrest. The only urgency came from the dwindling of its allotted time. Except for the pride of individual commissioners in achieving a successful conclusion to their work, there was no real necessity for compromise. Consequently, Commons' method did not apply. And the failure, although lamentable, was rather inconsequential.

The failure did have a personal consequence for Commons. One of his investigators, Robert Hoxie, after being dropped by Walsh, came to Commons in distress. Commons described Hoxie as "in a nervous and incoherent state of mind."[84] Yet the material he submitted to Commons was such that it was "the first really scientific study of scientific management, and it would be a serious misfortune if he did not publish as much of it as was already prepared."[85] Commons promised to find a publisher for him, and after being encouraged, he "went home seemingly cheerful."[86]

Although the manuscript was not in the finished shape Hoxie wanted it to be, Commons urged him to publish it anyway. Apparently, fearing criticism for publishing an imperfect book, but not feeling up to finishing it, Hoxie was in a dilemma.[87] Shortly afterwards he committed suicide.

Somehow Commons felt responsible for the tragedy. He said that it "burned" into his life.[88] Despite Hoxie's death, he went

---

84 Commons, *Myself*, p. 179.
85 *Ibid.*
86 *Ibid.*
87 *Ibid.*
88 *Ibid*, p. 177.

ahead with plans to obtain a publisher for Hoxie's book on *Scientific Management*.[89] Then he aided Hoxie's wife in editing a large number of articles and unpublished manuscripts for another book, *Trade Unionism in the United States*.[90] Both of these books became classics in their fields.

Commons did not escape the effects of tension either. In the spring of 1916 he suffered another of his nervous collapses, the first in ten years. To recuperate, he left Madison shortly before examination time for Lake Tenderfoot on the Wisconsin-Michigan border. There he spent a leisurely summer, followed by a long visit at his sister's (Clara) home in Mt. Vernon, New York. Finally, in February, 1917, he returned to the university to resume teaching his classes.

89 Hoxie, *Scientific Management and Labor.*
90 Hoxie, *Trade Unionism in the United States.*

PART III | COMMONS'
THOUGHT

JOHN R. COMMONS,
STUDENT OF THE LABOR MOVEMENT

JOHN R. COMMONS' influence on the thinking of students of the labor movement continues even in contemporary writing. While his works on general economics gather dust, his *History of Labor* remains a classic often quoted in its field.[1] No adequate substitute exists for its detailed coverage of the earlier years, so it is likely to remain an important history. Yet his influence on current thinking is due to much more than this one contribution. Commons wrote widely on the subject of labor and his works had wide circulation. Although some of what he wrote is of historical importance only, his conceptions of the nature and origins of the labor movement have relevance today.

His ideas on the labor movement are imbedded in the body of thought of what is often called the "Wisconsin School." This school includes Commons and a number of his students who specialized in labor economics.[2] Not only did this group trace the origins of the American labor movement, but the members developed theories explaining the behavior of unions. In general, their theories painted the unions as organizations compatible with the capi-

---

1 Commons, *History of Labor*.
2 Selig Perlman, John B. Andrews, Don Lescohier, Ira Cross, Edwin Witte, Elizabeth Brandeis, Frank Carlton, David Saposs, Russell Bauder, Philip Taft, and Milton Derber.

talistic system. Unions with revolutionary aims were pictured as deviations from the normal. Working people, according to the "Wisconsin School," are more interested in immediate gains than in revolutions. Although radical "intellectuals" have at times seduced the rank and file, they have not been able to prevail permanently over the workers' natural conservatism.

Commons and his students were among the earliest scholarly observers of the American labor movement. They reported their observations accurately and convincingly. Because of the slow pace of change in the labor movement, their facts on the behavior of unions still are generally accepted. What have been challenged often, then and to this day, are their theories as to why unions behave as they do. Both the widespread acceptance of their theories, and the continuing challenges, demonstrated the degree of influence the "Wisconsin School" has enjoyed.[3]

This founding of a continuing school of thought climaxed a successful career as a labor economist for Commons. It is fortunate he turned to the subject of labor. Until he focused his attention on this subject, his scholarly efforts were unsuccessful. Furthermore, his constant dabbling into unpopular reforms had kept him in trouble. The study of labor enabled him to combine his zeal for reform, his ability to stimulate students, and his capacity for hard work in such a way that he became one of America's outstanding labor economists.

Commons' background and experiences shaped his views

Commons' theories and analysis always drew heavily from his experiences and contacts. In his day there was perhaps no way to become an authority on labor problems other than by studying them directly. There was no substantial amount of authoritative material written on such subjects. He and his students pioneered the digging up of facts from the past, and his conceptions grew out of his experiences.

Although most of his firsthand knowledge of labor unions came from his contacts with labor leaders while attempting to solve labor problems, Commons did have a limited amount of experience as a union member. During his college days, he spent four summers as a compositor in Cleveland. Because the shop where he worked was a union shop, while the one across the street where his brother worked was not, he had an opportunity to compare con-

---

3 See below.

ditions. In general, there was no great difference. Both shops had
the same piece rates and the same working hours. What was different was the method of distributing the easier and more lucrative
type of work. In the nonunion shop the foreman gave such work
to his favorites. In the shop where Commons worked the workers
were permitted to bid for it, and on the process, earnings were
equalized and the possibilities of discrimination minimized. Such
differences in particular practices between union and nonunion
printing shops may not have been typical, but to Commons they
were significant. He valued his experience highly and in 1891 accepted an honorary membership in Typographical Union Local No.
53 of Cleveland, Ohio.[4]

More important than any direct experience as a worker were
his contacts with labor leaders. In 1897 and 1898 the *Federation-
ist* published a series of articles written by Commons, entitled, "A
Comparison of Day Labor and Contract System on Municipal
Works."[5] In view of the number of articles, the contact between
Commons and the *Federationist* editor must have been extensive.
At least Gompers specifically mentioned in his autobiography that
he knew Commons dating from this contact. They met on other occasions later when Commons was working for the National Civic
Federation, and when he was a member of the United States Com-
mission on Industrial Relations.

Commons greatly admired Gompers. In the Gompers obituary
he wrote, Commons declared, "Samuel Gompers was, in my opinion, one of the ten or twelve great Americans." He went on to
claim, "It is now twenty-seven years ago that I became personally
acquainted with Gompers, and I have counted myself since among
his followers."[6]

Just how far Commons meant to go in this last statement is
subject to conjecture, but Commons' views on the labor movement
closely paralleled those of Gompers. Even their methods of thinking displayed similarities. Yet the extent to which Commons was
influenced by Gompers is impossible to know. He may have found
in Gompers a labor leader who thought as Commons thought a
labor leader should think, or Gompers may have been the direct
source of his ideas. Gompers was the first prominent labor leader
Commons knew. In any event, the similarity of thinking is striking.

---

4 Commons, *Myself*, p. 19.
5 Commons, *American Federationist*, Vol. 3, pp. 229-32, 252-54; Vol. 4, pp. 3-6, 27-29,
49-51, 71-73, 88-90, 111-13, 150-54, 183-86, 207-209, 229-31; Vol. 4, pp. 252-53.
6 Commons, *Current History*, Vol. XXI, p. 670.

Gompers was described as "more intuitive than intellectual, more motor than reflective."[7] Even Commons conceded that, "His mind seemed to be rather slow in action rather ponderous and heavy . . ." Yet Commons claimed that Gompers " . . . thought in terms of experiment," with particular attention to facts and their applications.[8]

Although Gompers perhaps was incapable of sustained analysis, he had developed intuitions based on experience. To Commons, the pragmatist, Gompers' type of thinking was not inferior to that of glib-tongued theorists who commanded superior logic. Rather, he could be expected to believe it led to insights necessary for understanding the labor movement. He argued that Gompers, the empiricist, "knew that life and the experiences of life outran logic."[9]

Both Commons and Gompers viewed "intellectuals" in the trade union movement with suspicion. Each pointed to labor movement difficulties caused by such individuals. Often intellectuals led the unions into the labyrinth of politics. Such futile expenditure of energies often led to neglect of the important function of unions— improvement of wages and working conditions. Workers have tended to prefer immediate gains rather than wait for ultimate results from political efforts. Intellectuals often misjudge the psychology of the worker and at times are amazed when he fails to share their enthusiasms. Sometimes this failure to understand the worker has contributed to failure in organizing and holding members in unions, especially during crucial times. When intellectuals went so far as to make stable collective bargaining difficult or even impossible, they were particularly dangerous to the labor movement.

Commons and Gompers especially disagreed with radical "intellectuals" who believed members of the labor movement should work towards overthrowing the capitalistic system. It made little difference to the two of them whether the radicals proposed destroying capitalism by violent revolutions or peacefully by radical legislation. Accepting capitalism, they opposed radical changes. In fact, they both feared rapid changes of any sort. They believed in a step-by-step evolutionary process that would avoid a host of unforeseeable troubles. When each step of progress becomes rooted in successful experience, the basis for the next step would be created.

---

7 Harvey, p. 213.
8 Commons, *Current History*, Vol. XXI, p. 670.
9 Harvey, p. 116.

In promoting progress, the two men stressed the importance of forging institutions based on voluntary agreements. In Gompers' words:

> To my mind only development based on voluntary institutions holds promise of permanent progress, for such development is responsive to developing technology and cultural advance of individuals and group activity.[10]

The American Federation of Labor under Gompers remained a voluntary institution. Lacking centralized control, Gompers used moral power to direct the efforts of his union to organize labor. In spite of serious jurisdictional conflicts, he relied on voluntary compromises in trying to hold his organization together.

Gompers also believed that capital and labor had no basic conflicts that could not be resolved with voluntary agreements. Such collective bargaining, he claimed, rendered governmental intervention unnecessary.[11] He completely rejected compulsory arbitration and instead insisted that the role of government should be neutral in labor disputes.

Although Gompers did not expect labor to be neutral in politics, he was reluctant to commit the A. F. of L. to any political party. He was willing to use his influence to defeat known foes of labor or to elect friends. Yet he tended to minimize union involvement in politics. Because he believed that few gains for labor could be obtained by legislation, he was content when government maintained a laissez-faire policy toward unions. Then they would be free to win their gains through economic pressure on employers.

To a large extent, Commons shared Gompers' view as to the relation of unions and the government. He felt that unions should be wary of too much political action. Yet he was quite willing to utilize government to insure the welfare of the workers. In social legislation he was willing to go much further than Gompers. However, he agreed with Gompers that the government should not interfere with the bargaining between labor and capital. Like Gompers, he held the belief that workable compromises can be achieved through negotiations.

How many of his ideas on labor Commons borrowed from Gompers is impossible to know. In addition to studying the history

---

10 Gompers, p. 24.

11 In a few cases which he apparently saw as special cases, he advanced legislation to protect workers' rights. For example, he urged the passage of LaFollette's Seamen's Act of 1915, and he backed the miners in their efforts to obtain legislation requiring adequate safety precautions in mines.

of the labor movement, which he believed confirmed such views, Commons could have derived some of his views from his experiences with some of the other labor leaders.[12] In his autobiography and elsewhere, he described such experiences much more minutely than he did those he shared with Gompers.

After Commons was dismissed by the University of Syracuse, his work for the next five years caused him to meet many of the leaders of the American labor movement. The first position was with the Industrial Commission appointed by President Mc-Kinley; his job was to finish a report on immigration. In making his investigations before writing the report, he met members of both organized and unorganized labor.

During his investigation he became acquainted with Abraham Bisno, who, he claimed, introduced to him the ideas of Karl Marx and also added to his knowledge of labor unionism. His sessions with Bisno constituted a daily seminar for six months. Bisno, an immigrant, had escaped at the age of twelve with his family from the pogroms of Kiev, Russia. With very little schooling, he was brought up in the sweatshops of the American clothing industry. Working in these shops, he developed a philosophy Commons described as an American form of syndicalism. During busy seasons in the clothing industry Bisno worked in the sweatshops while organizing workers so they could obtain higher piece rates. As soon as the busy season was over he was the first to be laid off. His organization would collapse, and he spent the dull season as a real estate agent. With such a background, he was a stimulating as well as useful assistant.

In addition to using it to make his report for the Industrial Commission, Commons used his material to write a series of articles entitled, "Racial Composition of the American People," published during 1903 and 1904 in the *Chautauquan*.[13] Later, in 1907, he again used it for a book, *Races and Immigrants in America*.[14] He consistently campaigned for restrictions on immigration until they finally were provided. He maintained that unlimited immigrations resulted in accentuating the business cycle by permitting employers to overexpand by using cheap labor. In the meantime, high tariffs would prevent imported goods from providing a check on rising domestic prices. With wages held low by the competition

---

12 Commons, *Myself*, p. 69.
13 Commons, Vol. XXXVIII, pp. 33-42, 118-125, 223-34, 333-40; Vol. XXXVIII, pp. 433-43, 533-43; Vol. XXXIX, pp. 13-22, 115-24, 217-25.
14 Commons, *Races and Immigrants in America*.

of immigrant labor, price increases widened profit margins, providing irrestible incentives for business men to expand their operations. Yet lagging purchasing power foredoomed the expansion.

Commons' study of problems resulting from unlimited immigration also caused him to meet union leaders. During this study he visited about half of the national trade union headquarters and became acquainted with most of the prominent union leaders.[15]

When he visited the bituminous coal miners he was greatly impressed by their methods of collective bargaining. For about a week he observed the national joint conference of mine workers and their employers. He said that on one side of a great hall were nearly a thousand elected delegates from local unions. On the other side were seventy employers who owned coal mines. Such an arrangement reminded Commons of the British Parliament with a House of Commons and a House of Lords. He recognized it also as a variation on his own idea of representation of interests. The collective bargaining procedure required no third party. Yet this voluntary organization of representatives from conflicting interests could solve their mutual problems by creating working rules. In his enthusiasm, Commons wrote an article which he named, "Constitutional Government in Industry." However, the editor of the *Review of Reviews,* in which it was published, changed the name to "A New Way of Settling Labor Disputes."[16] Later Commons drew on this experience in the formulation of advisory boards for the Industrial Commission of Wisconsin.

While he was getting acquainted with labor leaders and their problems, he also came across a book that stimulated his thinking. For reading on the train between visits, he took a copy of the Webbs' *Industrial Democracy.*[17] He was particularly impressed with their analysis of the "Common Rule" and "working rules." These concepts he further developed and combined under the name of the "Working Rules" of collective action, by which workers protect themselves against competitive menaces.[18]

When Commons completed his work with the Industrial Commission, he took a position as a conciliator with the newly formed National Civic Federation. As a member of this organization, Commons shared in some very important developments affecting the

15 Commons, *Myself,* p .71.
16 John R. Commons, *American Monthly Review of Reviews,* Vol. XXIII, pp. 328-33.
17 Sidney and Beatrice Webb, *Industrial Democracy.*
18 Commons, *Myself,* p. 71.

labor movement. The National Civic Federation had been organized in 1900 when the Chicago Civic Federation was moved to New York for the purpose of increasing its scope to cover the nation. At that time the federation selected influential Senator Marcus A. Hanna of Ohio as its president. Besides being a leading politician of his day, Hanna, a powerful business leader, operated coal mines, shipping concerns, docks, and public utilities. Labor leaders respected and trusted him because he had dealt with them fairly.[19] Unlike many business men of his day, he believed in collective bargaining. Consequently, in view of his reputation among business men, labor leaders, and politicians, he was an ideal choice to head the federation.

Perhaps the most important part of the federation was the Division of Conciliation and Mediation. Its membership included representation from employer groups, labor leaders, and distinguished citizens to represent the public. On the roster for the division were ex-President Grover Cleveland, Charles Francis Adams, Charles W. Eliot, Archbishop Ireland, Marcus Hanna, Charles M. Schwab, Theodore Shaffer, Daniel J. Keefe, James O'Connell, James M. Lynch, John Mitchell, Samuel Gompers, Ralph Easley, and a number of others.

In a day when labor unions were considered not quite respectable, such an organization was unusual, indeed. Respected political, educational, religious, and industrial leaders co-operated with labor's top leadership to channel industrial disputes into peaceful collective bargaining. Yet both industrialists and union leaders found their participation hotly opposed by other members of their own sides. The National Association of Manufacturers' "open shop" movement was in sharp contradiction with the federation's objectives. At the same time, the participating labor leaders found some of their members accusing them of selling out to the employers. Socialists, in particular, attacked Samuel Gompers, who served as the National Civic Federation's vice president. They accused him of being "chloroformed by the capitalists."[20]

When Commons accepted the offer made by its executive secretary, Ralph Easley, of a position with the National Civic Federation, he joined a novel experiment in industrial relations. As Easley's assistant, he arrived just in time to participate in one of labor's most historically important struggles. In 1902 a strike in the anthracite coal fields attracted national attention and resulted

19 Gompers, Vol. II, p. 106.
20 Gompers, Vol. I, p. 400.

in what Gompers called "the most important single incident in the labor movement in the United States."[21]

Leading up to this strike, the United Mine Workers had staged an organizing campaign pointing out the miserable conditions among the miners. While such conditions might be expected to create public sympathy for the miners, the mine operators counter-propaganda only tended to increase that sympathy. Not only were the operators uncompromising at a time when the public was concerned about its coal supply, but also some of their statements were tactless. George Baer, who was president of the Philadelphia and Reading Railroad, which controlled some of the mines, made the classic remark, "The welfare of the working men would be cared for, not by the agitators but by the Christian men to whom God, in his infinite wisdom, had entrusted the property interest of the country."[22]

To prevent this strike the National Civic Federation offered its services. Commons' role was that of meeting the miners' leaders and interpreting their side to the federation, while Ralph Easley, the executive secretary, Senator Hanna, and others tried to reason with the operators. On May 12, 1902, the mine workers left their jobs and remained on strike until October 23, 1902. In the meantime, while the operators refused to deal with the strikers, the reserves of anthracite coal dwindled. By the beginning of the winter season the per ton price of coal had risen from six to twenty dollars. With colder weather approaching, the public became concerned over its fuel supply for the winter. At that time coal was the chief fuel for heating homes.

On October 3 President Roosevelt summoned both sides to a White House conference, where he urged arbitration. Although the miners agreed, the operators refused to compromise, and at the same time, insisted that they could resume production if they were given adequate protection. Yet when the governor of the state of Pennsylvania provided additional troops, the operators were unable to increase production significantly. Meanwhile, public anxiety mounted until on October 9 the mayors from 139 cities met in Detroit to discuss the problem. Feeling reached such a pitch that the mayors went on record in favor of governmental control of the anthracite coal mines. President Roosevelt did not go that far, but he continued to search for a solution. Finally, with the aid of J. P. Morgan, he got the operators to agree to arbitration by a

21 *Ibid.*, Vol. II, p. 126.
22 John Mitchell, p. 384.

commission appointed by the President, provided that no labor leader or former labor leaders would be included. The union agreed and the men went back to work in the mines on October 23, 1902.

Although President Roosevelt did not appoint a labor leader to be on the commission, he did appoint an ex-labor leader by calling him a "sociologist." This was commissioner Edgar E. Clark of the Interstate Commerce Commission. Formerly, Clark had headed the Railroad Conductors Brotherhood.

The Anthracite Commission held hearings for several months and received testimony from hundreds of witnesses. When the commission issued its report on March 18, 1903, it awarded the miners a ten percent wage increase, provided for check weighmen to safeguard miners' interests, and created a board of conciliation to adjudicate all disputes. However, it did not require the operators to recognize the union.

Yet the victory was a significant one for the workers. They had held out for five months until governmental pressure forced the operators to compromise. Although the public was deprived of the coal used in heating homes, it remained sympathetic with the miners who were struggling against what they had characterized as "uncompromising monopolists."

During this strike, Commons spent five months with John Mitchell, president of the coal miners. Mitchell was a labor leader who sensed the value of maintaining satisfactory public relations in an industry whose product was essential to the general public. By cautious and careful strategy he was able to base labor's cause on the principles of "fair play," which were sure to win public support. Although demanding justice, his reasonableness won the sympathy and support of members of the clergy and other influential men. He at least won Commons' sympathy during the negotiations carried under the National Civic Federation. To Commons he appeared to be the ideal kind of labor leader—a skillful negotiator, a powerful leader, and possessor of the psychology of the rank and file from which he had risen.

Not all the labor leaders Commons met were like Mitchell. Some he described as "intellectuals" who had not arisen from the ranks. One such man Commons met in 1901, during the strike against the United States Steel Corporation.[23] He was T. J. Shaf-

---

23 Commons, *Myself,* p. 86.

fer, president of the Amalgamated Association of Iron, Steel and Tin Workers. In Commons' opinion, Shaffer was responsible for the failure of that strike, which nearly destroyed the union.

The situation was a critical one for the union and it sorely needed better leadership. In 1901 it was faced with the problem of how to deal with the newly formed United States Steel Corporation. In the process of its creation the corporation combined union and nonunion companies into one big organization. Yet the officials did not want the power of the unions to be extended to any of its companies not yet unionized.

On the other hand, union leaders feared that the presence of nonunion firms within the same organization would be dangerous to the union. They had experienced the shifting of production by some companies to their nonunion plants, while using harassing tactics to drive unionism out of all their plants.

In the inevitable struggle that took place the union had a few advantages. The most important was that because the steel company was newly formed, many of its securities remained in the hands of the underwriting companies. Furthermore, the possibility that it might be charged as a monopoly made its officials reluctant to become involved in an unpopular strike.

Although the time was opportune for such a strike, the union was in no condition to carry it out. Ten years before, the strike at Homestead had nearly decimated its ranks, and it had never been able to regain its lost members. An even greater disadvantage was that it lacked proper organization and leadership. Its president, Shaffer, was a poor negotiator to whom the "Civic Federation of 'Capitalists' was anathema . . ."[24] He lead his union into "the strike without funds, or organization, or negotiational leadership, or attempts toward a trade agreement."[25]

Not even Samuel Gompers nor John Mitchell could reason with Shaffer. Commons described him as an "intellectual" and "an unsuccessful or dismissed minister, who entered by a side door, as it were, into the union."[26] Because of this man's incompetent leadership, the corporation succeeded in both crushing the strike and in suppressing unionism among the steel workers for many years.

Commons concluded from this experience that the "intellectual" misunderstands the desires of laborers. What workers want

---

24 Commons, *Myself*, p. 87.
25 *Ibid.*
26 *Ibid.*

are bread and butter, here and now. Changes in the economic system as envisioned by the "intellectuals" have no reality for the worker. Better wages, shorter hours, and better working conditions are goals the common man can understand. Because he has been one himself, the union official who has risen from the ranks realizes what the workers want and how many sacrifices they are willing to make. Such an official feels the same anxiety as to risks that the workers do, because if he is beaten he cannot turn to some other line of work. Furthermore, he knows that the desires of reformers are not always compatible with the immediate objectives of the workers. Consequently, union leaders such as Gompers and Mitchell, who have been workers themselves, favor what is called "business unionism," which is essentially the concentration on immediate objectives of workers. These and other experiences while working for the National Civic Federation gave Commons a picture of sharp contrasts between "wage conscious" union leaders and those "intellectuals" with ideologies to sell.

Commons' experiences during this five years produced a burst of writing. Although he had written a few articles on labor before, he now began what was an impressively long list of books and articles on the subject. At first many were short unsigned editorials written for the *Independent,* but his contributions to scholarly journals also were impressive.

Commons' history of labor

In 1904 Commons' former teacher, Richard T. Ely, obtained for him a position at the University of Wisconsin. In addition to teaching, Commons was to write a history of labor. Up to this time, labor history had been a comparatively untouched field.[27] In 1886 Richard T. Ely had published his book, *Labor Movement in America,* which was intended to be a preliminary to a larger and more comprehensive work. To this end he had collected a considerable amount of materials and notes. His collection included a large number of rare documents he had obtained at considerable expense. After bringing Commons to Wisconsin to work on the labor history, Ely finally turned the entire project over to him.

Another beginning of a labor history came into Commons' care when Colonel Carroll D. Wright, commissioner of the Bureau of Labor, died. Colonel Wright had been working on a history of labor for the Department of Economics and Sociology of the Carnegie Institute of Washington. His contribution on labor was to be

---

27 See below for earlier histories.

the fourth in a contemplated series under the title, *Contributions to American Economic History.* By the time of his death he had obtained a considerable amount of monographic and documentary material he intended to use in his history. To carry on the work of Wright, the Carnegie Institute turned to Commons.

In addition to the materials to which he fell heir, Commons and his students scoured the libraries of the nation for more. To five hundred libraries they sent printed finding lists containing a list of one hundred and sixty labor papers and papers sympathetic to labor, published before 1872. For three years Commons spent one semester in Madison and eight months traveling with some of his graduate students to libraries for research. The documentary material he and his associates published in an eleven-volume work, *A Documentary History of American Industrial Society.*[28] They published the history itself in the *History of Labor in the United States.* Except for the introduction which he signed himself, Commons gave credit for each part of the history to the student working on it. However, the history is not just a book of readings. Rather, it is a co-ordinated work done under Commons' careful direction. The task was so large that the first two volumes were not completed until 1918. Finally, in 1935, Commons' students finished two more volumes.

The *History of Labor in the United States* is the pioneer classic in American labor history. With the *Documentary History,* it brought together fragmentary sources to provide labor historians with a basis on which to build their subsequent histories. Along with his many other writings on labor and his teaching of labor courses at the University of Wisconsin, Commons' *History of Labor* established him as an authority in the field.

Recognition came first in the form of glowing reviews for the two works. Ernest Bogart, the economic historian, in reviewing the *Documentary History,* declared:

> Now that the series have been completed, and it is possible to estimate the work as a whole, only the highest praise can be given the editors for the scholarly and able fashion in which they have performed their task; criticism of minor features must give way at this point. The result is a noteworthy collection of the most valuable documents, which fully justifies the large expenditure of time and money involved in their publication; many of these must soon have been completely lost but for their timely rescue and preservation in this form by Professor Commons and his coeditors.[29]

---

28 Commons and associates, *A Documentary History of American Industrial Society.*
29 Bogart, pp. 75-77.

Reviewers also hailed the *History of Labor* as an important achievement. George Barnett of Johns Hopkins University testified that:

> The work is more, however, than merely the best available account of the events in the history of the labor movement. Careful attention has been paid throughout to the general economic background and to the labor philosophy of each period.[30]

In addition to his praise, Barnett suggested that an additional volume on the theory of the labor movement be written. While also making this suggestion, Ira Cross claimed, "This study is unquestionably the greatest contribution thus far made to our literature dealing with the field of labor in the United States."[31] Frank Carlton, also the writer of a history of labor, indicated both Commons' stature and the importance of this contribution when he said:

> This first fairly complete and authoritative history of American labor movements is the result of the combined efforts of the best-known student of the American labor history and his students from the time he went to the University of Wisconsin in 1904 to the date of publication . . . Over thirty investigators having access to the collected materials have written monographs and articles which have been used in connection with the two volumes under consideration.[32]

Commons' *History* was not the first important history of labor; Ely's work had that honor.[33] A year after Ely published his book, George McNeil, a labor leader, edited (in 1887) a book studying a number of phases of labor history.[34] Later (in 1911) Frank Carlton completed his *History and Problems of the Labor Movement*.[35] All of these books added to the knowledge of labor history, but none were as complete as the Commons book.

By gathering a great mass of heretofore unaccessible material, Commons and his students were able to assemble the first complete labor history. Especially for the early years, it is the richest single source of information.

The development of the labor movement

Commons and his students intended to do more than provide a chronicle of events. They intended to explain the origins and

---

30 Barnett, "Review," p. 340.
31 Ira Cross, pp. 667-76.
32 Carlton, "Review," p. 981.
33 Ely, *Labor Movement in America.*
34 McNeil.
35 Carlton, *The History and Problems of Organized Labor.*

course of the development of the labor movement. In doing so, they found themselves studying the problem of economic development.

Because of Ely's influence, Commons held the German historical school of economists in high respect. Possessing a reading knowledge of German, he naturally explored their works before formulating any theory of his own. In reading some of the writings of Karl Bücher, Gustav Schmoller, and Werner Sombart, he ran across the concept of economic evolution propelled by extension of markets. He thought their data on European economic history prevented them from developing the idea as completely as they might have. Certain considerations, he said, "obliterated or confused the economic facts."[36] In America, to the contrary, the absence of feudalism, militarism, ecclesiastical and guild regulations and restrictions allowed economic development to unfold in a manner much easier to trace.

Commons adopted the principle of extension of the markets to explain economic development. He then explained unionism as a reaction of workers against their relations with their employers. Because the relationships changed with the extension of markets over wider areas, the nature of the reaction changed over the years. These changes, he said, explain the development of the labor movement.

The heart of his explanation is that unions are formed among workers for the purpose of protecting themselves against menacing competition. They are engaged in a class struggle with their employers but not in the sense used by Karl Marx. They do struggle with their employers, but not necessarily to overthrow capitalism. Instead, they strive to preserve or enhance their own status in the existing capitalistic society.

The early unions arose when some new development threatened the security of the workers. When extending markets brought workers new sources of competition, they united to protect themselves. There was nothing sinister or subversive about such action. It was merely what might be expected of any group of people facing the same problems.

Commons found that the application of the principle of the influence of extending markets easier to demonstrate in the case of single unions than for the entire labor movement. Long before he

---

[36] Commons, *Labor and Administration,* p. 260.

published the *History,* he illustrated his thesis by writing an article on "The American Shoemakers, 1648-1895." In this work he traced the growth of unions in the shoe industry from the time itinerant workers went to customers' homes to make boots, until finally shoes were mass-produced in factories.[37]

Organizations among shoemakers began soon after they started to make shoes in their own shops. At that time they faced the competitive menace from shoemakers who produced inferior products. Consequently, to control the quality of work done, the better workmen set up craft guilds with the power to discipline their members. Although very few guilds were established in America, the shoemakers of Boston had such an organization in 1648.

Soon the American shoemakers entered the stage when part of their work was for stock in addition to custom work for specific customers. At this time the master shoemaker might have a journeyman or two working for him, but no real conflict existed between employers and employees. The relationship remained a very personal one with both master and workman working side by side. In this retail stage the serious competitive menace came from those retailers who advertised or did cheap work for auctions or public markets. To combat this menace the masters organized the equivalent of a retail merchants' association. An example of this kind of organization in Philadelphia was called the "Society of Master Cordwainers."

When waterways made the transportation of goods easier, the markets expanded beyond the boundaries of the local community. Some of the master shoemakers began taking wholesale orders from retailers in distant cities. It was in this stage that the conflict between masters and the journeymen began. Facing competition from producers in other communities, masters found it necessary to compete on the basis of keeping wages down. Such action brought into existence protective organizations for journeymen. Temporarily, such organizations transferred the weight of bargaining power from employer to employees. However, when employers found themselves at a disadvantage in bargaining, they transformed their own retail merchants' associations into employers' associations. Without such organizations, an employer who had a wholesale contract to make a large number of shoes might find the profits squeezed between the contract price and the in-

---

37 *Ibid.*

creased costs from the journeymen's demands. Yet a strike could cause disastrous losses for him. Consequently, he used his organizations, the courts, and anything else at his disposal to win over the journeymen's organizations. Thus, both types of organizaitons, those for employers and those for the journeymen, resulted from the extension of markets.

In time wholesalers developed their business to a stage Commons called "wholesale speculative." Instead of merely producing for orders, the wholesaler accumulated stocks of merchandise to fill orders later when they might be received. Rather than make shoes themselves, the wholesalers bought shoes on contract from master shoemakers. Now the merchant function was separated at the wholesale level from either producing or retailing merchandise. The retailer, instead of making his own shoes, began to buy all he sold from the wholesaler, who in turn had bought them from the manufacturer.

When the wholesaler accumulated inventories by buying wherever he could buy cheapest, shoemakers were faced with competition from shoes produced either in prisons or in sweatshops. Competition reduced the master shoemaker to little more than an employer of journeymen. His ability to take profits was concentrated in the possibilities of keeping down costs. Because in this age (before the introduction of complicated and expensive machinery) the chief cost was labor, shoemakers were forced to keep wages down and to work their workers as much as possible. Today their simple factories would be called "sweatshops."

In this wholesale speculative stage, the antagonism between employer and employee was increased. Employees continued to rely on their journeymen's associations as employers did on their organizations, but both groups became increasingly dependent on a growing merchant class that controlled both sources of materials and the distribution of finished shoes to consumers. It was during this stage that associationism became an important goal in America. Working men dreamed of co-operative warehouses and co-operative purchases of raw materials. They aimed at freeing themselves from the merchant capitalism so they could be independent producers.

The introduction of machinery into the shoe industry, such as the pegging machine in 1857 and the McKay sewing machine in 1862, coincided with the broader extension of the market brought on by the completion of railroad networks. No longer could the factory be a simple sweatshop without machinery. As factories grew in size owners began to see possibilities of freeing themselves from the domination of the wholesaler. Larger manufacturers began to sell directly to retailers. Instead of depending on orders from wholesalers, they developed sales forces of their own to build markets. In some cases they even bought their own retail stores. To further increase their independence, some manufacturers also acquired facilities for producing their own raw materials.

Not all the development of integrated firms came from expansion by manufacturers. In many cases wholesalers possessing adequate capital could buy factories more easily than the manufacturer could build up new marketing organizations. At first the older type wholesaler retained his dominance, but as time wore on the new integrated manufacturing firms gained dominance regardless of from which source they had developed.

Commons called the earlier part of this stage before the manufacturer gained dominance, the wholesale speculative stage. By then, rails extended markets to the nation's borders. To protect themselves from nationwide competition, it was necessary for unions to organize on a nationwide scale. The shoemakers accomplished this organization with a national union they called the Knights of St. Crispin. But as this wholesale speculative stage developed, the competitive menace from introduction of machinery overwhelmed the Knights. Green hands using new machinery displaced skilled journeymen shoemakers. Eventually, such competition eliminated the Knights from the shoe industry.

In this stage, which Commons called the factory order stage, the workers turned to the industrial type of unionism. Instead of excluding the semiskilled or unskilled workers as competitors, they were brought into the union. They called their organization the Boot and Shoe Workers' Union. Commons ends his article about the shoemakers by describing this union.

In his *Institutional Economics* he continued his analysis of the development of capitalism.[38] He added one more stage: banker capitalism. Again he illustrated this development with the shoemakers' case. For shoe manufacturing, banker capitalism meant the regulation of the industry by control of the necessary machinery. The United Shoe Machinery Company owned the basic patents on crucial machinery. It would not sell this machinery; instead

---

[38] Commons, *Institutional Economics*, pp. 763-73.

it rented machines on condition that the renter use only those belonging to the United Shoe Machinery Company. Hence, all companies that made shoes were forced to meet the machinery company's terms.

The shoe manufacturing industry remained competitive. Even small firms could obtain the necessary machinery through leases. Capital requirements therefore were low and plants could be moved easily to new locations. Consequently, this possibility of employers moving away from union territory was a constant threat to unions. Therefore, although the industry in the earlier stages was highly unionized, unions lost much of their power and membership in this last period.

Problems resulting from the lease of machinery was not common in other industries. But with the development of multiplant manufacturing firms, an analogous threat developed. Firms could shift production from unionized plants to those not yet under union control. They also had other means of defeating unions. As Commons reported:

> . . . the unions have practically disappeared from the trusts, and are disappearing from the large corporations as they grow large enough to specialize minutely their labor. The organized workmen are found in the small establishments like the building trades, or in the fringe of independents on the skirts of the trusts; on the railways, where skill and responsibility are not yet displaced by division of labor; in the mines where strikebreakers cannot be shipped in; on the docks and in other places where they hold a strategic position.[39]
>
> . . . especially after employers have consolidated in great corporations and trusts, their capacity for united action exceeds that of organized labor. Their tactics are directed, not so much toward winning of strikes as toward preventing strikes and disintegrating unions. By wise promotions, by watchful detectives, by prompt discharge of agitators, by an all round increase of wages when agitation is active on the outside, by a reduction only when the menace has passed or when work is slack, by shutting down a plant where unionism is taking root and throwing orders to other plants, by establishing the so-called "open shop," these and other masterful strategems set up a problem different from what unionism has heretofore met. It does not seem possible under such conditions that organization will get a footing in the great consolidated industries.[40]

Writing these words in 1906, Commons could not foresee that the mass-production industries eventually would be unionized with the help of legislation. His words give the impression that he was

---

39 Commons, *Labor and Administration*, p. 75.
40 *Ibid.*, p. 80.

very pessimistic over the development of the labor movement. However, he actually never was a pessimist. Writing in his *Institutional Economics* in 1934, he maintained that although the American trade unionists included only fifteen percent of the wage earners, they were more powerful than their European counterparts who made up sixty to seventy percent of their wage force.[41] He claimed that "big business" was attempting to forestall unionism by voluntarily giving their employees all the advantages that might be gained by joining unions. He observed that pay often was higher and working conditions often were better in these mass-production industries than in those that were unionized. By merely existing as a threat to potentially selfish businessmen, unions could serve their function. Consequently, he was optimistic over the continuing influences of unions, even if he doubted that they could grow much larger.

Applying the formula

Commons provided a preview of his theme for his *History of Labor* in his article on the shoemakers, which he published in 1909. His reading about other theories of economic development, his experience with labor leaders, and his survey of historical material convinced him that he should stress the consequences of expanding markets. By the time he had formulated his theory by testing it with an analysis of the shoemakers, he had much of his material on the labor movement available. In the following year he and his students published much of this data in the *Documentary History of American Industrial Society*. They included the article on the shoemakers as a preface. At that time the job ahead was to test the theme with their data.

The job of combining a complete labor history with a theory of the development of the labor movement proved difficult. In the process of providing a rich variety of materials to complete the history, the theory was so submerged that it is difficult to find.

Commons wrote the introduction and then parceled out the rest to his students. He stated the theme but sandwiched it in between discussions on the conditions peculiar to the American environment for labor. Torn between a desire to summarize what his students actually wrote and the desire to remain faithful to his prearranged schedule, he compromised. The result was that few recognized the importance he placed on the concept of expanding markets.

---

41 Commons, *Institutional Economics*, p. 888.

A close study of the *History of Labor* will disclose the fact that every single writer somewhere in his discussion included an analysis of the expansion of markets. A fair history of American transportation could be drawn from their accounts. They also described the changing market patterns. Over and over again they mention competitive menaces similar to those described in Commons' "Shoemakers."

David Saposs, whose assignment covered the first labor unions in America, displayed most prominently the theme of extending markets and the struggle against competitive menaces.[42] He also discussed the theories of Marx, Schmoller, and Bücher, as did Commons in the "Shoemakers." His language and his analysis followed closely the pattern of Commons' article. Because he had to explain the beginnings, he perhaps needed to follow the theory closer than the others did.

The second writer, Helen Sumner, in her second page explained that economic pressures from extension of markets (based upon turnpike and canal) were affecting labor. A few pages later she declared:

> The decreasing bargaining power of mechanics, resulting from the revolution in the means of marketing the product, coupled with the horrors of the depression, was doubtless sufficient to account for a labour movement.[43] [sic]

However, she spent very few words following the theme. Instead, she wrote on the politics of the working class and called her section "Citizenship."

Shortly after beginning the third section, "Trade Unionism, 1833-1839," Edward B. Mittelman launched into a discussion of the growth of the merchant capitalist and the extension of markets.[44] He then went on to describe competitive menaces and the local organizations created to combat them. Later when he discussed national unions, he described the developments in transportation that stimulated them. Yet these elements of Commons' theme did not stand out in Mittelman's contribution. They are almost lost in a mass of details concerning the activities of labor unions.

In the work of the next writer, Henry E. Hoagland, the theme was almost lost. His section on "Humanitarianism (1840-1860)"

---

42 Commons, *History of Labor,* Vol. I, pp. 25-165.
43 *Ibid.,* Vol. I, p. 175.
44 *Ibid.,* Vol. 1, p. 338.

concerned the retreat away from job-conscious unionism. During the early years, depression swept away many of the unions. The working people, and the intellectuals who tried to lead them, turned to schemes of speculative reform.[45] Consequently, Hoagland concentrated on such schemes and the people who devised them. But in the end when he reached the period when unions on a national scale were organized, he explained, "The rapid extension of the market in the years immediately preceding the Civil War showed the necessity of a wider organization."[46]

The job of explaining "Nationalization (1860-1877)" fell to John B. Andrews.[47] In doing so, he kept closer to the Commons' theme than any other writer, except Saposs. He began by bringing up to date the history of transportation. Then he went on to explain that the extension of markets stimulated the growth of national unions. He illustrated this proposition by describing the origins of a number of such organizations. But he had much more to say about unions than their origins. Consequently, even in his contribution, the theme was submerged until it was barely noticeable.

The last writer, Selig Perlman, in his section, "Upheaval and Reorganization (Since 1876)," took many pages before touching on the theme.[48] Much of his early discussion involved the Knights of Labor, socialism, and political activities of unions. When he reached the development of more wage-conscious unionisms, he was close to it. Finally, in his description of new economic conditions in the eighties, he brought up the subject of extension of markets and the changing methods of marketing.[49] Like the other writers, he included a discussion of the history of railroads in the country. After this brush with the theme, he moved on to other developments in the labor movement.

However, the theme was not so buried that critics failed to notice it. Frank T. Carlton, one of Commons' students and a writer of labor history in his own right, complained that he did not think any such single-track explanation of the evolution of the labor movement was sufficient.[50] He then went on to add that, indeed, other explanations had crept into the work in question.

---

45 *Ibid.*, Vol. I, pp. 487-623.
46 *Ibid.*, Vol. I, p. 620.
47 *Ibid.*, Vol. II, pp. 3-191.
48 *Ibid.*, Vol. II, pp. 195-537.
49 *Ibid.*, p. 358.
50 Carlton, "Review: *History of Labor*," *op. cit.*

George Barnett took substantially that same position taken in this publication.[51] Undoubtedly, the authors of the various parts built on the foundation of theory outlined by Commons in his preface. However, the amount of detail was so great that the theory was not closely knit with the facts. Yet the theory did not conflict with the facts.

Barnett was right in saying that Commons' theory of the labor movement was obscured by the mass of other information. And Ira Cross, a Commons' student, was also correct when he claimed that the work might have had more unity if it had been written by one person instead of by many. Whether Commons would have pulled it closer together is another question; and whether he should have is still another. He never felt compelled to write a clean logical theory if it meant leaving out pertinent information. At any rate, he did not sacrifice the history by dogmatically sticking to his theory.

The effect of special American conditions on labor's goals

While the *History of Labor* did not contain a theory of the development of the labor movement, it was a history of the ideas and goals held by labor leaders. Commons and his students were anxious to explain the nature of the labor movement and its implications for this country's society.[52] Individual unions, structures of unions, their policies, and labor legislation were secondary. Furthermore, such supplementary information not always was available for many cases. Consequently, they centered their history on the philosophies of labor developing within a changing environment.

They might have extended their analysis on the effect of fear of competitive menaces to explain the attitudes of labor leaders. Later on, one of the students, Selig Perlman, developed this analysis rather thoroughly. However, at the time of the writing of the *History,* Commons and his group used other conditions in American society to explain the thinking of labor leaders.

In tracing the development of ideas by laboring people and their leaders, Commons and his associates included a considerable amount of the economic, and some of the political history of the United States. They were drawing together all the various condi-

---

51 Barnett, *op. cit.*
52 Mark Perlman labels Commons' approach a "Social-Institutional Theory," *op. cit.*, p. 226.

tions in American environment that influenced the ideas of influential members of the labor movement on unionism, class struggles, and humanitarian goals.

They believed that the existence of vast amounts of unoccupied land had flavored the thinking of the working people in the early days.[53] For many years the struggle over how the vast public domain would be distributed was a contest between those who attempted to gain large holdings and those who thought the land should be given to homesteaders. In the eyes of the laboring people, it was a struggle between the monopolists and the people. According to them, big interests bought land from the government at extremely low prices to resell at higher prices to settlers. Working people had a stake in the outcome of this struggle because many of them were potential settlers themselves. The possibilities of sharing in greater job opportunities or of obtaining their own homesteads in the West caused them to side with the settlers. Furthermore, laborers were interested in encouraging some of their numbers to emigrate westward and thus reduce competition among those remaining.

Hence, the class struggle of the early days of the country tended to be between producer classes, consisting of an alliance between laborers and small farmers, and the classes that had large holdings.[54] Such a class struggle had quite different implications than that later envisioned by Karl Marx. Instead of trying to abolish private property, the producer classes were attempting to increase their opportunities to gain some property for themselves.[55] Their aim was not equality, but rather greater equality of opportunity. Hence, they saw monopolists as their prime enemies rather than employers as such.

Because many workers thought in terms of acquiring businesses or farms, they were slow to develop class consciousness. Because of abundant business opportunities constantly opening up in the expanding economy enough workers became independent farmers or businessmen to provide credence to these aspirations. Furthermore, no feudal traditions barred the way for workers to better themselves. Consequently, in the absence of class consciousness, the revolutionary type of unionism found in some European countries could not gain much of a foothold in America.

---

53 Commons, *History of Labor*, Vol. I, pp. 4, 234, 362, 522, 562; Vol. II, pp. 122, 447.
54 *Ibid.*, Vol. I, pp. 175, 193, 218, 261, 304, 462; Vol. II, pp. 122, 169, 240, 440.
55 *Ibid.*, Vol. I, p. 4.

Class consciousness in America also was limited because very early the working man received his right to vote.[56] By missing the struggle for suffrage the American working men were not made conscious of class status while their unions were in the formulative stages. American laboring men turned naturally to politics, but they never achieved a feeling of class solidarity sufficient for the formulation of successful labor political parties. Politicians, always quick to bring minority groups into the older parties, managed to take advantage of this lack of solidarity. They made promises assuring laboring groups that more could be gained through coalitions than by forming minority parties. Although working men formed many political organizations during their history, they found that minority parties seldom were effective in America. The major parties were far too effective and often sensitive to labor's desires.

Yet America's governmental structure made it difficult for labor unions to achieve goals through legislation.[57] The federal system, with each state creating, maintaining, and administering laws applying to labor, multiplied the problems involved whenever any group tried to introduce reforms. Because the areas of competition for business and industry spread far beyond the borders of each state, the obtaining of laws for any one state could not be effective. A reform law in one state could, and sometimes did, drive businessmen across state boundaries. Yet until sometime after Commons wrote his history, the national government lacked power to regulate labor conditions.

Although the legislative branches of government could not effectively intervene on behalf of labor's causes, the judicial branch did enter the picture.[58] Employers used the courts to veto as unconstitutional legislation benefitting labor on one hand, and then used them to restrict labor on the other. Even the federal courts were used to obtain injunctions that would hamper unions in their operations. Consequently, labor's experiences with government were not happy. It failed to achieve much in the way of reform through legislation, and it found the courts dangerous enemies. Hence, thought Commons, it was natural that many labor leaders in America came to prefer a laissez-faire policy on the part of government.

---

56 *Ibid.*, p. 5.
57 *Ibid.*, p. 5.
58 *Ibid.*, p. 9.

But labor demanded that government put an end to unlimited immigration.[59] Wherever the stream of new workers from abroad competed with native labor, unions found organization difficult. Employers could replace union members with foreigners who were not yet organized. By choosing workers who had diverse backgrounds and who spoke different languages employers could delay the time when the newcomers' docility would wear off.

Workers isolated by difficulties in languages could not be as independent as the native-born workers. Furthermore, the immigrants, often fleeing from extreme poverty abroad, usually accepted wages that were low by American standards. Hence, the immigrant caused a two-fold problem for unions: he made organization difficult, and his competition made maintenance of union standards even more difficult.

In prosperous times immigrants came to this country in greater numbers than during depressions. During prosperity the supply of cheap labor enabled employers to overexpand their operations so that productive capacity expanded faster than purchasing power. While increases in wages were retarded by the influx of immigrant workers, prices were not held in check by increased imports. Tariffs prevented the inflow of goods that might have been competitive with those manufactured in the United States. Thus, the employer had his protection from competition, but the worker only could agitate. In the meantime, according to Commons, unlimited immigration aggravated the movement of the business cycle.

The labor movement developed differently in each stage of the business cycle.[60] In periods of rising prices, when cost of living rose faster than wages, union organization grew lustily. Where unions formerly did not exist workers formed new ones, while the older unions experienced new and rapid growth. In boom times, when employers made good profits and labor was scarce, unions provided workers with considerable bargaining power. Hence, their union organization and strikes could be aggressive.

On the other hand, during depressions unions were on the defensive. In the face of rising unemployment, union leaders experienced difficulties in holding their organizations together. If they failed to provide protection to their members from wage cuts, they faced a withering away of their membership. Yet if they

---

59 *Ibid.*, p. 10.
60 *Ibid.*, p. 10.

maintained their struggle with employers by sponsoring desperate and defensive strikes, the remaining core turned to politics, panaceas, or schemes of universal reform.[61] Desperation and failure bred radicalism just as prosperity formerly had stimulated wage-conscious unionism. During depression years only a small group of leaders kept labor organizations together. Often such leaders were the "intellectual" type who had means other than union activity of making a living.[62] Thoroughly convinced of the futility of adjusting to the present social order, they maintained their zeal for radical measures even under difficult circumstances. As leaders they might be excellent speakers who could sway mobs to action, but their faithfulness to radical causes interfered at times with obtaining the objectives of wage-conscious unionism. Although they might hold power during depressions when unionism tended to be ineffective, their power was diluted by the influx of new union members when prosperity returned. Little by little more practical union leaders, rising from the rank and file, crowded them out of places of leadership.

At times the radical actually might grow into a wage-conscious unionist who concentrated on immediate gains instead of impending revolutions. The day-to-day problems of maintaining a union pressed on him sufficiently for his revolutionary ideas to fade further into the vague future. Eventually, he even might become a conservative unionist. Such, at least, was the fate of Samuel Gompers and some other well-known union leaders.

Commons and his students filled their *History* with lengthy accounts of the various pressures on unions and union leaders. In general, the sum total of these pressures was consistent with the one chosen as the theme: the extension of markets. But the links between the theme and the various special American conditions are not well worked out. Instead, it appears as if the *History* offers a number of explanations for details of the development of the labor movement. In the process the theme is subdued. The work is one of history and not theory.

Perlman's theory of the labor movement

John R. Commons never labeled his ideas concerning the formation and growth of the labor movement as a theory. Although he certainly had expounded a theory in his article on the shoemakers and in his *History*, he encouraged his student, Selig Perl-

---

61 *Ibid.,* p. 11.
62 *Ibid.,* p. 19.

man, to write a theory of the labor movement.[63] Hence, credit for the creation of such a theory went to Perlman for his book, *A Theory of the Labor Movement.*[64]

Although some authorities refer to the Commons-Perlman theory of the labor movement, others declare the two men's theories to be quite different. John Dunlop reported:

> . . . A rather sharp cleavage emerges, however, between writers such as the Webbs and Commons, who look upon the labor movement primarily as the manifestation of economic developments, and those, such as Perlman and Hoxie, who choose to emphasize the habits of wage earners.[65]

At the third annual meeting of the Industrial Relations Research Association, J. B. S. Hardman insisted that ". . . I am not all of the opinion that the Commons-Perlman axis is really of one piece."[66] He referred to the fact that Commons had asserted that ". . . the labor movement is always a protest against capitalism." Furthermore, he doubted that Perlman fully underwrote Commons' position as to the interaction between the labor movement and the social, economic, and political milieu.

At the same conference Russell Bauder agreed that " . . . the so-called Commons-Perlman theory is not all of one piece."[67] Instead of being identical, they are complimentary. Bauder went on to suggest that " . . . Commons was seeking to explain the varied forms of the program and structure while Professor Perlman has sought to find their permanent common characteristics."[68]

Bauder is correct when he argues that Commons' and Perlman's theories are complementary. Yet the relationship between their theories is no coincidence. Theirs was a long association with much cross-fertilization of ideas. Extensive examination of both of their works shows that they finally draw close together. To demonstrate any sharp distinction between the theories of the two men the comparison must be limited to Commons' theory in his "Shoemakers" and Perlman's theory. Further reading reveals many statements of Perlman echoing those of Commons.

---

63 Mark Perlman, *op. cit.*, p. 191.
64 Selig Perlman, *A Theory of the Labor Movement.*
   Selig Perlman, *The History of Trade Unionism.*
65 Dunlop, p. 173.
66 Hardman, *Proceedings of Third Annual Industrial Relations Research Association,* 1950, p. 9.
67 Bauder, p. 31.
68 *Ibid.*

In 1900 as a nineteen-year-old Marxist refugee from Russia, Perlman joined Commons at the University of Wisconsin.[69] There his training was financed by William English Walling, who was one of Commons' financial backers. Walling had found Perlman in Europe and had brought him back to help with the writing of a book on Russia.[70] After finishing his work with Walling, which continued while he was at the university, Perlman began to work with Commons on the *History of Labor.*

Under Commons' influence, Perlman gradually lost his enthusiasm for socialism and decided that radical movements were not good for either the labor movement or the working man. In his assigned portion of the labor history, Perlman followed Commons' theme of the extension of the markets and the reaction of the labor movement. So far he clearly displayed Commons' influence. Yet as time went on he began developing ideas of his own. Finally, he had something he could label *A Theory of the Labor Movement.*[71] Although consistent with Commons' ideas, it was clearly an extension beyond what Commons had done either with his "Shoemakers" or in his *History of Labor.* From his contribution, Perlman derived a considerable amount of favorable recognition.

Commons' influence in Perlman's earlier work is noticeably obvious, but the lines of influence seem to have been reversed in Commons' later writings. In Commons' article on "Jurisdictional Disputes"[72] and in his contribution, "The Labor Movement," in the *Encyclopedia of Social Sciences*[73] can be found many of Perlman's arguments. This latter article might not have been very different if it had been written by Perlman. Who influenced whom? In all probability, they influenced each other during their long years of intimate and cordial association.

---

69 Commons, *Myself,* p. 81.

70 Commons, *Myself,* p. 81. Dr. Witte disagreed with this account: "That Selig Perlman was brought to the United States to help William English Walling to write a book on Russia which he finished after he came to Wisconsin is different from the account which Perlman always gave. Perlman grew up in Bailystock, then in Czarist Russia, now in eastern Poland. He left Poland because the Jews were persecuted and he had no opportunities in Russia. He went to the University of Naples and while a student there read an advertisement in which Mrs. William English Walling asked for someone to teach her Italian. Perlman had a command of many languages including both English and Italian. As you state, the Wallings were millionaires. They brought Perlman to the United States and at their insistence, he went to the University of Wisconsin. . . . He came here as an undergraduate, but got a B.A. degree in one year. Then he became Commons' assistant and was connected with this University until his death this past year." Edwin E. Witte, letter of February 9, 1960.

71 Perlman, *A Theory of the Labor Movement.*

72 Commons, *Wertheim Lectures on Industrial Relations,* pp. 93-98.

73 Commons, *Encyclopaedia of the Social Sciences.*

Perlman's theory of the labor movement is centered on the psychology of the working man as contrasted with that of the businessman and intellectual. Working men, or "manualists" as Perlman calls them, tend to fear that opportunities for jobs are scarce. They are aware of their shortcomings, so discount the possibility of being able to rise out of their class by their own efforts. Although they may oppose the bosses, they do not have enough self-assurance to believe they can replace them. Hence, the conflict between the "manualists" and the employer settles down to a struggle over immediate benefits such as better wages, shorter hours, and better working conditions, and above all, greater job security.

Believing job opportunities scarce, workers prefer to submit to union control of job opportunities rather than to bargain individually. By doing so, they are released from pressure of competition with each other and hence are able to create "a solid bargaining front against the employer." "Checking the race for employment opportunities tends to equalize security among the members, and simultaneously safeguards or raises the standard of life, establishes industrial liberty, protects future earning power, and increases leisure."[74]

Union leaders, responding to demands of the rank and file, recognize the feeling of scarcity of job opportunities. Consequently, many efforts of such union leaders are directed at gaining control over those opportunities. By increasing such control, unions may protect those opportunities and, at the same time, ration them in a manner desirable to the membership. Attempts to get union security clauses in collective bargaining contracts demonstrate this tendency. When such a clause approaches that calling for a "closed shop," control over jobs is almost complete.

Although control over jobs may not be complete, the stronger it is, the easier it is for the union to impose its working rules. Many of these rules either aim to spread work among the workers or to provide them with greater job security. Rules tending to shorten hours or to restrict output are examples of the first, while seniority rules or provisions for appeals to grievance machinery are examples of the latter.

Although the worker prefers that his unions seek for him immediate and narrow gains, leaders of unions sometimes have other ideas. Such leaders are those which Perlman, as well as Commons, described as "intellectuals." Usually these leaders have risen from

---

74 Perlman, *Theory of the Labor Movement*, p. 243.

sources other than the rank and file and they do not share the psychology of the workers. Instead, they tend to hold radical views which they wish to implement with the aid of the workers. Although grasping part of the psychology—the desire of the worker for solidarity—they fail to realize that the worker has no desire to take part in co-operatives or in self-governing workshops. Rather than share the risks of management, the worker understands and seeks only those union policies that will provide more and better jobs. Furthermore, the worker has no dreams of a postrevolutionary society that would be a heaven on earth. Instead, the worker seeks only that which possibly can be attained earlier. He will seek higher wages and better working conditions, but not utopia.

Following Marx or other radicals, intellectuals look on labor as a vehicle by which a new social order can be attained. Consequently, a struggle takes place between the intellectuals and "organic labor." Perlman pointed to this struggle in European countries as well as in the United States. He concluded that in mature labor movements the "wage conscious" rank and file eventually wins over the "class conscious" intellectuals.

The radical trying to run a trade union runs into conflicts between his carrying on of class warfare and trying to bargain with employers for improvement in wages and working conditions for the workers. Successful bargaining requires at least the expectation that agreements will be carried out. The making of such agreements and the implementing of them implies at least a temporary suspension of hostilities. Unless the employer is unusually weak, he will not submit to an irresponsible union. His resources and determination usually are adequate for prolonged resistance. Under such circumstances, workers who are more interested in providing for their families than in improving conditions tend to desert their unions in times of crisis. They may fight fiercely for immediate union objectives, but they will lose interest quickly in a fight for changing the social order.

The intellectual also misjudges the power of capitalists to resist. Not only are capitalists prepared to defend their control with use of physical force, but they also defend themselves by convincing the other classes that they alone "know how to operate the complex economic apparatus of modern society on which the material welfare of all depends."[75] Except under such unusual conditions,

75 *Ibid*, p. 4.

as with the lack of a strong capitalistic class in Russia's case, the radical intellectual is not likely to succeed in changing the social order by a successful revolution. Even when he tries revolution he may find that the labor movement, instead of aiding him, actually opposes him, as in Germany after World War I. Hence, the labor movement, instead of being a threat to capitalism, is actually a conservative influence.

In addition to the revolutionary type of intellectual, Perlman described two others: the "ethical" and the "efficiency" types. The "ethical" intellectual seeks to replace capitalism with self-governing workshops. By freeing the workers from wage-slavery, he would destroy the fetters that have inhibited full development of workers' personalities. Means of implementing programs vary from revolutionary activity down to creating small producer co-operatives. Or the intellectual may rely on political means. In any case, his program will run into conflicts with union activity.

The third type of intellectual, the "efficiency" type, believes that capitalism is inefficient and gradually can be transformed into some form of socialism. Like the other two types, he thinks as an outsider and misjudges the worker's psychology. Usually he seeks his goals by political means. In doing so, he is forced to buck the workers' apathy and sometimes even antagonism growing into active opposition. Such a case might arise when a strike required by strategic necessity might conflict with the need for industrial peace before a crucial election. Any leader trying to combine political action with union activity would thus risk sacrificing the interest of at least one of them. Even in less crucial situations, such a leader might be accused by his labor union followers of neglecting their interests while he was playing politics. Furthermore, the injection of political issues into the proceedings of labor meetings and conventions provides more sources of possible disagreement. Except when some issue attains unusual urgency in the minds of working men, political activity tends to be a liability to the union leader.

The union leader free from political commitments uninhibited by any ideological loyalties in his bargaining with employers, and willing to concentrate on immediate issues of unionism holds a considerable advantage over his intellectual rival. Furthermore, when he has risen from the ranks he has no stigma of the outsider. The workers feel they know him, and what is also important, he knows them. He knows intuitively how workers will react to each step of union or employer strategy. In a time of crisis he knows how firmly his men will hold before giving way to the employer's pressure. He can maintain a strike long enough to exert maximum counter-pressure on the employer without allowing it to continue so long that the resistance of the membership collapses.

Perlman demonstrated that in several countries "wage conscious" leaders struggled with "class conscious" intellectual leaders. He believed the tendency was for the "wage conscious" leaders to win and eventually crowd the radical rivals from their positions. In addition to pointing to the American experience, he described the German trade unions' struggle to free themselves from domination by the Social Democratic Party. Even in England, trade unionists endeavored to maintain their independence from socialists. Here, in view of the developments subsequent to the publishing of Perlman's theory, the case seems a little weak. Yet even today considerable conflict exists between English trade union and party officials.

This conflict between intellectuals and socialism has been noted by numerous observers other than Perlman. Even Lenin declared that the working class, if left to its own forces, can attain only trade union consciousness.[76] George Bernard Shaw declared, "Trade Unionism is not Socialism; it is Capitalism of the Proletariat."[77] More recently, Schumpeter has referred to "the fundamental antagonism between socialist intellectuals and labor."[78]

To Perlman, this antagonism between the "manualists" and the "intellectuals" was crucial to the development of the labor movement. The degree to which each type of leader is able to dominate labor unions determines relative development. Successful bargaining favors "manualists," while frustration provides opportunities for "intellectuals." Finally, when successes of unionism demonstrate the efficacy of "wage conscious" unionism (as opposed to the conflicting tactics of the "intellectuals"), the movement matures under the dominance of "manualists."

At this point it might be wondered just how Perlman's ideas differed from those of Commons. The difference was only one of emphasis for they did not conflict. If such a comparison is limited to that between Commons' theory as shown in his "Shoemakers" and his *History* with that displayed in Perlman's *A Theory of the Labor Movement,* there are differences. Commons emphasized the

---

[76] Lenin, p. 90.
[77] Shaw, p. 186.
[78] Schumpeter, p. 315.

effect of extension of markets on workers. By creating competitive menaces, extension stimulated workers to form unions to protect themselves. Numerous other circumstances shaped the development, but Commons never wove them into a theory. He was quite content to view with favor numerous explanations of the development of the labor movement without feeling any compulsion to unify them.

Perlman emphasized the psychology of the worker as contrasted with that of the intellectual. This psychology did not differ from Commons' except that it was explicit. Perlman's concept of the workers' consciousness of job scarcity also could be explained in terms of their fear that market and technological developments might destroy the value of their skills. However, Commons did not use the concept of the scarcity of job opportunities in describing the labor movement until after Perlman did. Yet this concept fits perfectly with Commons' general institutional framework. Commons in his *Institutional Economics* stressed the fact that conflicts in this country arise from existence of scarcity. To overcome these scarcities men engage in collective action to bring order out of conflict. They create working rules to provide means of settling conflicts in a way to determine patterns for future action. Perlman's concept, using the worker's belief in the scarcity of job opportunities coupled with the creation of unions with their working rules, is closely parallel to Commons' general institutional analysis. Considering that Commons derived his theoretical approach from his experiences and research as a labor economist, this parellel is not surprising. The two men, in close association, were studying the same phenomenon, weighing the same facts, and sharing many common experiences.

The second point of difference between Commons and Perlman is in the latter's use of the role of the intellectual. Certainly, Commons shared Perlman's views on intellectuals in the labor movement, but initially he did not give them as large a role. In his introduction to the *History of Labor,* he referred to the failure of the intellectuals to dominate permanently the American labor movement. Yet this failure he explained in terms of special circumstances in American history.

In contrast, Perlman demonstrated the failure in terms of psychology of the "manualists" who eventually frustrate the "intellectuals." Such a psychology could be applied to European, as well as American labor. Much of Perlman's book on the *Theory of the Labor Movement* consisted of analysis of European labor movements, whose workers had a type of psychology similar to their American counterparts.

Because Commons was writing a history of American labor and not a theory, he refrained from claiming more than was necessary for his own purposes. In his "Shoemakers," which he wrote with a still narrower purpose, he did not even mention the special circumstances in America that shaped the labor movement. Instead, he confined his discussion to the effect of the extension of markets.

When Commons wrote his article on the "Labor Movement" for the *Encyclopedia of The Social Sciences* he had the broader purpose of explaining the labor movement. He retained his own previous explanations, but added some of Perlman's as well. Beginning with his own theory of economic development, he discussed various stages in the growth of capitalism. When he arrived at what he called Banker Capitalism, he began to branch off into the problem of unemployment. From the working man's fear of unemployment, he moved to a discussion of the psychology of laborers. At this point he brought in Perlman's concept of the workers' consciousness of job security. He then explained work rules (as did Perlman) as attempts to ration jobs among workers, and then mentioned that when workers are successful in protecting their jobs and in getting gains from collective bargaining, they choose "business type" leaders. In earlier years, in depressions, or in countries where collective bargaining is handicapped, radical "intellectuals" emerge as leaders. Commons went on to discuss unionism in a number of countries. He returned to an explanation of why American unions have concentrated on economic rather than political or reform activities. Near the end of his article he treated efforts to organize labor on an international scale. Finally, he cautioned that the labor movement is "amazingly complicated and diverse," and that no single principle or permanent trend seems to underlie it, except that it usually encroaches on the domain of capitalism. In short, he shied away from any theory of the labor movement.

Nothing in the article is incompatible with Perlman's work. In fact, the only real difference is in his rejection of any general theory. He incorporated Perlman's concepts, such as the role of consciousness of job scarcity, the conflict between intellectuals and the workers, and the nonpolitical nature of American unions. The differences between Commons and Perlman were always more of emphasis and manner of presentation than of substance. In this work the difference becomes so slight that it can be said there is a Commons-Perlman thesis which is one piece.

Over the years, the Commons-Perlman thesis has maintained its prominence as a theory of the labor movement. Whenever writers have written on various theories of labor movement, they invariably have included that of Commons and Perlman. Sometimes they treated them separately, while other times they treated them as one, that of the "Wisconsin School." Shortly after the appearance in 1928 of Perlman's *Theory of the Labor Movement,* Lyle W. Cooper reviewed five then recent books on the subject, including Perlman's.[79] In 1943, Russell Bauder again included a review of the Commons-Perlman theory along with two others.[80] Then in 1948 John Dunlop included separate reviews of Commons' and Perlman's works in a collection of six specimens of theories of the labor movement.[81] Finally, in 1955 Clark Kerr and Abraham Siegel lumped Commons' and Perlman's analysis with other popular versions as "traditional" theories that should be broadened so they could explain labor movements in noncapitalistic countries.[82] This lumping together of diverse theories drew objections from Milton Derber, who particularly defended Commons and Perlman.[83]

In late years, the Commons-Perlman thesis, itself, has received renewed discussion. After a reprinting in 1949 of Perlman's *Theory of the Labor Movement,* Philip Taft reviewed it along with a discussion of Commons and Hoxie.[84] He found that it continued to deserve reading by students of the labor movement. In 1950 Adolf Sturmthal wrote: "The tremendous influence which this has exerted on the minds of American students, however, creates the obligation for subsequent generations to look back upon it from time to time and to re-examine its assumptions and conclusions."[85] However, in following his own advice, Sturmthal concluded that, while Perlman's theory seemed to fit the American scene, it was inadequate when analyzing labor movements abroad.

More interest in the *Theory of the Labor Movement* appeared again in the December, 1950, meeting of the Industrial Relations

---

79 Cooper, pp. 154-170.
80 Bauder, *Social Forces,* Vol. XXII, pp. 215-24.
81 Dunlop, pp. 163-93.
82 Kerr and Siegel, pp. 151-68.
83 Derber, pp. 114-18.
84 Taft, *Industrial and Labor Relations Review,* Vol. 4, pp. 70-77.
85 Sturmthal, *Industrial and Labor Relations Review,* Vol. 4, pp. 483-96.

Research Association which met jointly with the American Economic Association in Chicago.[86] There one of the panel discussions centered on Perlman's work. While two of the speakers claimed the *Theory* had not been substantiated by events since its first publication, four of the speakers found that it continued to have validity.

The *Theory* continued to show enough prominence to be a target for attack. In 1953 Simon Rottenburg insisted that workers are more interested in jobs at good wages than in job security as such.[87] During the same year, C. A. Gulick and M. K. Bers, while describing Perlman's *Theory* as " . . . one of the relatively few attempts we have 'to devise a general theory of the labor movement . . . which will apply to all areas and times,' " denied that it is even a theory. Instead, they said it is a system of definitions.[88] They claimed that because the terminological properties of such a system are flexible, Perlman's *Theory* would appear to be correct under almost any conditions.

The mere fact that Gulick and Bers should launch such a vigorous attack on Perlman's *Theory* twenty-five years after its publication testifies as to the impact it has had on American thought. Although not all writers on the theory of the labor movement have referred to either Perlman's or Commons' work, most of them have. Few alternative theories have received attention approaching that given those of the leaders of the "Wisconsin School."

None of the critics have disposed of the Commons-Perlman thesis. They have made some effective criticisms, but so far no satisfactory replacement has been made. Truly satisfactory theories of the labor movement are as difficult to devise as theories of the behavior of the American people. Interesting analytical frameworks can be devised, but the cramming of the innumerable variables into a manageable theory is perhaps impossible. No one has done the task satisfactorily yet, not even Perlman.

An alternate formulation would need to explain the "job consciousness" of American labor, its apparent rejection of radicalism, its attitudes towards "intellectuals," and other facts that Commons and Perlman reported. Not only should it explain origins of labor unions, but it should account for their patterns of growth and their forms of organization. It should explain the dis-

---

86 *A Theory of the Labor Movement, A Reappraisal,* Reprinted from *Proceedings of Third Annual Industrial Relations Research Association,* Chicago, December, 1950.
87 Rottenburg, pp. 346-52.
88 Gulick and Bers, pp. 510-31.

crepancies in behavior between labor movements of various countries. Such a theory should go much further into the role of unions
in our society than did the expositions of Perlman and Commons.
The economic effects should be explored more fully than they explored them. Finally, the theory should indicate the relations of
unions to the future of capitalism. Commons and Perlman considered this relationship, but it needs more analysis.

The task of writing a theory of the labor movement is a formidable one. Until someone succeeds in weaving all the elements
together into such a theory, the Commons-Perlman thesis remains
the classic approach.

Commons publicized labor's conservatism

Perhaps the reason the Commons-Perlman thesis has retained
its vitality is that it was modeled after what labor leaders themselves thought. Commons certainly drew on his firsthand knowledge of labor leaders and their activities when he wrote of the
labor movement. His student, Selig Perlman, in close association
with him, shared some of the same experiences. It is no coincidence that their analysis bears considerable resemblance to these
words of Gompers:

> The ground-work principle of America's labor movement has
> been to recognize that first things must come first. The primary
> essential in our mission has been the protection of the wage-
> worker, now; to increase his wages; to cut hours off the long work-
> day, which was killing him; to free him from the tyrannies, petty
> or otherwise, which served to make his existence a slavery. These,
> in the nature of things, I repeat, were and are the primary objects
> of trade unionism.
>   Our great Federation has uniformly refused to surrender this
> conviction and to rush to the support of any one of the numerous
> society-saving or society-destroying schemes which decade by decade
> have been sprung upon this country. A score of such schemes,
> having a national scope, and being for the passing day subjects to
> popular discussion, have gone down behind the horizon and are
> now but ancient history. But while our Federation has thus been
> conservative, it has ever had its face turned toward whatever re-
> forms, in politics or economics, could be of direct and obvious bene-
> fit to the working classes. It has never given up its birthright for a
> mess of pottage. It has pursued its avowed policy with the conviction
> that if the lesser and immediate demands of labor could not be
> obtained now from society as it is, it would be mere dreaming to
> preach and pursue that will-o'-the-wisp, a new society constructed
> from rainbow materials—a system of society on which even the
> dreamers themselves have never agreed.[89]

---

[89] Gompers, *Labor and the Common Welfare*, p. 20.

Although most responsible leaders prominent in the American labor movement agreed with Gompers as to the objectives of the labor movement, the public retained some scepticism. For many persons the labor movement had a slightly revolutionary taint. Radicals, of course, insisted that labor unions existed as an institution training workers for the predicted revolution. William Z. Foster, the communist, even protested that unionists' pious protestations against radicalism were merely "protective coloration" to conceal their real purposes, which he implied were revolutionary.[90] Unionists of the Gompers variety denied this, and insisted that their real purposes were to improve the workers' wages and working conditions without destroying the capitalistic system.

What Commons and Perlman did was provide a plausible theory in defense of the unions' point of view. Naturally, those who have shared the sentiments of union leaders have tended to grasp at such a theory, and as the number of sympathizers of labor has grown, so has the acceptance of the theory.

The psychology of the worker may or may not be interpreted with complete accuracy by Commons or Perlman, but much of it corresponds to common experience. The implications of the psychology may or may not lead to the conclusions drawn by these writers, but the conclusions have fitted the operations of American labor unions. Undoubtedly, they had the conclusions before they drew up their premises. Yet because they derived their theory from a study of the operations of the labor movement, their reasoning seems to be a plausible picture of unionism in America. Because the labor movement evolves slowly, conditions have not changed sufficiently to invalidate their theory completely. Even if correctness of the theory did not explain why their picture of the labor movement is not dated, this slowness of evolution would. When viewing the labor movement of today through their theory, we may yet recognize what we see.

Much of the time their theory has competed with radical points of view derived from Marxian principles. Such competitors predicted consequences unpleasant to all except revolutionaries. With the obvious failure of unions to turn to revolutionary activity in America, it has seemed not only pleasanter but also more realistic to turn to a view such as the one by Commons and Perlman. Yet this theory had to come from someone not connected with the labor

---

90 Foster, *The Great Steel Strike and its Lessons*, p. 258.

movement. Coming from distinguished scholars, this view of the labor movement carried far more weight than the utterances of union leaders.

Commons' efforts at spreading the word that labor was not naturally radical began somewhat earlier than those of his student, Perlman. By drawing on his experience with labor leaders, Commons drew a picture of unions which matched that of the leaders themselves. His contribution was not one of originality, but rather it was one of justifying labor's cause before previously hostile scholars. As the Beards claimed:

> . . . John R. Commons, much to the dismay of several college presidents, was distributing the news abroad that the organization of labor was as natural as flowing water—a means of raising the standard of life for the masses and a procedure worthy of approval in polite society.[91]

Indeed, Commons did distribute the news abroad that the labor movement was no sinister threat to society. Not only did his works on labor history trace the maturation of the labor movement into a responsible partner in the U. S. economic society, but he also made numerous other favorable contributions to the literature on labor problems. In addition to writing numerous articles on labor problems, he published a number of significant books on the subject. With his former student, John B. Andrews, he wrote the popular textbook, *Principles of Labor Legislation.*[92] Through four editions, from 1916 until 1936, the textbook served as one of the most important in the field. Using articles by many outstanding labor economists, Commons edited two series of readings in labor problems entitled *Trade Unionism and Labor Problems.*[93] On the subject of employee representation plans, Commons and his students made an extensive study while visiting the establishments of thirty firms. Of these, they wrote accounts of eighteen in the book, *Industrial Government.*[94] On his own, Commons described the role of psychology and industrial morale in *Industrial Goodwill.*[95] In this work his ideas on the theory of wages are not very different from those of the conservative economists of his day. A few of his important short articles were reprinted in *Labor and Administration.*[96] Many of his other books, including *The Distribution of*

---

91 Charles and Mary Beard, Vol. II, p. 238.
92 Commons and Andrews.
93 Commons, *Trade Unionism and Labor Problems.*
94 Commons, *Industrial Government.*
95 Commons, *Industrial Goodwill.*
96 *Labor and Administration.*

Wealth,[97] *Social Reform and the Church,*[98] *Proportional Representation,*[99] *Races and Immigration,*[100] *Legal Foundations of Capitalism,*[101] *Can Business Prevent Unemployment?*[102] *Institutional Economics,*[103] and *The Economics of Collective Action*[104] all have a
bearing on labor problems.

In addition to being a prolific writer on the subject of labor,
Commons was also a doer. His activity in labor relations projects
did not end when he left the National Civic Federation to join the
staff of the University of Wisconsin. During vacation and leaves
of absence, he participated in many activities involving labor relations. In addition to drafting labor laws, including the act creating
the Wisconsin Industrial Commission, he served as one of the
first commissioners. Here his skill in bringing together both employers and union leaders contributed to the conspicuous success
of this pioneer commission.

In 1916 Commons served on the United States Commission
on Industrial Relations. This group dramatically placed labor's case
before the public.[105] Another pioneer experiment in labor relations
included Commons as an important participant in 1924. Employers in the men's clothing industry and the dominant union in that
industry, the Amalgamated Clothing Workers of America, jointly
sponsored an unemployment compensation fund. Because they recognized Commons as "the foremost authority on the subject in the
country," they chose him to head the various boards administering
the program.[106] Thus, Commons shared in this example of
employer-union co-operation that might very well have symbolized
his ideal of "reasonable capitalism." It was class partnership for
the purpose of achieving security for the worker without sacrificing production.

Commons' many activities with labor unions demonstrated
that a university professor could recognize labor without losing
respect. In addition to writing about unions in an academic way, he

97 *Distribution of Wealth.*
98 *Social Reform and the Church.*
99 Commons, *Proportional Representation.*
100 *Races and Immigration.*
101 *Legal Foundations of Capitalism.*
102 Commons, Lewisohn, Draper, Lescohier.
103 *Institutional Economics.*
104 *The Economics of Collective Action.*
105 "Report of Commissioners John R. Commons and Florence J. Harriman," in
*Industrial Relations: Final Report and Testimony Submitted to Congress by the Commis-
sion on Industrial Relations,* Vol. I, pp. 171-230.
106 Quoted from the *Chicago Sun* in *American Labor Legislation Review,* Vol. XIV,
No. 1, March, 1924, p. 135.

lead the way for professors to participate actively in solving problems in labor relations. He even urged his students to take menial jobs in industry, as he had in his younger days, to learn how workers actually live and think.

In the process of making the study of labor and labor problems respectable, Commons probably made his greatest contribution as a teacher. At the University of Wisconsin, he created a "school" of labor economists. In 1904 he began teaching labor subjects with twenty-five or thirty students. Later on, from among former students of Commons, additional specialists in the field of labor were added to Wisconsin's Economics Department. Eventually, five taught labor subjects, including Commons himself. Over the years, the University of Wisconsin trained a host of students in the field. Many other universities, as they added labor economists to their staffs, hired these Wisconsin products. Numerous other Wisconsin-trained labor economists found positions with state and national governments. Thus, the University of Wisconsin's "school" of labor became a leader among universities in the study of such problems.

When John R. Commons, around the turn of the century, began to study labor problems more intently than he had any other problem up to then, he found his medium. His studies, his many activities, and his teaching of labor relations and economics combined gave him an outlet for his zeal for reform, his restlessness, and his desire to be a scholar. He succeeded in becoming one of the greatest authorities on labor problems in his day. At the same time, his encouragement to others to follow the subject pushed studies in this field beyond his own considerable contributions.

JRC

COMMONS' APPROACH TO ECONOMICS

JOHN R. COMMONS called his kind of economics "institutional economics." He defined an institution as collective action in control, liberation, and expansion of individual action.[1] To many persons, such a definition does not even sound as if it might refer to economics, but to Commons it was a reformulation of economic theory along new lines. Such a reformulation was not to supplant traditional economic theory, but rather it was to broaden the base of economic investigation.

Commons derived institutional economics from his experiences

Although a reading of his masterpiece, *Institutional Economics*, might not so convince a reader, Commons was a practical man. To him the acquisition of economic understanding had one purpose; it should be used to solve economic problems. He rejected the argument of laissez-faire and appeals to natural laws in economics. According to him, men adopt and adapt economic institutions to solve economic problems. Consequently, as an institutional economist, he always addressed himself to the economic problems of the day. In Wisconsin he was the drafter of laws to

---

1 John R. Commons, "Institutional Economics," *American Economic Review*, XXI, p. 648.

aid the governors and legislatures in their work. Labor unions and corporations turned to him to help them solve economic problems. Even Congress sought his advice by hiring him as a special investigator. Most of his work as a writer was in the exploration for solutions for economic problems.

Although he respected the economists who preferred deductive or historical approaches, he himself tried to practice what he called the pragamatic inductive method for most of his work. He seemed to feel that the men concerned with economic problems often have insights that may be overlooked by the logical deductive thinker. For example, even supposedly ignorant and uneducated workers often may contribute ideas valuable to their employers. Business men, bankers, and government officials in their attempts to cope with economic problems often gain insights before economists have allowed for them in theories. Consequently, Commons constantly advised his graduate students to gain practical experience in addition to their studies. Many of his students followed this advice and became eminent applied-economics practitioners. They filled many important positions in government. Among his students who rose to prominence were many who frankly admitted that they did not understand Commons' theoretical structure in institutional economics. The emphasis on public policy and practical economic problems was enough for them.

Yet for Commons the inductive approach to a science of economic behavior required "analysis into similarities of cause, effect, or purpose, and a synthesis in a unified system of principles."[2] All the time he worked with economic problems he was gathering material for his "great work," which would be this synthesis, the *Institutional Economics* became almost a lifetime project. Parts of it were rewritten many times, but with each revision only the corrected copy was kept. Finally, when he was almost seventy-two, he published his *Institutional Economics*.

He derived his economic theories from a study of institutions. His method of study was a byproduct of his problem solving. Each time he worked on a particular problem he collected material to be used as a basis for creating theories. Finally, when he had sufficient material, he tried to tie it together as a "synthesis in a unified system of principles."[3] To analyze the vast amount of data,

---

2 Commons, *Ibid.*, p. 648.
3 Commons, *Ibid.*, pp. 648-657.

he looked for similarities or common elements. He particularly looked for a problem and its possible solutions. Because most of these problems involved reforms and the means of selling them, many diverse elements in addition to economics crept into his analysis.

Reforms seldom are sold on the basis of economics. Indeed, in Commons' day the teachings of economists tended to inhibit reform. The prevailing laissez-faire doctrine implied a presumption against governmental participation in any economic reform. Collective action from labor unions or other groups also was condemned as unhealthy interference with free competition. To a considerable extent, Commons sold his reforms not with economic arguments, but in spite of them.

If reforms could not be sold on the basis of economic arguments, they could on humanitarian grounds. By spotlighting what he believed to be injustices, he could effectively bring ethical and moral arguments to bear on the subject. He could point to the victims of industrial accidents, women working extremely long hours, the disaster to a family when a member contracts a long and serious illness, or the tragedy of a family whose wage earner loses his job. When the remedy conflicted with established rights of employers, he had to demonstrate the justice of his recommendations. He was required to prove that employers should have responsibilities toward their employees, which must be considered even at the sacrifice of some rights. Yet to make his proposals palatable, he contended that the benefits of reform would accrue even to the employers. Happier and more secure workers, he asserted, were more productive. Finally, as the clincher to his arguments, he brought in economics to prove that if the costs were applied to all employers, much of the ultimate burden would fall on the consumers.[4] Because he believed that all costs necessary to maintain the working force in health, decency, and comfort should be part of the costs of business, he could see no reason why the employers or their customers should not bear them. Otherwise, he argued, the public faces expenses in caring for the destitute, either in the form of some sort of charitable relief or custodial care. To Commons, the orderly prevention of distress through employer or public responsibility was far more preferable than the haphazard relief after distress had been caused.

---

4 Commons, *Industrial Goodwill*, p. 56.

In some of Commons' reforms, such as workmen's compensation for accident victims and unemployment compensation, he devised means by which employers might avoid part of the costs. Those employers whose employees drew the least on the workmen's compensation or unemployment compensation funds would pay the least under the programs. Hence, they would be given incentives to attempt to prevent accidents and unemployment among their workers.

Furthermore, the program aimed at fostering a sense of responsibility on the part of the employers. Not only would they be given incentives to establish good records, but they could have the feeling that they were paying only for their own workers and not for the employees of the less responsible employers. Hence, the employers who were in a position to avoid much of the costs could take pride in the humanitarian aspects of the program. Because of the small cost, they would provide less opposition to the introduction of the reform in question. In fact, many of them, under the influence of Commons' propaganda, even helped sell the program.

Yet the economic arguments were always the negative ones. The effective arguments were the moral and ethical ones. The public particularly tended to react more favorably when such humanitarian arguments were stressed. Sympathy for the unfortunate convinced more people than did dry economic arguments.

As soon as Commons' reforms reached the stage when they were about to be adopted, the legal and administrative aspects gained importance. During much of his time, constitutional barriers to reforms presented formidable problems. Consequently, careful drafting of legislation required as much attention as did the actual selling of an idea. To be able to predict what would be constitutional, he turned to an extensive study of the law and its history. This history he felt to be an evolution of economic institutions. Combining his ideas of ethical, moral, legal, and administrative aspects of economic institutions, he had the beginnings of his theories.

Because he intended that his theories be a systematic synthesis of his studies of economic institutions, it was natural that they stress the ethical, moral, legal, and administrative principles. Yet the use of these principles took him far across the borders of what usually is considered economics, combining into the fields of philosophy, psychology, sociology, and law. However, he made no superficial references in fields in which he was not familiar. Rather, he studied extensively until he felt at home in other fields. In doing so, he apparently neglected to keep up on the economic theories of his more orthodox colleagues. Except for some of the monetary theory, Commons used little of contemporary economic theory.

Yet, in his theoretical works, he intended to write books on economics. He did not intend for his work to replace current economic theory. Rather it was to supplement by providing an understanding of the development of economic institutions. By explaining the role of economic decisions in this development, he then brought his thinking back to reforms in which he had participated. By encouraging reasonable decisions, the economy would develop in a way to provide high productivity, and hence stable and fair incomes for the people.

Commons' theories had little influence

Although Commons spent years writing and rewriting his works on this theories, he failed to achieve much influence either on the professional economists or even on his own students. He left no "school" of thought to carry on his work. With a few exceptions, most of his students have done little with his type of analysis. They displayed the benefits of his influence in many ways but not by developing his kind of theory.

In judging Commons it must be admitted that the nature of his task presented considerable difficulties. Although he seemed to be addressing economists, his work contained little of what usually is discussed today on the subject by those in the profession. Rather, he was discussing the philosophical, psychological, legal, and organizational foundations of the U. S. economy. A mere economist, not feeling too much at home in fields other than his own, might prefer gaining his understanding of philosophy from a philosopher, his knowledge for psychology from a psychologist, and his legal principles from a lawyer. At least he would be on the comparatively safe ground of learning what generally is accepted by specialists in these various fields. It is no wonder that when an economist found understanding of everything in Commons' exposition difficult (except the rather obvious economics), he suspected Commons was to blame. He might well conclude that Commons was a muddy thinker who tried to verbalize without understanding. As his friendly critic, Wesley Mitchell, explained:

> . . . all books which lie on the borderlands cover some territory that is strange to most of their readers. Economists will find the legal distinctions difficult, lawyers will be puzzled by the economic theory, few historians have patience with any sustained analysis, and I fear many reformers will find everything strange except a few wrong-headed legal decisions which they know only too well.[5]

Mixing the various fields, as Commons did, presented difficulties in exposition. Using the various vocabularies and nomenclatures burdened his exposition. Furthermore, whenever a term had a restricted meaning in one field, differing from its usage in other fields, the chance for misunderstanding increased. Even when Commons carefully defined a term, the reader was faced with the burden of remembering its special use.

In addition to difficulties arising from divergent vocabularies, the mixing of various fields precluded the using of conventional methods of exposition. In each field special methods of expressive meanings have developed. Galbraith expressed this idea by explaining:

> Economics has developed a shorthand terminology which, however baffling it may be to the layman, has great advantages in speed and ease of communication for the initiated. It also requires a certain precision of thought and statement which is a protection against careless thinking and which places critics on firm ground in recognizing and protesting error. It also assures the critics that the author is learned in the terminology of his subject.[6]

By mixing several fields, Commons denied himself the use of conventional methods of exposition. Even if he had tried to use the conventional method of each discipline, he would have been frustrated by the fact that most of his readers would have been familiar with the terminology of only one field.

Commons' difficulties in organization cannot be blamed entirely on the nature of his material. Clearly his weakest point was his tendency to be unsystematic. He confessed and his students complained that his lectures were not systematic. When he wrote on subjects of limited scope or those possessing natural means of

---

5 Wesley C. Mitchell, *American Economic Review,* XIV, pp. 240-253.
6 Galbraith, p. viii.

organizing, his exposition was adequate.[7] He could argue eloquently and well for his reforms; but when he began to write on his theories, his exposition began to wander. Mitchell, in his review, described how a reader might react:

> He may feel that the ripe scholar who writes this book has much in common with the young instructor who failed when he tried to give a systematic course of lectures at Wesleyan in 1890. . . . The reader must do his own systematizing of the rich materials before him, but the result will amply reward the effort.[8]

Commons' poor exposition definitely limited the influence of his theoretical works. Most economists ignored his work completely. The reviewers of his *Institutional Economics* were confined to a few economists who had been influenced by the kind of institutional economics taught by Thorstein Veblen. The similarity of their ideas, in spite of their differences, provided them with a background enabling them to understand what Commons was trying to do. Furthermore, being nurtured on Veblen's works, tough reading did not discourage them.

Of these institutional economists, Wesley C. Mitchell gave the most sympathetic and understanding account of Commons' theories. Besides reviewing *Institutional Economics,* Mitchell also wrote a very respectful analysis of Commons' *Legal Foundations of Capitalism.*[9] Included in his lecture notes, published by August Kelly, was an excellent section on John R. Commons.[10]

Some of the other institutional economists had certain reservations as to Commons' work. He tended to be somewhat more conservative than others of that brand of economics. Morris A. Copeland, in his review of *Institutional Economics,* praised Commons' scholarship but complained that he had limited the possibilities of economic planning.[11] In a like manner, Clifford L. James thought his method of economic reform unworkable.[12] Rather than Commons' gradualism, he advocated considerably more governmental controls. Then, as mentioned earlier, the most compre-

---

7 Leona Spilman writes of Commons' style: "When Commons was writing *Institutional Economics,* which was published in 1934, he was equipped with so much experience that many of the passages of his book read as if he had put a multitude of pregnant ideas into a basket and then tramped them down to get more in. As a result, his delightful style which appears again and again in magazine articles and books, not dealing with extensive theories, is often weighted down by compressed thoughts. However, this book of his later years is worth careful study, especially by those who consider that theory and history of economic thought is the core of economics." Spilman, p. 99.

8 Mitchell, *American Economic Review,* XXV, pp. 635-652.
9 Mitchell, *American Economic Review,* Vol. XIV.
10 Mitchell, *Lecture Notes on Types of Economic Theory,* pp. 270-288.
11 Copeland, *Quarterly Journal of Economics,* Vol. 50, pp. 333-346.
12 Clifford L. James, pp. 61-75.

hensive treatment of Commons' work was that by Allen G. Gruchy. In his *Modern Economic Thought, The American Contribution,* Gruchy included Commons as one of six important contributors to a "holistic" school of economists.[13] His extensive analysis of Commons' theories demonstrated both an understanding and a reminder that they are not forgotten. Yet from the main body of economists Commons' theories received very little attention.

It is even difficult to criticize Commons' theories after laboring conscientiously over his meanings. Unlike most works in economics that use a familiar terminology and then follow a step-by-step sequence of logic, Commons' writings, with their strange terminology, follow no such pattern. Lacking definite check points, Commons' analysis does not offer ready points of attack. A reader can complain about his exposition, reject his policy recommendations, find a few faulty statements here and there, but he cannot easily find any vulnerable point crucial to the entire system. Commons' very looseness in exposition makes criticism difficult. Consequently, few economists have tried; most of those who might have objected to his analysis decided to ignore his work.

Yet Commons' theory of institutional development does deserve study, especially for those interested in the study of economic history. Although his analysis of the evolution of this country's economy is perhaps not so comprehensive as to exclude alternatives, it does provide a convincing explanation. It provides an interesting picture of social behavior explaining how men create institutional structures to resolve their conflicts and, in doing so, set up working rules to determine future conduct. Commons' theories are not neat, but they do deserve consideration from serious students of economic and social evolution.[14]

Common's theoretical works

Commons' theory is concentrated in five works. In addition, numerous articles, reviews, and sections of other books he wrote contain fragments of his theories, but the five works provide a

---

13 Gruchy, *Modern Economic Thought,* pp. 133-243.
14 For other versions of economic and social evolution, see: Marx, Karl, *Capital,* 1889.
Sombart.
Weber, Max.
Tawney.
Veblen, *The Theory of the Leisure Class.*
——————. *The Theory of Business Enterprise.*
Schumpeter.
Simons.
Lindblom.
Galbraith.

substantially complete picture. Of these five, the first two were written before he had formulated many of his ideas and methods. These were *Distribution of Wealth*[15] (1893) and the series, "A Sociological View of Sovereignty," published in the *American Journal of Sociology* during 1899 and 1900.[16] His major theoretical works were *Legal Foundations of Capitalism*[17] (1924) and *Institutional Economics*[18] (1934). His final work, *The Economics of Collective Action*,[19] was finished shortly before his death in 1945 with the aid of his student, Kenneth Parsons. This last book, in which he aimed to clarify his previous writings, was published posthumously in 1950.

In all of his works, Commons chose the role of economic institutions, how they developed and functioned, as the core of his theories. The evolutionary development of this theory reached its full maturity in the two middle works, *Legal Foundations* and *Institutional Economics*. He explained the relations of individuals to each other and to society in such terms as rights, duties, liberties, and privileges. The roles of habits, customs, working rules, and laws were given prominence in the last three volumes, but in all five he gave laws and their development an important place.

In each work Commons displayed a concern over monopoly. Because he believed monopoly was inevitable, he did not intend to have society suppress it. Rather he intended to protect other members of the community from its abuses. Consequently, reform played a dominant role in both his writings and his own activities. He would equalize bargaining power by using collective action. He would bring together the various economic interests to resolve their conflicts by negotiation and compromise. Even in cases where the government might act unilaterally, as in the making of factory safety rules, he would use advisory commissions drawn from the interested parties to such an extent that the procedure would approximate collective bargaining.

His reforms included the right of labor to employment. From the very first work he noted the suffering caused by unemployment during depressions to workers and their families. He devoted a large amount of his time to finding methods to prevent depressions and to alleviate the suffering they cause. Even in his theoretical

15 Commons, *Distribution of Wealth*.
16 Commons, *American Journal of Sociology*, Vol. IV, pp. 1-15, 155-71, 347-66; Vol. V, pp. 544-52, 653-93, 814-25; Vol. VI, pp. 67-89.
17 Commons, *Legal Foundations*.
18 Commons, *Institutional Economics*.
19 Commons, *The Economics of Collective Action*.

works, he devoted considerable attention to such problems. When he advocated guaranteeing work to laborers in his first work (1893), he was radical; but by the last work, in 1945, the proposal was commonplace. Commons' own writing was one of the reasons for this change.

In his first major work, he attempted to develop economic theory along lines similar to the approaches of other economists of his day. When the work, *Distribution of Wealth,* was written (1893), the contributions of the Austrian school were popular. He took their marginal utility theory, developed a number of interesting diagrams, and then added his own ideas.

Commons' *Distribution of Wealth* might have been named the *Misdistribution of Wealth,* because it demonstrated how actual distribution departs from what would take place under perfect competition. As has been described in a previous chapter, he analyzed monopoly in terms of marginal productivity theory and in terms of rent. He even unsuccessfully attempted to show how a monopolist might maximize his profits, by combining a marginal revenue product curve with a constant average cost curve.[20] Where they crossed, the quantity sold at the prices on the corresponding demand curve would bring the maximum amount of profits. However, Commons lost his way when he tried to use increasing costs and practically admitted as much.[21] His other analyses were not completely successful either. Yet Commons' theory of maximizing profits had value. Later, under other sponsors, and differently developed, it became a significant part of monopoly theory.

The *Distribution of Wealth* failed to make a good impression on the economic profession. In addition to its analytic crudities, it also had a radical tone. Commons insisted that "All industries except agriculture and retail merchandising have become monopolies, and these are rapidly on the road to monopoly."[22] Following this disconcerting assertion, Commons suggested drastic safeguards against monopoly. Consequently, his reviewers emphasized his radicalism rather than his shortcomings in analysis.

Not only did the interesting part of the analysis in the *Distribution of Wealth* fail to survive its bad reception from economists, but it failed to sustain Commons' interest. Never again did he attempt to approximate the type of analysis which inter-

---

20 Commons, *Distribution of Wealth,* p. 151.
21 *Ibid.,* p. 148.
22 *Ibid.,* p. 81.

ested his fellow economists. Instead he attempted to develop his own approach, which he finally explained in his *Legal Foundations of Capitalism* and his *Institutional Economics.*

The part of the *Distribution of Wealth* that did survive in Commons' thinking involved his discussion of the rights of property. In this discussion he examined the legal aspects of property and their relation to monopoly. In doing so he was examining institutional aspects of the economy as he would later on. This first attempt was incomplete and was almost in the nature of a digression from his main analysis of monopoly. Only this embryonic institutional economics survived.

Much of Commons' interest in the legal aspects of economics goes back to his teacher, Richard T. Ely, who had a similar interest. The interest of Ely finally culminated in the publishing of his book, *Property and Contract in Their Relations to the Distribution of Wealth.*[23] After studying in Germany, Ely passed on to his students an enthusiasm for the historical approach with its emphasis on the entire social environment of an economy. This approach showed up in Commons' preoccupation with the legal aspects of property. Commons, like Ely, turned to German writers in his early ideas. He particularly praised Bohm-Bawerk's *Rechte und Verhaltnisse vom volkswirthschlaftlichen Standpunkte.* This earlier work of Bohm-Bawerk had explored the nature of property and the limitation of property rights. For the economic significance of property, Commons turned to Wagner's *Lehrbuch der Polischen OeKonomie* and Samter's *Das Eigentum.* Commons complained that British and American writers had neglected the subject of property except from a legal point of view. He did use many quotations from an English writer, T. E. Holland, *The Elements of Jurisprudence.*[24]

Besides his training under Ely, there were other reasons why Commons was interested in the legal aspects of economics. His heritage from his father included a tendency to view human activity from an evolutionary point of view. The elder Commons had been a devotee of Herbert Spencer and his ideas. Of those ideas, John R. Commons inherited the belief that all social phenomena should be viewed from a dynamic evolutionary standpoint. The clearest connection with this point of view was development of the economic system as it became recognized in the courts

23 Richard T. Ely, *Property and Contracts.*
24 Holland.

of law. In *Distribution of Wealth* he displayed this interest which reached a fuller expression in the *Legal Foundations of Capitalism*, published thirty years later.

He had yet another reason why legal analysis should be included in a book on distribution theory. His reason was that he was writing about monopoly with its legal and economic considerations. He maintained that monopoly power arises from the ownership of property rights. The ability to withhold from others what they may desire gives the owner of property bargaining power. Such ability can exist only when the coercive power of the state guarantees property rights. One type of property that by its very nature is monopolized is that of land. Other monopoly privileges created by the government are patents, copyrights, trade-marks, and franchises. Commons found it necessary to remind his readers of all these legal possibilities of monopoly as well as others. To a reader of today, such a discussion seems to be laboring the obvious.

This interest in legal aspects of economics and in monopoly continued to be present in all of his theoretical works. He centered his attention on the means of protecting the public from effects of monopoly and protecting the worker from insecurities of employment. His method of analysis changed slightly but his basic interests persisted because in addition to being a theorist he was above all a reformer.

Commons' interest in institutions, as shown in the *Distribution of Wealth,* also was displayed in a series of articles he contributed to the *American Journal of Sociology* in 1899 and 1900.[25] This series, entitled "A Sociological View of Sovereignty," was a conjectural history of the development of society. It contained the embryo of his later work, *Institutional Economics.* Although he was concerned with institutions and their development, his treatment in this earlier work is much different from that in the later one. In this series he maintained that institutions developed as men organized themselves to escape from the static customs and conventional and ceremonious methods. Men passed from stages where they blindly followed the set ways of the past to stages where reason opened the way for more freedom of choice.

Just why men should pass from one stage to another he did not adequately explain. Such an explanation was supplied later when he became familiar with the pragmatism of C. S. Peirce.[26]

---

25 Commons.
26 Peirce, *Popular Science Monthly,* Vol. XII, pp. 286-302.

Then he developed the psychology necessary to explain better the development of institutions. This psychology included a concept of thought processes. Men experience repeated sensations and remember them. They begin to anticipate the end of a sequence of sensations by noticing the similarities in the beginning. When their expectations turn out to be wrong, they become aware of differences. Consequently, the mind can organize its impressions by verifying the expectations. By reacting to stimuli in the manner in which they have had previous successes, men form habits. Such habits substitute order for random activity in men's behavior.

Just as individuals follow habits, groups follow customs. To do so provides security of expectations. Yet because groups and their members have wide ranges of differences, habits and customs come into conflict with one another. These conflicts must be resolved either by the group or by its leader. Case by case, conflicts are solved in such a way that patterns are set up for the future. Customs are modified; and working rules and laws are created. As these customs, working rules, and laws are developed, the group concerned becomes part of a going concern, an institution.

Such a treatment of habits and customs, as shown in Commons' later works, is completely missing in this series on sovereignty. In this series habits and customs are something from which men are freed by reason instead of being the dynamic element in social development.

In this series of articles, "A Sociological View of Sovereignty," Commons devoted considerable attention to how the sovereign power of institutions forces the membership to co-operate in its activities. However, in this series he lacked the "common law" organic development of institutions, which was so important in his later writings. The development here comes only from (1) the drive to obtain the increased productivity by creating the institutions, and (2) the struggle for control of sovereignty in a series of stages beginning with primitive man up to recent ones.

Commons' "A Sociological View of Sovereignty" displayed a continued interest in monopoly, but he did not give it the prominence that he did in his *Distribution of Wealth*. He declared that monopoly is inevitable because it brings order and deliverance from chaotic competition. What is necessary is some check on the capricious use of power by men in charge of monopolies. He suggested that rights for minority stockholders and rights for workers be established. Particularly, he wanted to provide workmen with freedom from capricious discharge and provide them with the right to employment. Thus, the thread of continuity through Commons' works from the *Distribution of Wealth* becomes evident. Economic conflict causes a movement toward monopoly, which provides dangers for the workers.

Commons' theories take form

In the years that followed the publication of *Distribution of Wealth* and "A Sociological View of Sovereignty," Commons' ideas continued to develop. Yet his written works were addressed chiefly to specific economic problems. During this period he gained considerable recognition as a labor economist. He served in this capacity both as a participant in solving labor problems and as a writer. His list of writings on the subject of labor is an impressive one, indeed. Often related to labor, but not necessarily limited to it, Commons energetically pushed many reforms during this time, including those which involved him in the drafting of bills to aid Wisconsin's legislative committees. Because of possible disputes as to constitutionality, Commons found it necessary to exercise extreme care in the drafting of such laws. All over the country the greatest roadblock to reform was the possibility that the courts would declare any effective law unconstitutional. One constant issue was the determination of "reasonable value." Whatever they found "reasonable," the courts would also find constitutional. Commons explained:

> From the Court decisions it seemed that anything "reasonable" would be sustained, and so we had to use the words reasonable value, reasonable safety, reasonable wages, and fix up reasonable conduct for public officials and private citizens, whether we knew what it meant or not.[27]

To learn the meaning of reasonable, and particularly reasonable value, Commons turned to a study of the law. This he did both by reading and consulting legal authorities while drafting laws. In drafting the Wisconsin public utility regulation law of 1907, Commons had the aid of Harry L. Butler, one of the state's leading constitutional lawyers. Praising him, Commons said, "From him I learned to know in advance what the judges would do."[28] Such information proved extremely valuable in writing any reform law. Commons had other contributors to his legal education,

---

27 Commons, *Legal Foundations*, p. vii.
28 Commons, *Myself*, p. 122.

among whom was Senator A. W. Sanborn, who had been a judge in a circuit court. From this state senator, Commons testified:

> . . . I got the idea, thrilling to me at the time, of legal valuation in economics as always looking toward the future. From this point I worked for many years in making Futurity the main principle of economics, distinguished from all the schools of economic thought which based their theories on past labor or present feelings. Sanborn's futurity became my connecting link between law, ethics, psychology, and economics.[29]

A third lawyer who worked with him on the public utility regulation law also played an important part in Commons' legal education. This was M. S. Dudgeon, with whom Commons then taught a course on public utilities at the University of Wisconsin. Dudgeon took the legal aspects while Commons took the economic aspects of "reasonable value." In this course Dudgeon traced his concepts back to the earliest history of common law. Commons, himself, became interested in the techniques of tracing decisions of courts and incorporated the method into his own researches.[30]

In studying the law, Commons made use of an idea he had gained from Veblen. Veblen had insisted that an evolutionary theory of value should be constructed out of the habits and customs of social life. Although Veblen had not used court decisions for his studies of habit and customs, Commons found them a rich source. Here in the development of common law, Commons maintained, was the method by which many customs are tested for survival. In economic evolution new forms of behavior grow up in response to new needs or opportunities. Many of these new forms give rise to conflicts which must be settled by the courts. Those that are "reasonable" or good in the eyes of the law are accepted, while those that are "unreasonable" or bad are suppressed. Thus, case by case, common law produces standards for economic behavior. Hence, his study of the development of the country's economic system was to a considerable extent a history of the common law.

In addition to the public utility course, which he soon turned over to others, Commons used his legal studies in two courses he taught for years. One was a lecture course on "Public Value," and the other was a graduate research course on "Value and Valuations." In them he and his students worked out a comparison of legal and economic theories of value.[31] They "tried to reconcile the

---

29 *Ibid.,* p. 125.
30 *Ibid.,* p. 128.
31 Kirshen.

economists from Quesnay to Cassell with the lawyers from Coke to Taft."[32] As their study progressed it became clear to them that instead of merely studying "reasonable value," they actually were exploring the legal foundations of capitalism. Consequently, Commons developed material for two books, one focused on the legal decisions and the other on the development of economic thought leading up to institutional economics. The first became the *Legal Foundations of Capitalism,* published in 1924, and the second, published in 1934, was *Institutional Economics, Its Place in Political Economy.* Although appearing ten years apart, they belong together as two aspects of the same theme. By the time he finished the first book his thinking had jelled sufficiently so the theories did not change appreciably by the time he wrote the second. Furthermore, his last book, *The Economics of Collective Action,* can be considered but an amplification and clarification of these earlier works. Consequently, the theories contained in all three books can be analyzed together.

Commons believed traditional theory unrealistic

John R. Commons believed traditional theory of his time was unrealistic. Its focus on commodities and feelings about commodities caused it to be too mechanistic. In his own theory he shifted the focus to the transactions. His attention was centered on the process of bargaining and the psychology of the participants. On the other hand, traditional theory assumed that participants knew how much they would buy or sell at each possible price before any transactions took place. Given individual demand and supply curves, transactions for exchange of goods followed automatically and mechanically if each individual acted rationally. Commons did not repudiate traditional theory, but he believed it was limited in its usefulness because it followed the wrong analogy. He claimed the orthodox economists of his day were trying to compare economic with physical phenomenon.[33] They were trying to be too mechanical and hence were leaving out the dynamic elements in economics. Human beings have wills and are not so many atoms acting in a completely predictable manner.

By slavishly following a static mechanical analysis the orthodox economists wandered away from reality, Commons thought. They postulated perfect competition when evidences of monopoly were widespread. In his *Distribution of Wealth* Commons had

---

32 Commons, *Legal Foundations,* p. vii.
33 Commons, *Institutional Economics,* p. 56.

pointed to the monopoly elements in the economy. His analysis demonstrated a theory of how monopolists would determine prices and output by maximizing profits. By comparing the costs of additional increments of investments with revenues from those increments, the monopolist could determine where to set prices and output. Since Commons' time this theory has been refined and has gained acceptance under other sponsors. Yet even when he was proposing it he did not believe this was the way that monopolists actually make their decisions. He stated:

> In reality, a business man does not proceed in exactly this way. He knows nothing of different *rates* of profits on different increments of his investments, but he *averages* his total profits upon the basis of his total investments.
> . . . When profits get so low as to reduce his average returns, then he begins to retrench. This is the only way he has of calculating the returns to marginal investments.[34]

After confessing that businessmen did not follow the marginal analysis, he did not go on to answer, "Why pretend that they do?" Defenders of the marginal analysis have their answers, but Commons gave none. After the poor reception of his *Distribution of Wealth* he abandoned the marginal analysis as unrealistic.

He did concede that the usual price theory is adequate for analyzing such institutions as a stock exchange, a produce exchange, a board of trade, or some other organized market.[35] Because these markets are impersonal an individual cannot bargain (except in a limited sense) with anyone in them, as in the stock market, for example. His economic power, power of persuasion, or other characteristics are not pertinent to a transaction in this market. The individual merely reacts to the market conditions. Free competition in the market determines the prices.

Although the usual price theory is a fruitful one for analyzing transactions in highly competitive markets, Commons believed that "orthodox economists" used it in too many kinds of transactions where its usefulness was limited. His participation in labor problems caused him to reject this predetermined mechanical operation of the transactions as analyzed by "orthodox economists." To him, the participants in a transaction ordinarily do not approach an impersonal market with decisions made in advance.

The usual theory assumes that supply curves show what quantity of a commodity would be offered for sale at each pos-

---

34 Commons, *Distribution of Wealth*, p. 148.
35 Commons, *Institutional Economics*, p. 711.

sible price, and that demand curves show what quantity of a product could be sold at every possible price. Implicit in the construction of such curves is the fact that each seller or each buyer has determined (consciously or unconsciously) what he will sell or buy at each price. On these curves all changes while any transaction is taking place are ruled out except the interaction of the two variables. The entire process is mechanical and shuts psychology out of the picture at too early a stage in the analysis. Traditional theory uses psychology to determine original decisions made by buyers and sellers so that supply and demand curves may be constructed, but it stops short of analyzing what was particularly interesting to Commons. The whole psychology of negotiation with the use of persuasion, coercion, hesitations, and the interplay of many motives, he maintained, have as much to do with determination of prices and values as anything the more traditional economists use in their analysis.

In labor transactions involving collective bargaining nothing is predetermined. In the contest between the wills of the participants the final decision depends on many variables, the effects of which may not be foreseen. Although relative economic conditions might indicate the ability of each side to hold out to compel agreement by the other side, the purely psychological elements, such as the strength of each side's willingness to suffer sacrifices, cannot be measured. In a "war of nerves," the breaking point cannot be determined in advance. Powers of persuasion and skills of negotiators will affect transactions in ways that cannot be predetermined. Besides these mentioned, many other unforeseen variables also will act on the situation.

Reality in analyzing a collective bargaining transaction requires recognition of the fact that no single item, such as wages, is the only one usually considered. The scope of bargaining includes, besides wages, working conditions, hours of work, security conditions for the unions. With an extensive list of factors, with different weights as to importance, the number of acceptable combinations may be considerable. To analyze in what form the combination of these factors finally will be acceptable, the mechanical procedure of marginal analysis is limited in its usefulness.

The marginal approach also fails to provide a picture of the institutional framework within which the transactions take place. In this framework, customs (both those formalized into law and those established by common practices) set limits to bargaining.

Both the unions and employers are reluctant to bargain away rights that have been established by custom. Many of the methods of recruiting workers, paying them, and supervising them have become so habitual that change may be resisted. By following practices until they become habitual, both workers and employers build up a body of concepts concerning what is "fair" and what is "unfair."[36] Ideas of "fair pay" and a "just day's work," "fair pay differentials," and a host of other preconceived ideas enter into the bargaining picture. To assume these under supply and demand curves is assuming far too much of the problem of how wages are determined.

Customs that have become formalized into laws are also a part of the institutional framework within which the transaction takes place. The rights, duties, and privileges created by laws narrow the scope of bargaining to legally accepted limits. Pay below the minimum legal wage, work under unnecessarily unsanitary or unhealthy conditions, involuntary servitude, and numerous other conditions cannot be matters for bargaining. Also, laws stabilize conditions so that agreements are possible and enforceable. They protect employer's property and prevent workers from encroaching upon his rights. On the other hand, mechanics' lien laws protects workers' rights to pay they have earned. Laws both make transactions possible and limit the scope of their operations.

John R. Commons' focus on the transaction is particularly significant wherever bargaining is the dominant element. Collective bargaining is, of course, the important example. But he applied his approach to determination of values wherever competition was not perfect.

The role of the transaction

Commons considered the relationships of people and groups of people the key to economic activity. Hence, the transaction that brings people together was his unit of investigation. He said:

> In fact, transactions have become the meeting place of economics, physics, psychology, ethics, jurisprudence and politics. A single transaction is a unit of observation which involves explicitly all of them, for it is several human wills, choosing alternatives, overcoming resistance, proportioning natural and human resources, led on by promises or warnings of utility, sympathy, duty or their opposites, enlarged, restrained or exposed by officials of government or of business concerns or labor unions, who interpret and

---

36 Commons, *Institutional Economics*, p. 706.

enforce the citizen's rights, duties, and liberties, such that individual behavior is fitted or misfitted to the collective behavior of nations, politics, business, labor and the family and other collective movements, in a world of limited resources and mechanical forces.[37]

The transaction is the dynamic element in the functioning of this country's economy. It is the means by which people, individually and collectively, determine proportioning of resources, extent of output, and distribution of rights, duties, and benefits. In fact, Commons used the concept of the transaction for the same purpose other economists use the concept of the price system as a regulator of the economy. Yet he refused to follow very far into their theoretical structure of the price system. Their approaches were directed toward logical determinant solutions for value and distribution problems, while he probed human wills in action whether in concert or in conflict. Rather than finding precise objective valuations, he found judgments based on a multiplicity of factors.

Transactions are also the means by which economic problems are resolved. Transactions can take place in three ways. One method is by bargaining between the parties interested in the transaction. In the eyes of the law the bargainers are held to be equals, although in other respects they may in no manner be equal. Such bargaining may determine prices, wages, and other considerations in a contract.

A second method is by having a legal superior determine the conditions for a legal inferior, a situation Commons called a managerial transaction. The employer may issue an order the employee is obliged to execute. Any transaction taking place within a firm, or between branches of a firm, would come under this category.

The third type Commons used he called the rationing transaction. This rationing transaction is between a collective superior and individuals who are inferiors. Commons gave as illustrations the examples of the logrolling activities, taxation, and tariffs in Congress and the legislatures; the decisions of an arbitrator; and the decrees of a dictator. Such transactions involve the rationing of wealth or purchasing power to subordinates without their participation in bargaining. In the process of arriving at a decision, the superior may be subjected to pressures of the inferiors in arguments and pleadings. Yet the ultimate decision remains in

---

37 Commons, *Legal Foundations*, p. 5.

the hands of the superior. This particular type of transaction may include the laying down of "working rules" by a superior.

Commons described the three types of transactions in the following words:

> These three units of activity exhaust all the activities of the science of economics. Bargaining transactions *transfer ownership* of wealth by voluntary agreements between legal equals. Managerial transactions *create wealth* by commands of legal superiors. Rationing transactions apportion the burdens and benefits of wealth by *dictation* of legal superiors. Since they are units of social activity among equals, or between superiors and inferiors, they are ethical in character as well as legal and economic . . . These three types of transactions are brought together in a larger unit of economic investigation, which, in British and American practice, is named a Going Concern. It is these going concerns, with the working rules that keep them going, all the way from the family, the corporation, the trade union, up to the state itself, that we name Institutions.[38]

In Commons' analysis the bargaining transactions play the greatest role. He focused his attention on the two best buyers and the two best sellers in any market. By "best" he meant the sellers who are willing to sell at the lowest prices and the buyers who are willing to buy at the highest prices. As do other economists, he assumed that each side usually attempts to get as much as it can for as little as possible in each transaction. The buyer and the seller whose prices are closest bargain until they either reach an agreement or break off negotiations. In negotiations the next best seller and the next best buyer set the limits above which or below which the final price cannot go. The buyer will not agree to any price higher than that asked by his alternative seller. In like manner, the seller will not sell at a price less than that offered by his alternative buyer.

Commons used the following illustrations:

Actual (best)	Potential (next best)
$100 B (buyer)	$90 B' (buyer)
$110 S (seller)	$120 S' (seller)

The actual buyer, B, of say a horse or cow, comes upon the market hoping to buy at, say $100, the actual seller, S, hoping to sell at $110. The potential buyer hopes to buy at $90, the potential seller hopes to sell at $120. The other potential, or possible buyers and sellers will not ordinarily become actual buyers and sellers until those who are nearest together have first gotten off the market. They are possible exchangers. Hence the two best opportunities for

---

38 Commons, *Institutional Economics*, p. 65.

the actual seller, S, are the two offers of $100 and $90. Evidently the actual seller cannot be forced to sell for less than $90. On the other hand, the best two opportunities for the actual buyer are the offers to sell at $110 and $120. Evidently the actual buyer cannot be forced to pay more than $120. Consequently the actual price agreed upon by B and S will lie somewhere between $90 and $120. Between these two points may be said to be the field of persuasion and coercion, and at these points the opposite party has a costless alternative. Beyond these two points only persuasion can induce the exchange to be made.[39]

In perfect competition the gap between the limits of bargaining is negligible. Hence, neither buyer or seller may bargain, because each has many equally attractive alternatives. For Commons the analysis based on the concept of perfect competition is but a special case which he was happy to leave to the "orthodox" economists. Although he admitted cases exist where such an analysis is useful, he turned his attention to those in which he had maintained an interest from the first, where competition is less than perfect.

While the case of perfect competition ignores the process of bargaining and negotiation, Commons' institutional economics is centered on them. By introducing bargaining and negotiation, Commons' analysis is deprived of the precise conclusions the marginal approach provides even in some cases of imperfect competition. Commons visualized valuation as a matter of making judgments rather than following steps to a logical conclusion. His method of weighing nonadditive variables could lead only to approximations.

The parties to a transaction endeavor to induce each other to accept their offers.

In Commons' example, seller S tries to induce buyer B to buy for as close to $120 as possible, while the buyer attempts to persuade the seller to accept as close to $90 as possible. Just what the final agreed price will be depends on their powers of duress, coercion, and persuasion.

Duress depends on compulsion by physical force either directly or by threat. Except when the state is exercising its sovereign powers, contracts made under duress are not enforceable by law.

Coercion is the using of economic power to withhold something someone else wants. Thus, someone who has a monopoly

---

[39] Commons, *Legal Foundations*, p. 66.

over some essential commodity would have considerable power to coerce other individuals. Of coercion, Commons explained:

> It depends on the relative wants and resources of the opposite parties. But, since resources are but the means of satisfying the corresponding wants, and since the satisfying of wants exhausts resources in the course of time, the power of each to determine the ratios of exchange depends upon their relative power to wait for the other to give in. The one with larger resources or less wants can wait longer than the other. He has the larger power of abundance which gives him larger power of waiting and can eventually impose a higher value on his own product in terms of exchange for a larger quantity of services of the other.[40]

Persuasion is the use of moral power. In the absence of duress and coercion, each side is free to accept or reject the other's offer. Two bargainers may be unequal in their persuasive abilities. One may be a better salesman than the other. He may be intelligent and informed, while the other may be stupid or ignorant. Such information or ignorance may be general or just apply to the bargaining transaction under consideration. Fraud or misrepresentation may be another source of inequality between the bargainers which may influence the outcome.

In the background of every transaction stands the sovereign power of the state as exercised through the judicial system.[41] If physical coercion or duress were not suppressed by the state, transactions would be little more than robbery. Private property could not exist if the state did not create the rights and duties connected with this institution and then guarantee them with the use of physical force, if necessary. Ownership of property is the possession of certain rights connected with the property. Corresponding to these rights are the duties of other individuals to respect those rights. For example, the right to exclusive use of the crops of some land must be backed by the existence of the duty of others to refrain from appropriating those crops.

Although the state does not prevent all economic coercion, it does set upper and lower limits. For example, when an individual or organization has a monopoly of a commodity necessary to society, the state sets an upper limit on the price that may be charged. Public utility companies must gain permission from the state before raising their rates. At the same time courts prevent state governments from reducing the rates of public utility com-

---

40 Commons, *Institutional Economics*, p. 337.
41 Kirshen.

panies to the point where confiscation of property results. Between these points, rates or prices are considered "reasonable" by courts.

The state limits its interference with the exercise of persuasion to the prevention of fraud, misrepresentation, or unfair use of pressure. A minor, or someone not mentally competent, is protected from having someone else take advantage of his weakness. Furthermore, the state suppresses fraudulent advertising and requires sellers to list ingredients in the products they sell.

Where the state does not limit powers of persuasion and economic coercion, private associations in many cases are organized to equalize the power of the bargainers. Professional organizations develop sets of "professional ethics" which, to a considerable extent, are attempts to prevent unfair methods of persuasion by advertising or unfair pressure on the client. Business men have their business ethics, and trade union men have their union ethics.

To equalize economic bargaining power, workers form unions. Because individual workers must have jobs to support themselves and their families, they are individually in inferior bargaining positions. Usually opportunities for jobs for them are much more limited than the opportunities for an employer to find employees. Not having the worker's urgency, the employer can be more selective. His waiting power is greater. Only during boom times when the demand for labor is abnormally high is the relative bargaining power of employers and workers in comparative balance. Consequently, membership in strong unions becomes the means by which the economic power of the worker is brought up to a strength in collective bargaining comparable to that of employers.

Unions also provide means by which workers collectively attempt to control competition for job opportunities. According to Commons, control of competition has two directions. One is to equalize the bargaining powers of the buyer and the seller, that is, employer and employee. The other is to equalize the power of the competitors on one, or sometimes both, sides of the transaction. Trade unions owe their existence to the desire to control competition among workers as much as they do to equalize the bargaining power with that of the employers. Unions attempt to control workers so that employers may not take advantage of differences between workers. In this attempt, unions do not allow workers to make special agreements with the employers, because if they did, collective bargaining would be impossible. Furthermore, the unions do all in their power to prevent competition from immigrant labor.

The employers' association is for the employer the counter-part of the union. It, too, has the function of increasing bargaining power by maintaining the solidarity of its members. Yet the business men have other organizations, both formal and informal, to control competition. Trade associations, cartels (where the law permits), and the informal arrangement of tacitly following a price leader are all means to maintain equality among competitors.

In many cases the state has encouraged organizations whose purposes are to equalize the bargaining power of groups which otherwise would be inferior. Unions among working men, co-operative marketing organizations among farmers, and co-operatives among consumers have been encouraged. Yet the state has suppressed organizations whose primary purpose is to control competition. The antitrust laws aim at preventing combinations that would be in unreasonable restraint of trade. Such combinations would lead to greater inequalities in bargaining power. Thus, Commons observed that equality of bargaining power has been an important objective of the state. It encourages organizations that equalize, but discourages those that would increase the disparity in bargaining power.

Commons' ideal of equality of bargaining power can be applied with greater consistency than the ideal of perfect competition held by other economists of his day. At least the ideal of perfect, or even active, competition has not been applied consistently. While the antimonopoly laws attempted to increase the amount of competition, other laws permitted unions and farm co-operatives to control competition. Antitrust laws have even been interpreted so as to condemn aggressively destructive competition. Yet equality of bargaining power was an objective in each case.

Commons, as a labor economist, had his eye on the collective bargaining transaction. Disparities in bargaining power greatly impressed him. It is little wonder that an analysis of the inequalities of the bargainers and the methods to equalize them would play an important role both in his theories and his policy recommendations. Such considerations would not have the same emphasis for other economists who held to the ideal of perfect competition. But wherever it is recognized that either of the bargainers is limited as to alternatives, bargaining power becomes important. For Commons, this was much of the time.

The transaction as the dynamic element in society

The transaction is more than an exchange of ownership of property. It is the activity undertaken by individual groups organized as going concerns to resolve their conflicts in interests. Commons believed that conflicting interests are due to the existence of scarcity in the world. In some primitive societies where necessities of life are abundant everywhere, conflicts may be at a minimum. However, in most regions of the world, nature is not so bountiful. Man must combine in order to augment the natural products of nature. In doing so, he engages in collective action, and he is faced with two problems. One is that conflicts in interest will continue, because scarcity also will continue. Secondly, to the extent that his organization succeeds in reducing scarcity, mutual dependence is created. Consequently, man through his collective action must bring order out of the conflicts and stabilize his relations. Hence, "working rules" of the group (called a going concern by Commons) are created so that individuals and groups will have their rights which determine what they may expect from others. These working rules also will assign duties to others so that the assigned rights may be effective.

It is the transaction that provides the mechanism by which conflicts are resolved. Commons explained:

> In every economic transaction there is a Conflict of Interests because each participant is trying to get as much and give as little as possible. Yet nobody can live or prosper except by Dependence on what others do in managerial, bargaining, and ration transactions. Hence, they must come to a working agreement, and since such agreements are not always possible voluntarily, there always has been some form of collective compulsion to decide disputes. If these decisions are accepted as precedents and are conformed to as a matter of course in succeeding transactions, then the deciding authority need not intervene and does not usually intervene unless the conflict again reaches the crisis of a dispute between plaintiff and defendent. This process we name the Common-Law Method of Making Law by Deciding Disputes. To the entire process we give the name, Working Rules of Going Concerns, the purpose of which is to bring Order out of Conflict.[42]

The transactions that determine the pattern for others, Commons called "strategic." The rest he classified as "routine." These routine transactions are automatic and so are not given the attention given those that are strategic. The strategic ones become the basis for establishing customs, resolving conflicts of interests, and

---

[42] Commons, *Institutional Economics*, p. 118.

establishing working rules. By focusing on the strategic transactions, men can exert a leverage determining the pattern for all the routine transactions which follow as a result.

Thus, each transaction affects more people than the direct participants. Always in the background are the groups varying all the way from the family up to the state itself. Commons calls these groups that make working rules "going concerns." These going concerns enforce the rights and duties created in each transaction. In the case of the state, the courts enforce the rights and duties of the individuals through the exercise of force if necessary. It is the sovereign power of the state to exercise such force which makes private property possible. Other groups may use economic power to coerce or moral power to persuade persons to comply with their working rules.

Although the collective action of the group does place restraints on those it assigns duties, it expands the freedom of action of the individuals who are given rights. In Commons' words:

> Collective Action is more than control of individual action—it is, by the very act of control, as indicated by the auxiliary verbs, a *liberation* of individual action from coercion, duress, discrimination, or unfair competition, by means of restraints placed on other individuals.
> And Collective Action is more than restraint and liberation of individual action—it is expansion of the will of the individual far beyond what he can do by his own puny acts.[43]

Commons' concept of collective action reaches to the very fundamentals of social organization. He said:

> If it be considered that, after all, it is the individual who is important, then the individual with whom we are dealing is the Individualized Mind. Individuals begin as babies. They learn the custom of language, of cooperation with other individuals, of working toward common ends, of negotiations to eliminate conflicts of interest, or subordination to the working rules of the many concerns of which they are members. They meet each other, not as physiological bodies moved by glands, nor as "globules of desire" moved by pain and pleasure, similar to the forces of physical and animal nature, but as prepared more or less by habit, induced by the pressure of custom, to engage in those highly artificial transactions created by the collective human will. They are not found in physics, or biology, or by subjective psychology, or in the German Gestalt psychology, but are found where conflict, interdependence, and order among human beings are preliminary to getting a living. Instead of individuals the participants are citizens of a going concern. Instead of mechanical uniformities of desire of the hedonistic economists,

---

43 Commons, *Institutional Economics*, p. 73.

they are highly variable personalities. Instead of isolated individuals they are always participants in transactions, members of a concern in which they come and go, citizens of an institution that lived before them and will live after them.[44]

For the most part, human beings live and act as members of groups. The habits and customs of these groups are imposed on them. Yet customs are constantly changing, even if gradually. Groups repeat their activities of the past, but not precisely. Gradually changes take place which give rise to disputes over new conflicts in interests. When these disputes are settled by the group, a leader, or a judge the customs are given the precision of a "working rule." Such is the method of the development of "common law" in jurisprudence or development of union or company rules.

Hence, the transaction is the method by which collective action creates institutions. These institutions are not creations of nature, but rather they are made by men in their attempts to solve their problems. Consequently, there is nothing sacred in men's institutions. In fact, there is nothing definitely permanent. The processes by which men establish practices, customs, working rules, or laws (with their accompanying going concerns and institutions) go on indefinitely. Commons would not try to develop, therefore, a system of deductive economics based on unchanging human behavior. He would leave the elaborately logical systems to others.

Economic evolution

John R. Commons displayed his use of the transaction as a moving force in his article on the shoemakers. He traced the development of bargaining organizations used in the shoe industry in America from 1648 until 1895.[45] Although technological changes and extension of markets play important roles in the history of the shoemakers, Commons demonstrated that these factors changed bargaining conditions and thus brought about changes in organizations. He laid out a series of stages showing the effect of extensions in the markets on bargaining and economic organizations. In the first stage the craftsman had a direct relationship with the customer. With the extension of the market, made possible by transportation developments, middlemen hired the workers and then sold their products to the customers. As the various stages developed, the number of levels of middlemen increased to what they are today.

---

44 Commons, *Institutional Economics*, p. 74.
45 Commons, *Quarterly Journal of Economics*, XXIV, pp. 39-84.

Throughout each stage of development, workers faced one form of competitive menace or another. In some of the early stages, "bad ware" makers or "advertisers" were the menaces. Later on, scabs, prison labor, sweatshop, or immigrant labor were the menaces. Whatever the menace was, protective organizations were organized to fight them. These organizations began with craft guilds, and reached a climax with industrial unions and employers' associations. In each of the various stages the control of unfair competition was the motivating force behind all organizations. Workers strived to maintain their bargaining power in their transactions. To do this they even combined with their employers on occasions to protect themselves from what they believed were competitive menaces.

In his article on the shoemakers Commons used eight stages up to 1895. Later in his *Institutional Economics* he used an additional method of dividing the development of capitalism.[46] In each of three periods, he explained, there was a different form of capitalism. He called that before the industrial revolution Merchant Capitalism; that during the nineteenth century, Employer Capitalism; that in the twentieth century, Banker Capitalism. Commons admitted that no set dates could be used for these periods. Furthermore, not all industries enter the same stage at the same time. His criteria in defining a stage depended on who was dominant in the economy—the merchant, the industrial employer, or the banker.

When the merchant controlled it, he hired producers on contract. He had control over the markets while the competition among the producers gave him effective bargaining power. Gradually, with the introduction of the factory system, the producers reached toward their markets to become less dependent on the merchants. Finally, when the extension of markets had reached the stage where integration and consolidation of firms became the dominant economic activity, the banker stepped into the major role.

Commons characterized these three stages as those of scarcity, abundance, and stabilization. In the pre-industrial revolution period of scarcity, the community exercised a considerable amount of control over economic activity. Like cities under siege, communities facing serious scarcities protected themselves by this control. Local governments with their guilds of craftsmen and merchants made supervision of economic activities their business. With the growth

---

46 Commons, *Institutional Economics,* p. 763.

of nationalism, central governments following the principles of merchantilism replaced local regulation of industry with nation-wide control.

With the coming of the industrial revolution, the new pro-ductivity of industry replaced scarcity with abundance. Conse-quently, the nations could permit a maximum of individual liberty and a minimum of governmental control. Individuals could bargain effectively because of the abundance of alternative opportunities open to them. Under such conditions, while the economic units still were small, competition was an effective protection against exploitation.

Yet the period of "abundance" had its evil—competition was destructive, unfair, or cut-throat. Such competition, according to Commons, led to periods of oversupply followed by periods of undersupply. "These oversupplies led to destructive competition, price wars in manufactures and rate wars in transportation, the elimination of weak competitors, the consolidation or absorption of competitors into large combinations."[47]

A conflict between the goals of efficiency and scarcity created the conditions under which combinations appeared to be desirable forms of relief. Efficiency permitted businessmen to increase the quantity of goods they could sell in order to increase their wealth. Yet value depended on scarcity as well as quantity and useful-ness. Consequently, businessmen sought to increase their own sales, but at the same time, limit the total amount offered. Aggres-sive competition designed to drive out competitors resulted. The way out of these "price wars" was combination.

In their efforts to free themselves from destructive competi-tion, the businessmen turned to the bankers for money to accom-plish their consolidations. Then financiers, as the creators of the great economic combinations, superseded the production experts as the key men in the economy. Hence, Commons named this period the one of Banker Capitalism.

The period was also one of stabilization. The consolidations aimed at preventing overexpansion, which was thought to be the source of instability in the economy. To prevent the frantic com-petition which bred overexpansion, businessmen also developed a new morality. Their policy became "live and let live" by each firm following a price leader who set prices enabling all firms in an

---

47 Commons, *Institutional Economics*, p. 779.

industry to gain their fair share of the profits. Perhaps no firm could get all the business it wanted, but stability was preferable to "price wars." Morality censured "price chiseling," price cutting, and the initiating of price wars. Part of this development stemmed from the reactions of businessmen to the instability of the previous period, and part was derived from the operations of the anti-monopoly laws.

In the beginning, the antitrust law enforcement attempted to prevent combinations in restraint of trade, but as time went on it simmered down to a means of suppressing discrimination. These laws became a part of the code to preserve fairness in competition and to minimize destructive competition. They directed the control of industries toward the price leader principle rather than outright combination. To enjoy relative freedom from harrassment under these laws, large firms found it to their interest to tolerate the existence of many smaller competitors. Yet the mere possibility that the giant could use its economic power to crush them, would keep the smaller firms in line. When great and small firms in an industry became convinced of the fairness of the leader and that price leadership principle was in their mutual interest, direct combination became unnecessary.

Although businessmen and bankers strive for stability, they cannot achieve it alone. Commons believed that an unregulated capitalistic economy is unstable unless price fluctuations can be dampened. Once prices begin to move either up or down, expectations of further movements drive prices in the same direction. Businessmen expecting price rises will hasten purchases, but they will hurry sales or delay purchases when they anticipate price declines. Furthermore, because cost changes tend to lag behind price movements, profits are high while prices are rising, but are low, or are replaced by losses, when prices are falling. The stimulus of profit or loss anticipation drives the economy either to a boom which must give way to a depression or directly to a depression.

The banking system itself, according to Commons, plays an important part in the instability. During upward movements of the business cycle, businessmen seek loans from banks. Because these loans increase the money supply, additional purchasing power is thus created to accentuate the upswing in economic activity. During the downswing, the reduction in loans to businessmen causes a reduction in the money supply so that the forces working for deflation are aggravated.

Commons believed that monetary controls exercised through the Federal Reserve System could prevent price fluctuations to a considerable extent. If prices tended to go upward, he would have the Federal Reserve Banks restrict credit to prevent an uncontrolled boom. When prices tended to sag, he would ease credit to stimulate business. However, he had more confidence in preventing a depression by suppressing a boom than in efforts to cure the depression itself. Collective action by bankers acting through the Federal Reserve Banks is an important function in the era of stabilization under Banker Capitalism.

Yet Commons was not quite satisfied to limit stabilization to monetary controls. He wanted to stabilize employment for the workers. Such a goal developed from his proposed rights to employment which he featured in his *Distribution of Wealth*. For years, Commons campaigned in an effort to sell his state and the nation on the idea of unemployment compensation with its device designed to stabilize employment.

John R. Commons had considerable faith in the profit motive when properly organized. According to him, institutions should be fashioned in such a way that individuals are given incentives to behave in the manner that would be beneficial to society. Monetary controls and his unemployment compensation scheme were examples of such institutions. Bankers may be tempted to loan money if reserves are provided through open market transactions or if they can borrow at lower rates themselves from the Federal Reserve Banks. They would be acting in their own self-interests because they would be given incentives to earn profits. In a similar manner, the Federal Reserve System, by reducing reserves, could induce the bankers to loan less money. No direct compulsion would be necessary. Neither would any government orders for an employer to refrain from employment practices causing unemployment be necessary. Commons maintained that the incentives under the unemployment compensation plan would be effective if monetary controls kept the economy from violent fluctuations.

Institutions can be organized so that individuals react to the stimulus of profits. Because margins of profits, which represent the difference between the total revenues and total costs, are normally very slender, businessmen are sensitive toward any prospective changes. Unless it is passed on to the consumer or to someone else, a small percentage change in total costs can result in a very much larger percentage change in the profit margin. Although the possibility does exist that a cost may be shifted, he businessman views each possible additional cost in relation to the size of his profit margin. He focuses his attention on each possible cost as its prospects arise. Some may be shifted, but to do so may take time and incur resistance. The avoidance of the cost is the preferable course, especially if his competitors are not also to be burdened with it.

Consequently, Commons believed that changes in the interest rate or avoidance of unemployment compensation payments have a considerable value as incentives for businessmen to act. Such small changes with weighty impacts he called limiting factors. By selecting and acting through such limiting factors, man can influence a whole host of complementary factors to achieve a desired result.[48] Pressure of a man's foot on the limiting factor, the accelator, in his car will cause the other complementary factors in the engine to make it run at a desired speed. In the same way, a particular change in the interest rate can have far-reaching effects on the economy.

By making use of incentives which would have the leverage of limiting factors, Commons created his many schemes for economic reforms. From the very first, his work displayed a concern for what he believed to be the growing amount of monopoly in our economy. To reverse the trend, he believed, was neither possible nor desirable. The only feasible course he could see open was the protection of individuals from the arbitrary power of the monopolists.[49] Besides protection of the consumer by control of

---

48 See Barnard, pp. 202-211.

49 In all probability, Commons would have been enthusiastic over Galbraith's concept of the Countervailing Power. Certainly there was nothing in this concept that would have been inconsistent with what Commons believed. Yet Galbraith's analysis is much neater than Commons' rather vague "reasonable capitalism." Both men are optimistic in their pointing out that exploitation has not been great in spite of ever-increasing concentration of economic power. For the protection against such exploitation, both stress the role of bargaining. In both analyses there is a recognition that equalized bargaining power will not provide protection for the various groups if there is economic instability. For Galbraith the countervailing power breaks down under inflationary pressures and becomes a mechanism for spreading further inflation. Commons, being pre-Keynesian, lacked an adequate explanation of how purchasing power is generated in the economy; at least he would have been ready to apply tight monetary controls to prevent an inflation.

Commons certainly wanted to develop countervailing power, but his "reasonable capitalism" is not quite the same thing. Except for consumers' co-operatives or government regulation of prices, Commons' analysis tended to neglect protection for the consumer. He clearly saw the producers organized to protect their interests by collective bargaining, but unlike Galbraith, he did not clearly see the role of the powerful retailers. Such retailers, who make their money on volume sales of goods attractive to consumers, use their strong bargaining power to reduce the manufacturer's prices. Their use of countervailing power thus provides protection for the consumers. This and other parts of Galbraith's analysis is missing in Commons'. Yet it is likely that Commons would have been willing to accept them, at least until he had evidence to the contrary.

public utility companies, many of Commons' reforms centered on social security provisions. He was a leader in the accident compensation, health insurance, and unemployment compensation movements as well as supporting allied forms of protection for the workers.

In all of his reforms, John R. Commons was not a true radical. Unlike the utopians, socialists, communists, and other radical reformers, he had no consistent blueprint of any new economic order that could be installed at some future time. Rather he visualized our economic order slowly evolving to new forms. Because he was not sure where this evolution would lead, he was willing to push it in directions favoring security consistent with liberty. He had observed other economic societies attempt to solve the problems of security and stability by means which killed freedom for its members. Not only did he reject totalitarian methods, but he also distrusted all sudden changes unless they had roots in past experience. Preferable to such sudden changes has been the Anglo-American common law development of accepting customs that were reasonable while rejecting those that were unreasonable.

Progress for Commons consisted of selecting the best practices that had been proved practical and then making them standard. For example, in factory safety, the Wisconsin Industrial Commission (which he designed and served on for its first two years) would study the means that the most enlightened employers used to protect their workers. Gradually these methods would be required of all employers.

In his other reforms, as we have seen, he also would start with the most enlightened employers, gain their support, and then use them to sell the others. They and representatives of labor would be asked to work out details of the reform. Usually those who were to be reformed presented less opposition if they had an opportunity to participate in the planning. Yet they never could dictate the terms because conflicting interests also would be represented. Neither side would be completely satisfied, but they could have confidence in the reasonableness of the reform. Much of the history of American social security laws demonstrates the soundness of Commons' strategy.

If one were to describe the kind of economy Commons would view with favor, it might be characterized as a welfare state with rather complete social security coverage.[50] Yet individuals and

---

50 Such as described in Myrdal.

firms would have the maximum amount of freedom consistent with their charging "reasonable prices," and maintaining "reasonable labor relations." Although the meaning of "reasonable" is still vague in spite of Commons' efforts, its definition must imply forebearing from exercising the full weight of one's economic power. The economic giants, in Commons' scheme, would refrain from practices which would "exploit" the consuming and working public. Instead of maximum profits, the great firms would prefer satisfactory public relations. Instead of conflict, they would prefer harmony.

Commons also would equalize bargaining power by fostering collective bargaining for the workers. Besides labor unions, he would encourage organizations of farmers and consumers as methods of equalizing bargaining. These numerous going concerns he saw as bulwarks against seizure of totalitarian power. Conflicting though these different interests might be, Commons had faith that their differences could be resolved. Although he had dropped his earlier ideas of representation of interests by a scheme of government by proportional representation, he believed that conflicts could be resolved by the use of advisory boards working for governmental commissions. The Wisconsin Industrial Commission demonstrated this technique at its best.

Commons would have the state play the role of the wise and kindly father. It would jealously guard the welfare of its citizens by maintaining a healthy economic climate. By monetary means it would keep the economy on an even keel. Through all types of trouble it would protect the workers by providing them with security of incomes by means of a comprehensive social security program. Yet like the wise father, the state would limit its interference with the activities of its citizens. It would refrain from imposing such direct controls as would seriously reduce the area of the citizen's freedom. Thus, Commons was neither an advocate of state control nor a defender of laissez-faire. He was neither a radical nor a conservative. He kept one eye on the future and one on the past. He did his best to hurry along the economic evolution to levels of "stability and fairness to all."

JRC
9

THE INSTITUTIONAL
SCHOOL OF ECONOMICS

SUPPOSEDLY there is, or at least was, an institutional school of economics. Economists still exist who call themselves institutionalists. Although they disagree on who qualifies for membership, they insist there is such a school. They admit that it has lost some of its vigor, but they express confidence that their brand of economics has a future. Every few years they manage to induce the American Economic Association to include a discussion of their school on the agenda for an annual meeting. Occasionally one of them writes an article or a book on the subject. Yet to the outside observer, the attempts to restore the school to its former vitality appear unpromising.

The term "institutional" gained currency shortly after Walton H. Hamilton introduced it at the 1918 meeting of the American Economic Association.[1] He displayed wisdom by cautiously avoiding defining what would prove to be an elusive concept. Instead he provided five criteria for judging economic theory.[2] Traditional

---

[1] Hamilton, *American Economic Review*, Vol. IX, pp. 309-324. Allan Gruchy quotes A. B. Wolfe that Max S. Hardman first used the word institutional to describe Veblen's Works, Gruchy, *Modern Economic Thought*, p. 2.

[2] Characteristics of Institutional Economics: (a) Economic theory should unify economic science; (b) Economic theory should be relevant to the modern problem of control; (c) The proper subject-matter of economic theory is institutions; (d) Economic theory is concerned with matters of process; (e) Economic theory must be based upon acceptable theory of human behavior.

theory, he claimed, failed to meet these tests, but the institutional theory did.

Hamilton did not create institutional economics; he merely gave it a name. He explained that such Americans as Henry Carter Adams, Charles Horton Cooley, Thorstein Veblen, and Wesley Mitchell already had made significant contributions to this brand of economics. Hamilton might have named others, but their inclusion would have depended on the definition he failed to give.

Over the years, institutionalists and their opponents have struggled over a proper definition. J. M. Clark called the school that "elusive movement known as 'Institutionalism' which means so many different things to so many different people that doubt has arisen whether it has any definable meaning at all."[3] John R. Commons confessed difficulty in defining the term, though he managed to write a book on the subject.[4] At the American Economic Association annual meeting in 1930, two papers, one by Evelyn Burns[5] and the other by M. A. Copeland,[6] failed to give any definition. Yet the subject of their panel was "Institutionalism: What It Is and What It Hopes to Be." Mrs. Burns blamed some of the difficulties of the institutional school on the vagueness of the concept. At the next meeting in 1931, J. M. Clark also declined to make any definition while Paul Homan (who had been chairman of the meeting the year before) cast doubt on the possibility of arriving at any definition. He stated:

> . . . My correspondence and my reading have reached every known economist of supposed institutional proclivities, and they divide roughly into two classes, those who refuse to define institutional economics, and those whose definitions disagree . . .[7]
> . . . I may as well bluntly state my opinion that an institutional economics, differentiated from other economics by discoverable criteria, is largely an intellectual fiction, substantially void of content.[8]
> . . . If institutional economics be broadly defined, it is practically co-extensive with economics. If narrowly defined in connection with a Veblenian origin, it consists mainly in a few thin essays, critical,

---

3 J. M. Clark, p. 426.

4 Commons, *American Economic Review*, Vol. XXI, pp. 648-657. "We may define an institution as collective action in control, liberation and expansion of individual action." This defines the word institution, but not institutionalism.

5 Burns, *American Economic Review*, Vol. XXII, pp. 80-87. See also "Economic Theory—Institutionalism: What It Is and What It Hopes to Become," *American Economic Review*, Vol. XXI, pp. 134-141.

6 Copeland, *American Economic Review*, Vol. XXI, pp. 67-79. See also "Economic Theory—Institutionalism: What It Is . . . ."

7 Homan, p. 12.

8 *Ibid.*, p. 15.

hortatory, and hopeful. If not defined at all, it is a miscellaneous body of works associated with a group of economists reputed to be institutionalists.[9]

The lack of agreement on the definition of institutional economics (which has persisted to this day) also has obscured the origins of the school. Several contemporary institutionalists, Allan Gruchy,[10] Clarence E. Ayres,[11] and John Gambs[12] trace their economic school back to Thorstein Veblen. Joseph Dorfman concurs but adds the influence of Charles Horton Cooley, the sociologist who pioneered studies of institutions.[13] Although considerable opinion probably could be mustered to the view of the Veblenian origin, there is by no means unanimity. Hamilton, it might be noted, included Henry Carter Adams of a generation earlier than Veblen.[14] Another member of Adams' generation, Richard T. Ely, insisted that institutionalism began long before Veblen appeared on the scene.[15] Upon listening to the roundtable discussion on the subject in 1931, he declared that he had heard the same arguments in 1885. At that time he and others who were institutionalists (except in name) founded the American Economic Association.[16] Many of his colleagues were, at the time, young economists who had been trained in Germany. Upon coming home, they had found the field of economics dominated by an old guard steeped in the classical tradition. These younger men, in revolting against the conservatives, began the school of institutional economics.

Undoubtedly there is some truth in Ely's assertions. The revolt which began in the eighties did fuse with that sparked by Veblen after the turn of the century. But it was a milder one centering on methodology and some limited reforms. Furthermore, it lacked the influence of Veblen. He added a new intensity to the revolt, and some new grounds for dissent.

Although Veblen was not the only important institutionalist, his influence came close to dominating the movement. Institutionalism was the voice of dissent, and his voice was the strongest. Those who formed the new school often had little in common

---

9 *Ibid.*, p. 16. See also "Institutional Economics," *American Economic Review*, Vol. XXII, pp. 105-116.

10 Gruchy, p. 31.

11 Ayres, *American Economic Review Supplement*, Vol. XX, p. 47.

12 Gambs, p. 1.

13 Dorfman, *Proceedings American Economic Association Meeting*, Vol. XLI, p. 80.

14 Although Veblen was only six years younger than Adams, his influence came much later. Only after he published his first book, *The Theory of the Leisure Class*, did he gain any reputation. By then he was 42. While Veblen's productive career at that time was in the future, Adams had already distinguished himself.

15 Ely, *American Economic Review*, Vol. XXII, pp. 114-116.

16 Ely, *American Economic Review*, Vol. XXVI, pp. 141-150.

except their repudiation of orthodox economics. Occasionally economists with views at wide variance with Veblen joined the group. In time, it became easier to identify institutionalists by what they were against than by what they were for. Consequently, the difficulties over definition arose.

There was much to attack in the orthodox economics at the turn of the century. It presented a smug picture of an economy efficiently controlled by competitive forces. Members of society were assured by the theorists that competition guaranteed them incomes equal to the value of their respective contributions of services or property. Facts such as the cumulative growth of trusts for the purpose of suppressing competition were either ignored or minimized. Furthermore, the prevailing economics neglected the obvious fact that the economy was not stable. Because the economists assumed that the economy automatically could run efficiently and justly, there was no need for any government intervention. Governments could safely follow the policy of laissez-faire.

Just as the orthodox economist's view of the economy invited criticism, so did his methodology. In spite of the arguments that had been raging since the eighties, many economists followed what has been called the deductive approach. Those using it assumed that all of economics could be deduced from a few general assumptions which are self-evident to most intelligent people. Consequently, such assumption did not require empirical verification. What was worse, it often ignored facts at variance with its conclusions. Because such information was not readily available, economists failed to use statistical evidence. They even ignored historical information by assuming that their reasoning was valid in almost every period of time and in almost every country. Because their assumptions involved what they believed was unchanging human nature, they left out all cultural variations in their reasoning. Furthermore, their conception of human nature did not necessarily correspond to that held by the psychologists of their time. But perhaps the most noticeable methodological fault was the failure to analyze economic changes over time. They patterned their models after the static analysis of physics and consequently had been unable to incorporate dynamic elements. In an age when the most obvious fact about our economy was that it was undergoing rapid changes, the failure to account for them invited criticism.

The institutionalists agreed substantially on their criticisms of the orthodox economists' picture of the economy and the methodology used in arriving at it. Some emphasized certain portions of their common criticisms, others different ones. The gathering and evaluating of statistics became the job of some empirically minded economists. Some concentrated their studies on the business cycle and causes of instability in the economy. Many, in their revolt against the formal theory of orthodox economics, specialized in the study of special problems and institutions. A synthesizing theory they hoped might grow later from such studies.

Their studies often led to opportunities for participation in the creation of institutions. Consequently, many institutionalists worked with governments. Those interested in long-run problems studied the evolution of economic institutions and their prognosis for capitalism's future.

Although the various problems on which institutionalists worked created a picture of diversity, the nature of their concept of proper methodology bridged most of their differences. Yet there was one very fundamental dividing line between two groups of institutionalists: those who would substitute a planned economy for private enterprise, and those who would not. Those following Veblen tended to be in the first group while the followers of Commons tended to be in the second.

Veblen and Commons have much in common, even though their conclusions are different.[17] They both were impressed with the rapid economic changes they and their generation witnessed. Both believed that the tasks of economics includes the explanation for development. They watched the biological sciences accept the Darwinian explanation of evolution and, in doing so, found what they thought was a fruitful methodology for economics.

Both Commons and Veblen believed that men live by habits and customs. Not caring to think except under necessity, men prefer the security of established routines that develop into institutions. These institutions change but only when subjected to the influences of strong forces.

The two men differ in their explanations of the cause of change. With Commons it is the conflict of interests among individuals and among groups.[18] This conflict originates because there

---

17 David Hamilton, pp. 43-50.
18 Commons, *Institutional Economics*, p. 244.

is a scarcity of economic goods in the world. Yet conflicts must be resolved for men to organize production efficiently. Working together, men both increase the goods available and create an interdependence upon one another. Commons focused his theory on how men have resolved their differences in the past. He assumed that there is a good chance they would continue to be reasonable in the future. Although free enterprise would be somewhat limited by some reforms providing protection for consumers, investors, workers, and farmers, it need not be abandoned.

While Commons' evolution stressed institutional adaptation to changing conditions, Veblen's emphasized the reverse. He demonstrated how old habits and institutions inhibit adaptation to changes.[19] Old instincts, remnants from the days of savagery or barbarism, cause men to cling to practices and thoughts that would be ridiculous, if objectively viewed. But man is not rational. He is a creature of superstitious and anthromorphic propensities.

Yet some men do think more rationally than others, because their jobs condition their minds. These are the industrial workers and technicians who work with machines. By watching cause and effect sequences they begin to shed notions that ascribe Divine intervention, luck, magic, or other supernatural explanations as causes. They are practical men who take pride in good and productive workmanship.[20]

Unfortunately, the more rational industrial workers (or engineers) are not in control of economic institutions. Instead, a leisure class controls both government and industry. This class, whose members avoid productive labor as being beneath them, has been shielded from the processes that produce rationality. Hence, they tend to be conservative (except in consumption) and attempt to inhibit any changes in the status quo.

Being throwbacks to the predatory class that dominated barbarian cultures, the members of the leisure class are more interested in their own pecuniary gain than in production. They engage in fraud, chicanery, and other predatory practices that undermine the stability of the economy. During boom times their fierce competition, their speculations, and their credit manipulations cause them to overtax the economy. Inevitably the credit structure collapses under their excesses. Exogenous forces may restore prosperity temporarily but recovery cannot be permanent.

19 Veblen, *The Theory of the Leisure Class*.
20 Veblen, *The Instinct of Workmanship*.

The pecuniary interests seek relief by combining into huge monopolies for the purpose of limiting production. This measure of stabilization is helpful in maintaining profits only temporarily. Finally, it leads to a stalemate of declining production and employment. Veblen was not sure of the outcome. He thought the government might purchase enough armaments and other goods which might be produced with the excess capacity. By reverting to warlike imperialism, a nation might find relief from chronic economic stagnation.[21]

The sensible alternative, he thought, was unlikely to happen in the calculable future. If the technicians and engineers, who actually run the industrial enterprises, would revolt from their financial masters, the businessmen, they would free the economy of the fetters that limit production. By cutting out waste, eliminating selling costs, by canceling financial claims of the vested interests, and by putting the idle to work, the engineers could increase production many times. Unfortunately they "are a harmless and docile sort, well fed on the whole, and somewhat placidly content" with their lot.[22] Like most of the population, they are caught in a web of institutions which inhibit them from making drastic changes.

Thus, while Commons saw an evolution in which men constantly adapted their institutions to changing conditions, Veblen saw one in which such adaptation was incomplete and tardy. Although neither was certain of the future, Commons tended to believe in the possibility of progress, while Veblen could foresee only purposeless change. Commons' evolution provided him with incentive to be a reformer, while that of Veblen created only a critic.

It is but a short step from Veblen's reasoning to the acceptance of some form of a controlled economy, and some of his followers made that step. But their radical thinking did not significantly divide them from the other institutional economists. All institutional economists were rebels revolting against orthodox economics. For some, the revolt stopped at methodological considerations, for others at reforms for the purpose of providing security and stability in the economy, and for a few it did not stop short of advocating a complete change in the economic system. The extent of the revolt was not as important as the fact that they all had the same adversary, the orthodox economists.

21 Veblen, *The Theory of Business Enterprise*, p. 256.
22 Veblen, *The Engineers and the Price System*, p. 135.

Although the institutional school of economics did not succeed in replacing traditional economics, it did achieve a considerable measure of success. A number of institutionalists made significant contributions to economic knowledge and pursued highly successful careers. Their spiritual leader, Veblen, achieved the distinction of being America's most outstanding economist, at least in reputation. Yet it was not his positive contributions that gained him his eminence, but rather his provocative criticism. He wrote with a strange style, a blend of elements that attracted left-wingers, malcontents, nonconformists, intellectual snobs, and numerous other people who enjoyed his pungent phrase-making. The intention here is not to disparage his analytic ability, but to point out that his manner of writing probably was as influential as anything he said. His irony, which approached dead-pan humor, continues to fascinate his readers. Three of his books, *The Theory of The Leisure Class, The Higher Learning in America,* and *The Theory of Business Enterprises* today enjoy such wide circulation that they have been made available in paperback editions.[23]

Veblen set men to thinking, even when he did not convince them. His books began to appear at a time which favored their reception. Shortly after *The Theory of the Leisure Class* and *The Theory of Business Enterprise* were published, the magazines of the country erupted in a wave of criticism of business and politics. Although not connected with Veblen, the magazine writers who gained the name muckrakers seemed to add documentation to his assertions. On the political front, the progressive movement radiating out from Wisconsin also attacked the status quo. Here the link with institutional economics was through Commons and not Veblen, but the movement added fire to the revolt against traditional economics.

While Veblen served as a publicity agent for the revolt and Commons directed it into channels of reform, a third prominent leader of the institutionalists assumed a quieter role.[24] Wesley Mitchell limited his role to that of a scholar. Unlike his teacher, Veblen, he did not write speculative accounts of the evolution of capitalism. Neither did he step out of the role as an economist and assume the one of reformer or public administrator as Commons did. Instead, he patiently studied the operations of the economy while remembering the institutionalists' criticisms of orthodox methodology.

23 Veblen, *The Theory of the Leisure Class, The Higher Learning in America, The Theory of Business Enterprise.*
24 Arthur F. Burns.

Mitchell confined his studies largely to what he could verify. He wanted to test each hypothesis empirically before he would accept it. Consequently, he began with a subject that would lend itself to measurement, that of money. After publishing several articles on the subject, he completed his study with his *A History of the Greenbacks*.[25] In the process of writing it, he discovered that the available index numbers were not adequate. To remedy the situation he turned to developing some statistical techniques of his own. His interest in money and in statistics lead to a study of the business cycle. Originally this subject, which was to absorb so much of his interest, was to be covered in an introduction to a work on "The Money Economy." Instead, it grew into his classic book, *Business Cycles,* which he published in 1913.[26]

Shortly after World War I he became the director of the National Bureau of Economic Research. With the facilities of this organization, he was able to extend his study of business fluctuations even farther. He and his co-workers used their ever-growing arsenal of empirical techniques to gather facts on the numerous time series, composition, and changes in the national income, and anything they could find related to the operation of the business cycle. The National Bureau, in continuing this work, today stands as a monument to its founder, Wesley Clair Mitchell.

Veblen, Commons, and Mitchell each had a number of prominent students and followers. In the past, their common revolt against orthodox economics, and their determination to be identified as a school, have given these followers a measure of unity. The question now is, will there continue to be an institutional school of economics? Or will it pass from the scene when its distinguished but elderly adherents are gone? I believe that the institutional school is dying.

The one issue that held institutionalists together no longer has the force it once had. Revolts against the thinking of the main body of economists may break out in the future, but they are weak at present. Much of the faulty methodology of the older economists has been corrected. The manifold forms of today's empirical research stand out in marked contrast with the deductive techniques of fifty years ago.

25 Wesley Clair Mitchell, *A History of the Greenbacks.*
26 Wesley Clair Mitchell, *Business Cycles.*

Although much of the acceptance of the need for more empirical investigations has been on an intellectual basis, part of it has
stemmed from the comparative ease in raising money for such
projects. A considerable amount of Commons' success came from
his ability to promote such projects. He found it easier to raise
money for this type of work than for that of a more theoretical
nature. The trend which had its beginning with the institutionalists
has continued to this day.

Institutionalists were not the only ones who could be tempted
by research grants. Using such tools as statistical methods and
econometrics, the newer economists have come to do the lion's
share of empirical research. So the institutionalists won their
methodological battle, but in doing so lost one of their points of
dissension.

The battle against the rigid doctrine of laissez-faire also has
been won. The reforms Commons and others advocated in the
teeth of this doctrine have given individuals security against the
harsh operations of the economic system. Then, when the more
orthodox economist, Keynes, introduced techniques for stabilizing
the economy, much of the force of the institutionalists' revolt
was gone. When the Keynesian techniques met with apparent
success, proposals for a controlled economy also were effectively
shelved. Apparently this country could retain all the benefits of
free enterprise while at the same time claim the benefits of economic planning.

Institutionalists also have had much of their special subject
matter stolen from them. At one time they had the subject of
monopoly almost to themselves. Except as an aberation from the
norm of perfect competition, the subject remained an undigested
lump in the traditional theory. In time, different writers began
to deal successfully with the subject. Finally, Edward H. Chamberlin and Joan Robinson fitted it into price theory.[27]

Morris A. Copeland declared that a large part of the eclipse
of institutionalists in late years stems from the fact that other
economists have developed more realistic dynamic models.[28] Institutionalists had complained for years that their orthodox competitors thought along static lines. In contrast, Veblen, Mitchell,
and others of their school made use of what they called a cumulative sequence. Although today's models would not meet all of

27 Friday, "Veblen Versus Chamberlin."
28 Copeland, *American Economic Review,* Vol. XLI.

the criticisms, they do a neater job of analyzing the same problems that occupied the institutionalists.

Modern economists are showing an increasing interest in the field of economic development. In doing so, they are taking over the subject that has held the greatest interest of any for institutional economists. Veblen complained that the economics of his day was pre-Darwin in its orientation. Although "the phenomena of growth and change are the most obtrusive and most consequential facts observable in economic life,"[29] they clung to their static analysis. In contrast, Veblen, Commons, and other institutionalists made the evolution of the economy the central feature of their studies. Although some only gave lip service to this evolutionary approach, almost all institutionalists have agreed on its importance. Some such as Allan Gruchy declare "that Institutionalism is primarily a positive, creative movement which aims at broadening the nature and scope of economic science by pushing beyond basic theory to create a theory of our developing economic system."[30]

In recent years interest in undeveloped countries has provided incentives to explore the reasons why some economies have grown while others have not. The apparent stagnation of our economy during the thirties and its rapid postwar growth also have focused attention on economic development. Similarly, the strides with which the Soviet economy apparently has been catching up with ours have provided a compelling incentive to study the growth of our own.

Some of the studies in economic development have been limited to the creation of models constructed in such a way to demonstrate which combination of variables lead to economic expansion. Others have gone beyond to a study of each determinant that might be used in any model.[31] When economists begin to search for all the conditions that must be considered as prerequisites to economic growth, they find it necessary to cross the boundaries of their discipline. They follow in the steps of the institutionalists by studying all the psychological, cultural, and social factors revelant. In fact, if Gruchy's[32] or Ayres'[33] definition were accepted, many of those studying economic development

29 Veblen, in Wesley C. Mitchell, ed., *What Veblen Taught.*
30 Gruchy, *American Economic Review*, Vol. XLVII, p. 13.
31 Abramovitz, pp. 132-182.
32 Gruchy.
33 Ayres, *American Economic Review*, Vol. XLI, pp. 47-55.

are institutional economists. Yet the fact that their work is similar to the institutionalists' does not make them members of that school. Many of them would be surprised to be so classified. It is doubtful that the institutionalist had much of an influence on most of those studying economic development.

Perhaps the greatest jurisdictional encroachment has been in the study of institutions. While the study of the subject has languished in the hands of economists, it has undergone a considerable development in the hands of sociologists. Although Charles Horton Cooley provided inspiration for institutional economists, his influence among sociologists has been even greater. Beginning with him a substantial literature has accumulated on the subject of institutions. By now the study of institutions is one of the primary tasks of sociology. According to J. O. Hertzler, "one of the most important tasks of further conceptualization, classification and generalization in the field of theoretical sociology relates to social institutions."[34] Although sociologists, until recently, have dealt with economic institutions only incidentally, they are now entering this field. For example, Talcott Parsons along with Neil Smelser have attempted a new synthesis of sociology and economics in their *Economy and Society*.[35]

From the economists' side there have been a few skirmishes along the border of sociology. In the fields of labor economics, entrepreneural theory, organizational theory, marketing theory, economic history and development, such encroachments hardly can be avoided. Yet no general synthesis of economics and sociology, such as was envisioned by the institutionalists, has been attempted by economists.

What has happened on both sides of the border between economics and sociology might be taken by some as a neo-institutionalism. Certainly modern analysis is moving along the very lines which institutionalists had staked out for themselves long ago. Yet it is difficult to establish sufficient links to validate any claim to any continuous movement. At least to this observer, it appears that this is another case where outsiders have moved in to take over the institutionalists' subject matter.

The decline of institutionalism has been the result of more than the appropriation of its methodology and subject matter by the main stream of economics and sociology. The greatest cause

---

34 Hertzler, pp. 1, 2.
35 Parsons and Smelser.

of the decline of the school has stemmed from the centrifugal nature of its practical bias. Because institutionalists tended to be overly suspicious of theory, they tended to encourage their students to concentrate on practical problems. Hence, institutionalists became labor economists, public finance and taxation experts, agricultural economists, monetary theorists, transportation and public utility economists, and numerous other specialists. Although such economists might hold chairs at reputable universities, they did not pass on institutionalism to their students.[36] Instead they merely taught them subjects from their own fields. What theory the students learned often would be taught by noninstitutional faculty members. Even when an institutionalist did teach theory, his influence often was diluted by that of his other colleagues. Furthermore, the lack of textbooks, except on an elementary level, precluded teaching institutional theory except to a handful of graduate students. Even these few were not a total gain for the school. To find positions they often were forced to follow one of the special fields of economics and consequently did not pass on their special training.

In some cases institutional economists found a greater knowledge of orthodox economics necessary for their own studies. Men such as Alvin Hansen, a student of Commons, and Paul H. Douglas, a student of Mitchell, made significant contributions to the main stream of economics. Although such men might have held certain sympathies with institutionalism, their work tended to carry them out of the school. In this way it lost some of its ablest economists.

Another large number of students trained by institutional economists were drained into the government service. This was particularly true of Commons' students. The University of Wisconsin became a pioneer in the training of persons for public administration. Ostensibly, Commons and his colleagues were training economists, but in reality they were staffing government agencies.

Governments needed the type of persons trained by institutional economists. When governments began to enter the fields of economic regulation, they needed people who could dig up information; they did not need theorists. Often the success of administrative commissions depended on how well staff members

---

36 C. E. Ayres of the University of Texas and Allan Gruchy of the University of Maryland are among the exceptions.

could marshall facts to support their cases before both the courts and the public. In this kind of research, the Commons-trained students excelled. Consequently, many found positions in government and many became prominent administrators.

Today governments continue to require such persons, but do not insist they be trained as economists. A new field of training, that for public administration, has been developed to fulfill the same need. In this training, much of the study of economics has been replaced by that more closely related with governmental administration.

Economists continue to have roles in government, but in professional instead of administrative capacities. Because the type of economic problems has grown in complexity, the casual training in economics such as that possessed by those trained by institutionalists is no longer adequate in many cases. Government economists must be able to follow developments in their field. Because they are trained as scholars, they do not attempt to cope with the numerous administrative details that plague administrators. Instead the economists contribute professional advice on economic problems to administrators and legislators who make policy decisions.

This failure to develop unified institutional theory, because of members of the school becoming either specialists or government economists, is important. The writing of monographs on specific economic problems, or the elevation of men to high administrative positions, may create a distinguished membership, but it contributes very little to the long-run vitality of a school. Only Veblen and Commons made any significant contributions to the unification of the theory. Unfortunately, Veblen's contribution was a negative one, while Commons' did not appear until 1934, when the school was definitely on the decline. His insights were important and interesting, but they needed further work before they could contribute to unity in institutional theory.

Subsequent developments in both sociology and economics indicate that the institutionalists might have worked their vein of theory more profitably. The price of their failure was the loss of their subject matter to their competitors. While they continued to attack traditional economics, the justification for their revolt gradually vanished. The orthodox economists both corrected many of their methodological faults and extended their studies into the areas the institutionalists had accused them of neglecting. As

Kenneth Boulding claimed before the American Economic Association meeting in December of 1956, institutional economists were essentially dissenters. They had an important role in America's ideological development. But take away their reasons for dissenting, and their reason for existing is gone.

It is believed by some that the school is approaching its end. It may linger for some time, but it is doomed. This does not mean that individual institutionalists will not continue to wield an influence. People will continue to read Veblen and enjoy his works. There might even be a rediscovery of Commons. Books written by other institutional economists such as Ayres and Gambs will continue to be classics in their fields. Undoubtedly the subject matter of the school will be developed by other economists and sociologists. Some modern institutionalists may contribute to these further developments. But the number is not likely to be so many, or their approach so different, that they could be identified as a continuation of the institutional school of economics. The institutionalists broke off from the main stream of economics only to find themselves later swallowed up by that very stream.

Even though the institutional school of economics comes to an end, Commons' contributions should not be neglected. His contributions to the history and study of the labor movement have a secure place in economic literature, but his ideas on economics have not had the attention they deserve. In an age in which there is so much interest in the processes of economic development, Commons' insights should be re-examined.

Yet even more important than any of his contributions to economic thought, is his practical demonstration of how reformers can push along the evolution of society. What he did in the campaigns to establish public utility regulation, workmen's compensation, factory safety regulations, and unemployment insurance demonstrated his method of reform. Implicit in his reforms was the belief that men will be reasonable if presented with proper alternatives. Institutions can be created with incentives built in to ensure behavior consistent with the general interest. Economic and social evolution thus can be directed toward desirable ends instead of those dictated by blind chance or revolution. His plan of extending small voluntary projects into state programs and finally into nationwide ones contributed greatly to the development of the U. S. social security system. His influence in bringing about great changes in this country's economy entitles him to a permanent place of importance in history.

JRC

BIBLIOGRAPHY

Adamic, Louis. *Dynamite*. New York: Viking Press, 1931.

"A Barren Performance," *The World*. New York, August 23, 1915.

Abramovitz, Moses. "Economics of Growth," in Haley, Bernard F. (ed.). *A Survey of Contemporary Economics*. Vol. II. Homewood, Ill.: Richard D. Irwin, Inc., 1952.

"Agitation." *Harper's Weekly*. Vol. LXI, September 11, 1915.

Altmeyer, A. J. *The Industrial Commission of Wisconsin*. Madison, Wisc.: University of Wisconsin Press, 1932, University of Wisconsin Studies in Social Science and History, No. 17.

American Labor Legislation Review. Vol. L through XXV, 1911-1935.

Andrews, John B. *Administrative Labor Legislation*. New York: Harper & Brothers, 1936.

——————. *Labor Laws in Action*. New York: Harper & Brothers, 1938.

Armstrong, Barbara Nachtrieb. *Insuring the Essentials*. New York: MacMillan Co., 1932.

Ayres, Clarence. "Institutional Economics: The Coordinates of Institutionalism," *American Economic Review*. Vol. XLI, May, 1951.

——————. *The Divine Right of Capital*. Boston, Mass.: Houghton Mifflin Co., 1946.

——————. *The Theory of Economic Progress*. Chapel Hill, N. C.: University of North Carolina Press, 1944.

——————. *The Problem of Economic Order*. New York: Farrar & Rinehart, 1938.

Barbash, Jack. "Ideology and the Unions," *American Economic Review*. Vol. XXXIII, December, 1943.

257

Barber, Hollis William. *Development of Some of the Administrative Departments of the Government of Wisconsin from 1850 to 1930.* Unpublished Ph.D. thesis, University of Wisconsin, 1935.

Barnard, Chester L. *The Functions of the Executive.* Cambridge, Mass.: Harvard University Press, 1947.

Barnett, George E. "Review: John R. Commons' *History of Labor in U. S.,*" *American Economic Review.* Vol. IX, June, 1919.

————. "Review: *Principles of Labor Legislation* by John R. Commons and John B. Andrews," *American Economic Review,* Vol. VI, Sept., 1916, pp. 654-58; Vol. XI, June, 1921, p. 305; Vol. XVII, June, 1927, pp. 336-337; Vol. XXVIII, June, 1937, p. 382.

Bauder, Russell. "Three Interpretations of American Trade Union Movement," *Social Forces.* Vol. 22, December, 1943.

————. "Discussion," *Theory of the Labor Movement, A Reappraisal.* Reprinted from *Proceedings of Third Annual Meeting, Industrial Relations Research Association.* Chicago, Ill., December, 1950.

Beard, Charles A., and Mary R. *The Rise of American Civilization.* New York: MacMillan Co., 1930.

Beard, Charles A. *American Government and Politics.* New York: MacMillan Co., 6th ed., 1932.

Bernstein, Irving. "The Growth of American Unions," *American Economic Review.* Vol. XLIX, June, 1954.

————. "Union Growth and Structural Cycles," *Proceedings of Seventh Annual Meeting of Industrial Relations Research Association,* Detroit, Michigan, December, 1954, pp. 202-246.

Blackly, Frederick F., and Oatman, Miriam E. *Administrative Legislation and Adjudication.* Washington, D.C.: Brookings Institution, 1934.

————. *Federal Regulatory Action and Control.* Washington, D. C.: Brookings Institution, 1940.

Blaisdell, Thomas C. *The Federal Trade Commission.* New York: Columbia University Press, 1941.

Blanchard, Ralph H. *Liability and Compensation Insurance.* New York: D. Appleton & Co., 1917.

Bogart, Ernest L. "Review: John R. Commons and J. B. Andrews, *A Documentary History of American Industrial Society, 1860-1880,*" *American Economic Review.* Vol. II, March, 1912.

Boulding, Kenneth E. "Institutional Economics," *American Economic Review.* Vol. XLVII, May, 1957.

Boyd, James Harrington. *Workman's Compensation and Industrial Insurance.* Indianapolis, Ind.: Bobbs-Merrill Co., 1913.

The Bricklayer, Mason, and Plasterer, Vol. XVIII, September, 1915, p. 200.

Brinton, Crane. *The Shaping of the Modern Mind.* New York: Prentice-Hall, Inc., 1950; The New American Library of World Literature, Inc., 1953.

Brown, Ray Andrews. *The Administration of Workmen's Compensation.* Madison, Wisc.: University of Wisconsin Press, 1933, University of Wisconsin Studies in the Social Sciences and History, No. 19.

Bryce, James. *The American Commonwealth.* New York: MacMillan Co., 3rd ed., 1906.

Buck, Solon J. *The Agrarian Crusade.* New Haven, Conn.: Yale University Press, 1920.

—————. *The Granger Movement.* Cambridge, Mass.: Harvard University Press, 1913.

Burgess, John William. *Reminiscenses of An American Scholar.* New York: Columbia University Press, 1934.

Burns, Arthur F. (ed.). *Wesley Clair Mitchell, The Economic Scientist.* New York: National Bureau of Economic Research, 1932.

Burns, Eveline M. "Does Institutionalism Complement or Compete with 'Orthodox Economics'," *American Economic Review.* Vol. XXII, March, 1931.

—————. *The American Social Security System.* Boston: Houghton Mifflin Co., 1949.

Business Cycles and Unemployment, Report and Recommendations of A Committee of the President's Conference on Unemployment Including An Investigation Made Under The Auspices of The National Bureau of Economic Research. New York: McGraw-Hill, 1923.

Calder, John. "Scientific Accident Prevention," *American Labor Legislation Review,* Vol. I, No. 4, December, 1911.

Campion, G. F. M. *An Introduction to the Procedure of the House of Commons.* London: Philip Allan & Co., 1929.

Campion, Lord, and others. *Parliament A Survey.* London: George Allen & Unwin, Ltd., 1952.

Carlton, Frank T. *The History and Problems of Organized Labor.* New York: D. C. Heath & Co., 1911.

—————. "Review: *History of Labor in the United States* by John R. Commons," *Journal of Political Science.* Vol. XXVI, December, 1918.

Chamberlain, John. *Farewell to Reform.* New York: John Day Co., 2nd ed., 1932.

Clark, J. M. *Preface to Social Economics.* New York: Farrar & Rinehart, 1936.

Clark, Lindley. *The Laws of Employment of Labor.* New York: MacMillan Co., 1911.

Cochran, Bert, ed. *American Labor in Midpassage.* New York: Monthly Review Press, 1959.

Commager, Henry Steele. *The American Mind.* New Haven, Conn.: Yale University Press, 1950.

"The Commission on Industrial Relations," *The Outlook.* Vol. CIV, July 5, 1913.

Commons, John R. *Popular Bibliography of Sociology.* Publication of the Christian Social Union in the United States, No. 6. Baltimore, Md.: Guggenheimer, Weil & Co., 1892.

—————. *Distribution of Wealth.* New York: MacMillan Co., 1893.

—————. *Social Reform and The Church.* New York: T. Y. Crowell & Co., 1894.

—————. "A Comparison of Day Labor and Contract System on Municipal Works," *American Federationist.* Vol. 3 (January-February, 1897); Vol. 4 (March-December, 1897); Vol. 4 (January, 1898); also in Yale Review, Vol. V (February, 1897).

—————. "A Sociological View of Sovereignty," *American Journal of Sociology.* Vol. V (July-November, 1899); Vol. V (January-May, 1900); Vol. VI (July, 1900).

—————. "A New Way of Settling Labor Disputes," *American Monthly Review of Reviews.* Vol. XXIII, March, 1901.

—————. "Racial Composition of the American People," *The Chautauquan.* Vol. XXXVIII (September-December, 1903); Vol. XXXVIII (January-February, 1904); Vol. XXXIX (March-May, 1904).

—————. *Races and Immigrants in America.* New York: MacMillan Co., 1907.

—————. (ed.). *Trade Unionism and Labor Problems.* Boston: Ginn and Co., First Series, 1905; Second Series 1921.

—————. *A Documentary History of American Industrial Society.* Cleveland, Ohio: The Arthur Clark Co., 1910.

—————. "Constructive Investigation and Wisconsin Industrial Commission," *The Survey,* January 4, 1913, p. 440.

—————. "Government Agencies," *The Survey,* Vol. XXX, August 2, 1913, p. 578.

—————. "American Shoemakers, 1648-1895," *Quarterly Journal of Economics.* Vol. XXIV, November, 1909. Also in Commons, John R. *Labor and Administration.* New York: MacMillan Co., 1913, Chapter XIV.

—————. *Labor and Administration.* New York: MacMillan Co., 1913, 1923; "An Idealistic Interpretation of History," "Economists and Class Partnership," "Class Conflict," "Union Shop," "Restrictions by Trade Unions," "Unions and Efficiency," "European and American Unions," "American Shoemakers, 1648-1895." (All previously published articles.)

—————. "Review. Hoxie's Trade Unionism in the United States," *Quarterly Journal of Economics.* Vol. XXXII, February, 1918.

—————. *Industrial Goodwill.* New York: McGraw-Hill Book Co., 1919.

—————. *History of Labor in the United States.* New York: MacMillan Co., 1918.

—————. *Industrial Government.* New York: MacMillan Co., 1921.

—————. "Putting an End to Unemployment," *LaFollette's Magazine,* Vol. XIII, March, 1921, p. 38.

—————. "Unemployment: Compensation and Prevention," *The Survey,* Vol. XIII, October 1, 1921, p. 5.

—————. "Unemployment Insurance," *The Monitor* (official publication of Associated Industries of New York State), Vol. VIII, February, 1922, p. 2.

—————. "Unemployment Preventions," *American Labor Legislation Review,* Vol. XII, March, 1922, p. 15.

—————. "Unemployment: Prevention and Insurance—Chapter IV," *The Stabilization of Business,* ed. Lionel T. Edie. New York: MacMillan Co., 1923.

—————. "The Delivered Price Practice in the Steel Industry," *American Economic Review,* Vol. XIV, Sept., 1924, pp. 505-519.

—————. *The Limits of Unemployment Insurance.* Toronto: The British Association for the Advancement of Science, 1924.

—————. *Legal Foundations of Capitalism.* New York: MacMillan Co., 1924.

—————. "The Passing of Samuel Gompers," *Current History.* Vol. XXI, February, 1925.

—————. "The True Scope of Unemployment Insurance," *American Labor Legislation Review,* Vol. XV, March, 1925, p. 43.

—————. "Jurisdictional Disputes," *Wertheim Lectures on Industrial Relations.* Cambridge, Mass.: Harvard University Press, 1929, pp. 93-98.

——————. "Unemployment Compensation," *American Labor Legislation Review,* Vol. XX, September, 1930, p. 249.

——————. "Unemployment Reserves and Unemployment Insurance," *American Labor Legislation Review,* Vol. XX, September, 1930, p. 266.

——————. "Permanent Preventatives of Unemployment," an address delivered before the Conference on Permanent Preventatives of Unemployment, at Washington, January 26, 1931.

——————. "Should America Adopt a System of Compulsory Unemployment Insurance," *Congressional Digest,* Vol. X, August-September, 1931, p. 214.

——————. "Institutional Economics," *American Economic Review.* Vol. XXI, December, 1931, No. 4.

——————. "Unemployment Compensation," An address delivered at the Initial Conference on Unemployment, Madison, Wisconsin, February 11, 1932.

——————. "The Groves Unemployment Reserves Law," *American Labor Relations Review,* Vol. XXII, March, 1932, p. 8.

——————. "Unemployment Insurance," an address delivered over N.B.C. network on April 9, 1932, Economic Series Lecture No. 24. Chicago, Ill.,: University Press, 1932.

——————. "What is the Difference Between Unemployment Insurance and Unemployment Reserves?" *State Government,* Vol. V, May, 1932, p. 3.

——————. "Labor Movement," *Encyclopedia of the Social Sciences.* Edited by Edwin R. A. Seligman and Alvin Johnson. New York: MacMillan Co., 1932, Vol. 8.

——————. *Institutional Economics.* New York: MacMillan Co., 1934.

——————. *Myself.* New York: MacMillan Co., 1934.

——————. *Economics of Collective Action.* New York: MacMillan Co., 1950.

Commons, John R., and associates. *The History of Labor in the United States.* New York: MacMillan Co., 1918, 1935.

Commons, John R., and Andrews, John B. *Principles of Labor Legislation.* New York: Harper & Brothers, 1916, 1920, 1927, 1936.

Commons, John R.; Lewisohn, S. A.; Draper, E. G.; Lescohier, Don D. *Can Business Prevent Unemployment?* New York: Alfred A. Knopf, 1925.

Congressional Record. House of Representatives. Vol. 52, Part 4, 63rd Congress, February 10, 1915.

Congressional Record. Vol. 53, Part 1, 64th Congress, 1st Session, December 17, 1915.

Congressional Record. Senate. Vol. 53, Part 2, 64th Congress, February 3, 1916.

Congressional Record. Senate. Vol. 53, Part 5, 64th Congress, 1st Session, March 17, 1916.

Congressional Record. House of Representatives. Vol. 53, Part 6, 64th Congress, 1st Session, March 31, 1916.

Conrad, Frederick. *Agrarian Discontent.* Unpublished Ph.D. thesis, Stanford University, 1932.

Cooper, Lyle W. "Theories of the Labor Movement, As Set Forth In Recent Literature," *Quarterly Journal of Economics.* Vol. XLIII, November, 1928.

Copeland, Morris A. "Commons' Institutionalism in Relation to The Problems of Social Planning and Economic Planning," *Quarterly Journal of Economics*. Vol. L, February, 1936.

——————. "Economic Theory and the Natural Science Point of View," *American Economic Review*. Vol. XXI, March, 1931.

——————. *Fact and Theory in Economics*. Ithaca, N. Y.: Cornell University Press, 1958.

——————. "Institutional Economics and Model Analysis," *American Economic Review Supplement*. Vol. XLI, May, 1950.

——————. "Institutionalism and Welfare Economics," *American Economic Review*. Vol. XLVIII, March, 1958.

Cox, James M., *Journey Through My Years*. New York: Simon and Schuster, 1946.

Croly, Herbert. *The Promise of American Life*. New York: MacMillan Co., 1919.

Cross, Ira. "Review: Commons' *History of Labor in the United States,*" *Quarterly Journal of Economics*. Vol. XXXII, August, 1918.

Curti, Merle. *The Growth of American Thought*. New York: Harper & Brothers, 1943.

Curti, Merle, and Cartensen, Vernon. *The University of Wisconsin*. Madison, Wisc.: University of Wisconsin Press, 1949.

Cushman, Robert E. *The Independent Regulatory Commissions*. New York: Oxford University Press, 1941.

Davis, Horace B. "The Theory of Union Growth," *Quarterly Journal of Economics*. Vol. LV, August, 1941.

Derber, Milton. "Communications: Structuring of the Labor Force in Industrial Society," *Industrial and Labor Relations Review*. Vol. 9, October, 1955.

Derber, Milton, and Young, Edwin. (ed.). *Labor and the New Deal*. Madison, Wisc.: University of Wisconsin Press, 1957.

Dewey, John. *Experience and Nature*. Chicago, Ill.: Open Court Publishing Co., 1925.

——————. *The Quest For Certainty*. New York: Minton, Balch & Co., 1929.

——————. *How We Think*. Boston, Mass.: D. Heath & Co., 1931.

——————. *Reconstruction In Philosophy*. New York: Henry Holt & Co., 1920.

Dickinson, John. *Administrative Justice and Supremacy of Law in U. S.* Cambridge, Mass.: Harvard University Press, 1927.

Dimock, Marshall E. *Congressional Investigating Committees*. Baltimore, Md.: John Hopkins Press, 1929.

Doan, Edward N. *The LaFollettes and the Wisconsin Idea*. New York: Rinehart & Co., 1947.

Dodd, W. F. *Administration of Workmen's Compensation*. New York: Commonwealth Fund, 1936.

Dolnick, David. "History and Theory of The Labor Movement," *Employment Relations Research*, Industrial Relations Research Association, Publication No. 23. New York: Harper & Brothers, 1960.

Dombrowski, James. *The Early Days of Christian Socialism In America*. New York: Columbia University Press, 1936.

Dorfman, Joseph. *The Economic Mind In American Civilization*. Vol. III, IV, V. New York: The Viking Press, 1949, 1959.

_____. *Thorstein Veblen And His America.* New York: The Viking Press, 1934.

_____. *American Economic Review Supplement,* Vol. XLI, December, 1950, p. 80.

Douglas, Paul. *Social Security in the United States.* New York: Whittlesey House, 1936.

_____. *Standards of Unemployment Insurance.* Chicago: University of Chicago Press, 1932.

Downey, E. H. *Workman's Compensation.* New York: MacMillan Co., 1924.

Dunlop, John T. "The Development of Labor Organization, A Theoretical Framework," *Insights into Labor Issues.* Edited by Richard Lester and Joseph Shister. New York: MacMillan Co., 1948.

Dunn, Robert W. *The Americanization of Labor.* New York: International Publishers, 1927.

Dyche, John A. *Bolshevism in American Unions.* New York: Boni & Liveright, 1926.

Earnest, Ernest. *Academic Procession.* Indianapolis, Ind.: Robbs-Merrill Co., 1953.

Eastman, Crystal. *Work-Accidents and the Law: Pittsburgh Survey.* Russell Sage Foundations, 1910, Vol. V.

Eaves, Lucille. "Conference on Labor Legislation," *The Survey.* Vol. 27, October 14, 1911.

Eberling, Ernest J. *Congressional Investigations.* New York: Columbia University Press, 1928.

"Economic Theory—Institutionalism: What It Is and What It Hopes to Become," *American Economic Review Supplement,* Vol. XXI, March, 1931, pp. 134-141.

Edie, Lionel, ed. *The Stabilization of Business.* New York: MacMillan, 1923.

Eggleston, Edward. *The Hoosier Schoolmaster.* New York: Orange Judd & Co., 1871.

Elbert, R. G. *Unemployment and Relief.* New York: Farrar & Rinehart, 1934.

Ely, Richard T. *Ground Under Our Feet.* New York: MacMillan Co., 1935.

_____. "The Past and Present of Political Economy," *John Hopkins Studies in Historical and Political Science,* Second Series, III, March, 1884.

_____. *Labor Movement in America.* New York: T. Y. Crowell Co., 1886.

_____. *Property and Contract In Their Relations To The Distribution of Wealth.* New York: MacMillan Co., 1914.

_____. "Economic Theory: Institutional Economics," *Proceedings of The American Economic Association.* Vol. XXII, December, 1931.

_____. "The Founding and Early History of the American Economic Association," *Proceedings of The American Economic Association,* Vol. XXVI, December, 1935.

Epstein, Abraham. *Insecurity, A Challenge to America.* New York: Harrison Smith & Robert Haas, 1933; New York: Random House, 1938.

Feibleman, James. *An Introduction to Peirce's Philosophy.* New York: Harper & Brothers, 1946.

Feldman, Herman. "Applications of Merit Rating to Unemployment Insurance," *Social Security in the United States.* 8th National Conference of American Association for Social Security, 1935.

"The Fiasco of the Industrial Commission," *The Nation,* Vol. CI, August 26, 1915, p. 251.

Final Report and Testimony. Submitted to Congress by the Commission On Industrial Relations created by the Act of August 23, 1912, 64th Congress, 1st Session 1915-1916, Senate Documents Vol. 19, Document 415, Vol. I-XI.

Finley, John H., and Sanderson, John F. *The American Executive and Executive Functions.* New York: Century Co., 1908.

Fitch, John A. "Probing the Causes of Unrest," *The Survey.* Vol. XXXII, Vol. XXXIII, Vol. XXXIV, Vol. XXXV.

————. *The Steel Workers: The Pittsburgh Survey.* Russell Sage Foundation, 1911.

Fitzpatrick, Edward A. *McCarthy of Wisconsin.* New York: Columbia University Press, 1944. Chapter XIV.

Foner, Philip Sheldon. *History of Labor in the United States.* New York: The International Publishers, Vol. I, 1947; Vol. II, 1955.

Forsberg, Allen Bennett, ed. *Selected Articles on Unemployment Insurance.* New York,: H. W. Wilson Co., 1926.

Foster, William Z. *American Trade Unionism.* New York: International Publishers, 1947.

————. *The Great Steel Strike.* New York: B. W. Huebsch, Inc., 1920.

————. *Misleaders of Labor.* Trade Union Educational League, 1927.

"Francis Patrick Walsh—An Estimate," *United Mine Workers' Journal.* Vol. XXV, August 12, 1915.

Freund, Ernst, and others. *The Growth of American Administrative.* St. Louis, Mo.: Thomas Law Book Company, 1923.

Friday, Charles B. "Veblen versus Chamberlin on Monopolistic Competition," *Proceedings of The Twenty-Ninth Annual Conference of the Western Economic Association.* Eugene, Oregon, September, 1954, pp. 54-57.

Gagliardo, Domenico. *American Social Insurance.* New York: Harper & Brothers, 1949.

Galbraith, John Kenneth. *American Capitalism, The Concept of Countervailing Power.* Cambridge, Mass.: Riverside Press, Houghton Mifflin Co., 1952.

Galenson, Walter. "Reflections on the Writing of Labor History," *Industrial and Labor Relations Review,* Vol. II, October, 1957, pp. 85-95.

Gallie, W. B. *Peirce and Pragmatism.* Edinburgh: R. & R. Clark for Penguin Books, Ltd., 1952.

Galloway, George B. *The Legislative Process in Congress.* New York: T. Y. Crowell & Co., 1953.

Gambs, John. *Beyond Supply and Demand.* New York: Columbia University Press, 1946.

Gellhorn, Walter. *Administrative Law.* Chicago: Foundation Press, Inc., 1940.

Gill, Norman N. *Municipal Reference Bureaus.* Washington, D. C.: American Council on Public Affairs, 1944.

Glaeser, Martin G. *Outlines of Public Utility Economics.* New York: MacMillan Co., 1927.

Goldman, Eric F. *Rendevous With Destiny.* New York: Alfred Knopf, Inc., 1952; Vintage Books, Inc., 1956.

Gompers, Samuel. *Seventy Years of Life and Labor*. New York: E. P. Dutton & Co., 1925.

——————. "Industrial Relations Commission's Report," *American Federationist*. Vol. XXII, October, 1915.

——————. "Walsh, A Great Tribune," *American Federationist*. Vol. XXII, July, 1915.

——————. *Labor and the Common Welfare*. New York: E. P. Dutton Dutton & Co., 1919.

Goodrow, Frank J. *Politics and Administration*. New York: MacMillan Co., 1914.

Graham, George A., and Reining, Henry, Jr. *Regulatory Administration*, New York: John Wiley and Sons, Inc., 1943.

Green, Marguerite. *The National Civic Federation and the Labor Movement, 1900-1925*. Washington, D.C.: The Catholic University Press, 1956.

"Growth of the Job Insurance Program, an Evolutionary Program," *American Labor Legislation Review*. Vol. XXIII, September, 1933.

Gruchy, Allan G. *Modern Economic Thought*. New York: Prentice-Hall, Inc., 1947.

——————. "Discussion: Institutional Economics," *American Economic Review Supplement,* Vol. XLVII, May, 1957, pp. 13-18.

Gulick, C. A., and Bers, M. K. "Insight and Illusion in Perlman's *Theory of the Labor Movement,*" *Industrial and Labor Relations Review*. Vol. 6, July, 1953.

Haber, William, and Cohen, Wilbur J. *Readings in Social Security*. New York: Prentice-Hall, Inc., 1948.

Hadley, Arthur Twining. *The Education of the American Citizen*. New York: Charles Scribner's Sons, 1901.

——————. "Review: *The Distribution of Wealth* by John R. Commons," *The Yale Review*. Vol. II, February, 1894.

Haferbecker, Gordon M. *Wisconsin Labor Laws*. Madison, Wisc.: University of Wisconsin Press, 1958.

Haines, Charles G., and Dimock, Marshall E. *Essays on Law and Practice of Governmental Administration*. Baltimore, Md.: Johns Hopkins Press, 1935.

Hale, Robert L. *Valuation and Rate Making the Conflicting Theories of the Wisconsin Railroad Commission*. New York: Columbia University Press, 1918—Studies in History, Economics, and Public Law. Vol. LXXX, No. 1.

Hall, G. Stanley. *Life and Confessions of a Psychologist*. New York: D. Appleton & Co., 1924.

Hamilton, David. "Veblen and Commons: A Case of Theoretical Convergence," *Southwestern Social Science Quarterly,* Vol. 34, September, 1953, pp. 43-50.

Hamilton, Walton. "The Institutional Approach to Economic Theory," *Proceedings of the American Economic Association*. December, 1918.

Hansen, Alvin H., and Murray, Merrill G. *Unemployment Reserves*. Minneapolis, Minn.: University of Minnesota Press, 1933.

Hansen, Alvin H.; Murray, Merrill G.; Stevenson, Russell A.; and Stewart, Bryce M., *A Program for Unemployment Insurance and Relief in the United States*. Minneapolis, Minn.: University of Minnesota Press, 1934.

Hard, William. "A University In Public Life," *The Outlook.* Vol. 86, July, 1907.

Hardman, J. B. S. (ed.). *American Labor Dynamics.* New York: Harcourt, Brace & Co., 1928.

————. "From Job Consciousness to Power Accumulation," *A Theory of the Labor Movement, A Reappraisal.* Reprinted from *Proceedings of Third Annual Industrial Relations Research Association.* Chicago, Ill., December, 1950.

Harriman, Florence. *From Pinafores to Politics.* New York: Henry Holt, 1923.

Harris, Seymour E. *Economics of Social Security.* New York: McGraw-Hill Book Co., 1941.

Harvey, Rowland Hill. *Samuel Gompers, Champion of the Toiling Masses.* Stanford, Calif.: Stanford University Press, 1935.

Hearings before the Banking and Currency Committee. House of Representatives, 69th Congress, 2nd Session, on H. R. 7895, 1927. (*Congressional Record,* Vol. 68, Pt. 4, February 15, 1927, pp. 3834-3848).

Hearings before the Committee on Finance. U. S. Senate, 74th Congress, 1st Session, on S. 1130, 1935.

Hearings before the Committee on Ways and Means. House of Representatives. 74th Congress, 1st Session, on H. R. 4120, 1935.

Hearings before Subcommittee of Ways and Means Committee. House of Representatives. 73rd Congress, 2nd Session, H. R. 7659, 1934.

Hearings before Subcommittee of the Committee of Labor. 74th Congress, 1st Session, on H. R. 2827, 1935.

Henderson, Gerard C. *The Federal Trade Commission.* New York: Columbia University Press, 1932.

Henderson, Charles Richmond. *Industrial Insurance in the U. S.* Chicago: University of Chicago Press, 1908.

Hertzler, J. O. *Social Institutions.* Lincoln, Neb.: University of Nebraska Press, 1946.

Hicks, John D. *The Populist Revolt.* Minneapolis, Minn.: University of Minnesota Press, 1931.

Hoar, Roger Sherman. *Unemployment Insurance in Wisconsin.* South Milwaukee, Wisconsin: South Stuart Press, 1932.

Hofstadter, Richard. *Social Darwinism In American Thought.* Boston, Mass.: The Beacon Press, revised edition, 1955.

————. *The Development of Higher Education in America.* New York: Columbia University Press, 1952.

Hogan, John D., and Ianni, Francis A. J., *American Social Legislation,* New York,: Harper and Brothers, 1956.

Holland, Thomas Erskine. *The Elements of Jurisprudence.* London: Clarendon Press, 6th ed., 1890.

Holman, Graham R. "Probing the Causes of Unrest, XXII," *The Survey.* Vol. XXIV.

Holmes, Fred L. *Regulation of Railroads and Public Utilities in Wisconsin.* New York: D. Appleton & Co., 1915.

Homan, Paul T. "Appraisal of Institutional Economics," *American Economic Review.* Vol. XXII, March, 1932.

Hopkins, Charles Howard. *The Rise of the Social Gospel in American Protestantism, 1865-1915.* New Haven, Conn.: Yale University Press, 1940.

Howe, Frederic C. *Wisconsin, An Experiment in Democracy*. New York: Charles Scribner's Sons, 1912.

Hoxie, Robert Franklin. *Trade Unionism in the United States*. New York: D. Appleton & Co., 1917.

"Industrial Relations Commission," *The Survey*. Vol. XXIX, December 28, 1912.

"Industrial Relations Commission," *The Survey*. Vol. XXX, July 5, 1913.

"Industrial Relations Committee Report," *The Outlook*. Vol. CXI, September 1, 1915, pp. 7, 8.

Industrial Relations Counselors, Inc. *An Historical Basis for Unemployment Insurance*. Minneapolis, Minn.: University of Minnesota Press, 1934.

"Institutional Economics," *American Economic Review Supplement*, Vol. XXII, March, 1932, p. 12.

James, Clifford L. "Commons On Institutional Economics," *American Economic Review*. Vol. XXVII, No. 1, March, 1937.

James, William. *The Meaning of Truth*. New York: Longmans, Green & Co., 1909.

————. *Pragmatism*. New York: Longmans, Green & Co., 1909.

Jensen, Vernon H. "Notes on the Beginnings of Collective Bargaining," *Industrial and Labor Relations Review*, Vol. 9, January, 1956, pp. 224-234.

Jones, Eliot. *Principles of Railway Transportation*. New York: MacMillan Co., 1931.

Jones, Eliot, and Bigham, Truman C. *Principles of Public Utilities*. New York: MacMillan Co., 1931.

Jones, Eliot, and Vanderblue, Homer B. (ed.). *Railroads Cases and Selections*. New York: MacMillan Co., 1925.

Kaiser, Philip M. "Discussion," *A Theory of the Labor Movement, A Reappraisal*. Reprinted from *Proceedings of Third Annual Industrial Relations Research Association*. Chicago, Ill., December, 1950.

Kaplan, David. "Job Conscious Unionism As a Form of Economic Citizenship," *A Theory of the Labor Movement, A Reappraisal*. Reprinted from *Proceedings of Third Annual Industrial Relations Research Association*. Chicago, Ill., December, 1950.

Kassalow, Everett. "Discussion," *A Theory of the Labor Movement, A Reappraisal*. Reprinted from *Proceedings of Third Annual Industrial Relations Research Association*. Chicago, Ill., December, 1950.

Kelley, O. H. *Origins and Progress of the Order of the Patrons of Husbandry*. Philadelphia, Pa.: J. A. Wagenseller, 1875.

Kerr, Clark, and Siegel, Abraham. "The Structuring of the Labor Force in Industrial Society, New Developments and New Questions," *Industrial and Labor Relations Review*. Vol. 8, January, 1955; "Reply," Vol. 9, October, 1955.

Kirshen, H. B., "Essays in Legal Economics," *The Maine Bulletin*, Vol. XXXV, August, 1932, 73 pp.

LaFollette, Belle Case and Fola. *Robert M. LaFollette*. New York: MacMillan Co., 1953.

LaFollette, Robert M. *Autobiography*. Madison, Wisc.: The Robert M. LaFollette Co., 1911.

Landis, James M. *The Administrative Process*. New Haven, Conn.: Yale University Press, 1938.

Lang, Frank. *Workmen's Compensation Insurance.* Chicago: Richard Irwin, Inc., 1947.

Leek, H. J. *Legislative Reference Work A Comparative Study.* Philadelphia, Pa.: University of Pennsylvania, 1925.

Lenin, V. L. *What Is To Be Done?* Reprint from *The Iskra Period.* New York: International Publishers, 1929.

Lescohier, Don D., and Brandeis, Elizabeth. *History of Labor in the United States,* Vol. III. New York: MacMillan Co., 1935.

Leiserson, William M. "The Wisconsin Legislation of 1911," *The Survey.* Vol. 27, October 14, 1911.

————. "Will Industry Provide Security?" *Social Security in the U. S.* 6th National Conference of American Association for Social Security, 1933.

Lindblom, Charles Edward. *Unionism and Capitalism.* New Haven, Conn.: Yale University Press, 1949.

Lorwin, Lewis L., *The American Federation of Labor,* Washington: Brookings Institution, 1933.

Lovejoy, Allen Fraser. *LaFollette and the Establishment of the Direct Primary in Wisconsin.* New Haven, Conn.: Yale University Press, 1941.

Lyon, Richard Martin. *The American Association for Labor Legislation and the Fight for Workmen's Compensation Legislation.* Unpublished Master's Thesis, Cornell University, Ithaca, N. Y., June, 1952.

Machinists' Monthly Journal. Vol. XXVII. August, 1915, p. 682.

Marcy, Carl. *Presidential Commissions.* New York: King's Crown Press, 1945.

Martin, John Bartlow. *Indiana, An Interpretation.* New York: Alfred A. Knopf, 1947.

Marx, Karl. *Capital, A Critique of Political Economy.* Frederick Engels, ed., Translated from 3rd German edition by Samuel Moore and Edward Aveling, New York: Appleton, 1889.

Marx, Karl, and Engels, Frederick. *Letters to Americans.* New York: International Publishers, 1953.

Maxwell, Robert S. *LaFollette and the Rise of the Progressives in Wisconsin.* Madison, Wisc.: State Historical Society of Wisconsin, 1956.

Mayo, Elton. *The Human Problems of an Industrial Civilization.* New York: MacMillan Co., 1933.

Mayo-Smith, Richard. "Review: *The Distribution of Wealth* by John R. Commons," *Political Science Quarterly.* Vol. LX, No. 3, September, 1894.

McCabe, D. A. "Review: *A History of Trade Unionism in the United States* by Selig Perlman," *American Economic Review.* Vol. XIII, June, 1923.

————. "Review: *Industrial Government* by John R. Commons and others," *American Economic Review.* Vol. XI, December, 1921.

McCabe, James Dabney. *History of the Grange Movement.* Chicago, Ill.: National Publishing Co., 1874.

McCarthy, Charles. *The Wisconsin Idea.* New York: MacMillan Co., 1912.

McFeely, Otto. "Pullman Porters Railroad Shop Men and Stock Yard Hands," *The Survey.* Vol. XXXIV.

McGeary, M. Nelson. *The Developments of Congressional Investigative Power.* New York: Columbia University Press, 1940.

McNeil, George. *The Labor Movement*. Boston: A. M. Bridgeman Co.; New York: M. W. Hazen Co., 1887.

McVey, Frank. "The Populist Movement," *American Economic Association Economic Studies*. Vol. I, No. 3, August, 1896.

Mendelson, Wallace. *The Public Service Commission of Wisconsin, A Study In Administrative Procedure*. Unpublished Ph.D. thesis, University of Wisconsin, 1940.

Merriman, Christine. "Probing the Causes of Unrest, V," *The Survey*. Vol. XXXII.

Miller, A. C. "Review: *The Distribution of Wealth* by John R. Commons," *Journal of Political Economy*. Vol. II, June 1894.

Millis, Harry A. *Labor's Risks and Social Insurance*. New York: McGraw-Hill Book Co., 1938.

"Misleading Inquiries," *The Nation*. Vol. C, February 11, 1915.

Mitchell, Broadus. *Depression Decade*. New York: Rinehart & Co., 1947.

Mitchell, Wesley C. "Commons on *The Legal Foundations of Capitalism*." *American Economic Review*. Vol. XIV, No. 2, June 1924.

—————. "Commons on Institutional Economics," *American Economic Review*. Vol. XXV, No. 4, December, 1935, pp. 635-652.

—————. *Lecture Notes on Types of Economic Theory*. (A student's stenographic record). New York: August Kelley, Inc., 1949.

—————. *The Backward Art of Spending Money*. New York: McGraw-Hill Book Co., 1937.

—————. *Business Cycles*. Berkeley, Calif.: University of California Press, 1913.

—————. *What Veblen Taught*. New York: The Viking Press, 1936.

—————. *A History of the Greenbacks*. Chicago, Ill.: University of Chicago Press, 1903.

—————. *The National Bureau's First Quarter Century*. Twenty-Fifth Annual Report of the National Bureau of Economic Research, Inc. New York, May, 1945, pp. 5-10.

Mitchell, John. *Organized Labor*. Philadelphia: American Book and Bible House, 1903.

Moore, Wilbert E. "Notes for a General Theory of Labor Organization," *Industrial and Labor Relations Review*, Vol. 13, April, 1960, pp. 387-397.

Muelder, Walter G., and Sears, Laurence. *The Development of American Philosophy*. Cambridge, Mass. Riverside Press, Houghton Mifflin Co., 1940.

Myrdal, Gunnar. *Beyond The Welfare State*. New Haven, Connecticut: Yale University Press, 1960.

Newcomb, Simon. *Principles of Political Economy*. New York: Harper & Brothers, 1885.

The Painter and Decorator, Vol. XXIX, September, 1915, p. 457.

Parkinson, Thomas I. "Problems and Progress of Workmen's Compensation Legislation," *American Labor Legislation Review*. Vol. I, No. 1, January, 1911.

Parrington, Vernon Louis. *Main Currents in American Thought*. New York: Harcourt Brace & Co., 1927.

Parsons, Kenneth H. "John R. Commons' Point of View," *The Journal of Land and Public Utility Economics*. Vol. XVIII, No. 3, August, 1942; also in Commons, John R., *Economics of Collective Action*. New York: MacMillan Co., 1950.

Parsons, Talcott, and Smelser, Neil J. *Economy and Society.* London: Routledge and Kegan Paul, Ltd., 1956.

Peirce, Charles Santiago Sanders. *Collective Papers.* Edited by Charles Hartshorne and Paul Weiss. Cambridge, Mass.: Harvard University Press, 1934.

——————. "How to Make Our Ideas Clear," *Popular Science Monthly,* Vol. XII, January, 1878, pp. 286-302.

——————. *Chance, Love and Logic.* New York: Harcourt Brace & Co., 1923.

Perlman, Mark. "Labor Movement Theories: Past, Present, and Future," *Industrial and Labor Relations Review,* Vol. 13, April, 1960, pp. 338-348.

——————. *Labor Union Theories in America.* Evanston, Illinois: Rowe, Peterson and Co., 1958.

Perlman, Selig. "Perlman on Commons," Spiegel, Henry William, (ed.). *The Development of Economic Thought.* New York: John Wiley & Sons, Inc., 1952.

——————. *The History of Trade Unionism.* New York: MacMillan Co., 1922; August Kelley, Inc., 1950.

——————. *A Theory of the Labor Movement.* New York: MacMillan Co., 1928; August Kelley, Inc., 1949.

"Perlman, Selig," *Industrial and Labor Relations Review,* Vol. 13, April, 1960, pp. 335-337.

Perlman, Selig, and Taft, Philip. *History of Labor in the United States, 1896-1932.* New York: MacMillan Co., 1935. Vol. IV.

Perry, Arthur Latham. *Political Economy.* New York: Charles Scribner's Sons, 1888.

"Petition To The President For A Federal Commission On Industrial Relations," *The Survey.* Vol. XXXVII, December 30, 1911.

Pierce, Lloyd F. *The Activities of The American Association for Labor Legislation, In Behalf of Social Security and Protective Labor Legislation,* Unpublished Ph.D. Dissertation, University of Wisconsin, Madison, Wisconsin, June, 1953.

Platt, Chester C. *What LaFollette's State Is Doing.* Batavia, N. E.: Batavia Times Press, 1924.

Pond, Oscar L. *A Treatise on the Law of Public Utilities.* Indianapolis, Ind.: Bobbs-Merrill Co., 1913.

"Professor Commons at Seventy," *The Survey,* Vol. LXVIII, December, 1932, p. 674.

Quint, Howard H. *The Forging of American Socialism.* Columbia, S. C.: University of South Carolina Press, 1953.

Randall, John Herman. *The Making of the Modern Mind.* Cambridge, Mass.: Riverside Press, Houghton Mifflin Co., 1926.

Raney, William Francis, *Wisconsin, A Story of Progress.* New York: Prentice-Hall, Inc., 1940.

Ratner, Joseph. *The Philosophy of John Dewey.* New York: Modern Library, 1938.

Reder, Melvin W., "Job Scarcity and The Nature of Union Power," *Industrial and Labor Relations Review,* Vol. 13, April, 1960, pp. 349-362.

"Report of the Industrial Relations Commission," *United Mine Workers' Journal.* Vol. XXV, August 26, 1915, pp. 4, 5.

Report of Ohio Commission on Unemployment Insurance. Columbus, Ohio, 1932, 1933, Vol. 1 and 2.

Report of the Senate Committee on Finance on H. R. 7260, 74th Congress, 1st Session, Report No. 628, Calendar 661, 1935.

Report to the President, of the Committee on Economic Security. January 15, 1935.

Rhodes, J. E. *Workmen's Compensation.* New York: MacMillan Co., 1917.

Riley, Woodbridge. *American Thought.* New York: Henry Holt & Co., 1915.

Ripley, William Z. *Railroad Rates and Regulations,* New York: Longmans, Green & Co., 1924.

"Risks in Modern Industry," *Annals of the American Academy of Political and Social Science.* Vol. XXXVIII, No. 1, July, 1911.

Robinson, J. William. *Royal Commissions in England.* Unpublished Ph.D. thesis, Stanford University, 1936.

Ross, Edward Alsworth. *Seventy Years of It.* New York: D. Appleton & Co., 1936.

Rottenburg, Simon. "Wage Effects in the Theory of the Labor Movement," *Journal of Political Economy,* Vol. LXI, August, 1953.

Rubinow, I. M. *Social Insurance.* New York: Henry Holt & Co., 1913.

——————. "The Movement Toward Unemployment Insurance in Ohio," *Social Service Review,* Vol. VII, 1933.

——————. *The Quest for Social Security.* New York: Henry Holt & Co., 1934.

——————. *Social Insurance.* New York: Henry Holt & Co., 1913.

Saposs, David J. *Left Wing Unionism.* New York: International Publishers, 1926.

Schneider, Herbert W. *A History of American Philosophy.* New York: Columbia University Press, 1946.

Schumpeter, Joseph A. *Capitalism, Socialism, and Democracy.* New York: Harper & Brothers, 2nd ed., 1947.

Schwarztrauber, Ernes E. *Workers' Education.* Madison, Wisc.: University of Wisconsin Press, 1942.

Sharfman, I. L. *The Interstate Commerce Commission.* New York: Commonwealth Fund, 1931-1937.

——————. *Railway Regulation.* Chicago: LaSalle Extension University, 1915.

——————. "Commons' *Legal Foundations of Capitalism,*" *The Quarterly Journal of Economics.* Vol. XXXIX, February, 1925, pp. 300-312.

Shaw, G. B. *Intelligent Women's Guide to Socialism, and Capitalism.* New York: Bretano's, 1928.

Shister, Joseph. "The Logic of Union Growth," *Journal of Political Economy.* Vol. LXI, October, 1953.

——————. "Unresolved Problems and New Paths for American Labor," *Industrial and Labor Relations Review,* Vol. 9, April, 1956, pp. 447-457.

Simons, Henry C. *Economic Policy for a Free Society.* Chicago: University of Chicago Press, 1948.

Social Security in the United States. Records of the National Conferences 6 through 13, 1933-1940, American Association for Social Security.

Sombart, Werner. *The Quintessence of Capitalism.* London: T. F. Unvin, Ltd., 1915.

Spilman, Leona. *A Comparison of Veblen's and Commons' Institutionalisms.* Unpublished Ph.D. Dissertation, University of Wisconsin, Madison, Wisconsin, 1940.

Squires, B. M. "Review: *A Theory of the Labor Movement* by Selig Perlman," *American Economic Review*. Vol. XIX, March, 1929.

Staten, Francis Angevina. *An Appraisal of Public Utility Regulation in Wisconsin*. Unpublished Ph.D. thesis, University of Wisconsin, 1930.

Steffens, Lincoln. "Wisconsin Representative Government Restored," *The Struggle for Self Government*. New York: McClure, Phillips & Co., 1906.

Stephansky, Ben S., "Selig Perlman on The Role of Labor," *Proceedings of the Twelfth Annual Meeting of Industrial Relations Research Association*. Washington, D. C. December, 1959, pp. 15-19.

Still, Bayrd. *Milwaukee, The History of a City*. Madison, Wisc.: State Historical Society of Wisconsin, 1948.

Story, H. W. "Sound Unemployment Protection," *Nation's Business,* October, 1934.

Sturmthal, Adolf. "Comments on Selig Perlman's *A Theory of the Labor Movement*," *Industrial and Labor Relations Review*. Vol. 4, October, 1950.

Sumner, William Graham. *The Forgotten Man and Other Essays*. New Haven, Conn.: Yale University Press, 1918.

The Survey series on the U. S. Commission on Industrial Relations.

    Fitch, John A., "The Commons Report," *The Survey,* Vol. XXXV, January 1, 1916, pp. 401, 402.

    "Field Investigations of The Industrial Relations Commission," *The Survey*, Vol. XXXIII, February 27, 1915, p. 578.

    "Probing the Causes of Unrest," *The Survey,* Vol. XXXII, pp. 71, 85, 86, 92, 93, 230, 231, 252, 320, 321, 339, 340, 397-99, 538-40, 558-60, 593, 594, 609, 610, 632, 633; Vol. XXXIII, pp. 4-6, 284-88, 350-52, 389-92, 467-69, 477-80, 531-34; Vol. XXXIV, pp. 212, 230-35; Vol. XXXV, pp. 317-23, 326-33, 395-402, 432-36.

    Kellogg, Paul, "The Industrial Relations Commission," *The Survey,* December 28, 1913, p. 386.

    "Petition to the President for a Federal Commission on Industrial Relations Commission," *The Survey,* Vol. XXVII, December 30, 1911, pp. 1431-1439.

    "Commission on Industrial Relations," *The Survey,* Vol. XXIX, December 28, 1912, p. 381.

    "The Constructive Work Before the Industrial Relations Commission," *The Survey,* Vol. XXX, August 2, 1913, pp. 571-578.

    "Industrial Relations Commission," *The Survey,* Vol. XXX, July 5, 1913, pp. 452, 453.

    "Walsh Controversy," *The Survey,* Vol. XXXIII, November 14, 1914, pp. 175-181.

    "Survey Associates Statement of Paul U. Kellogg, Editor, Prepared for the New York hearings of the United States Commission on Industrial Relations, January 15, 1915," *The Survey,* Vol. XXX, February 20, 1915, pp. 561-564.

    "Charles McCarthy On Why He Is Out of Federal Inquiry," *The Survey,* Vol. XXXIV, April 10, 1915, p. 40.

Taft, Philip. "A Rereading of Selig Perlman's *A Theory of the Labor Movement*," *Industrial and Labor Relations Review*. Vol. 4, October, 1950.

—————. "Commons-Perlman Theory: A Summary," *A Theory of the Labor Movement, A Reappraisal.* Reprinted from *Proceedings of Third Annual Industrial Relations Research Association.* Chicago, Ill., December, 1950.

—————. "Professor Perlman's Ideas and Activities," *"Proceedings of the Twelfth Annual Meeting of Industrial Relations Research Association.* Washington, D. C., December, 1959, pp. 8-14.

Tannenbaum, Frank. *The Labor Movement.* New York: G. P. Putnam's Sons, 1921.

—————. *A Philosophy of Labor.* New York: Alfred A. Knopf, 1951.

Tarkington, Booth. *The Gentleman From Indiana.* New York: Doubleday & McClure Co., 1899.

Tawney, R. H. *Religion and the Rise of Capitalism.* New York: Harcourt, Brace, 1937.

Taylor, Carl C. *The Farmers' Movement 1620-1920.* New York: American Book Co., 1953.

Taylor, Graham R. "Probing the Causes of Industrial Unrest," *The Survey.* Vol. XXXIV.

Tugwell, R. G. (ed.). *The Trend of Economics.* New York: Alfred A. Knopf, 1924.

The Typographical Journal, Vol. XXXXVII, October, 1915, p. 441.

Unemployment Benefits and Insurance. National Industrial Conference Board. New York. 1931.

Unemployment Insurance in Theory and Practice. Research Report No. 51, National Industrial Conference Board, New York, June, 1922.

Veblen, Thorstein. *The Theory of The Leisure Class.* New York: MacMillan Co., 1899.

—————. *The Theory of Business Enterprise.* New York: Charles Scribner's Sons, 1904.

—————. *The Instinct of Workmanship and The State of The Industrial Arts.* New York: MacMillan Co., 1914.

—————. *The Higher Learning in America.* New York: B. W. Huebsch, Inc., 1918.

—————. *The Place of Science in Modern Civilization.* New York: B. W. Huebsch, Inc., 1919.

—————. *The Engineers and The Price System.* New York: B. W. Huebsch, Inc., 1921.

—————. *Absentee Ownership and Business Enterprise in Recent Times.* New York: B. W. Huebsch, Inc., 1923.

—————. "The Limitations of Marginal Utility," reprinted in Wesley C. Mitchell, ed., *What Veblen Taught.* New York: The Viking Press, 1936.

Walker, Harvey. *The Legislative Process.* New York: Ronald Press, 1948.

"The Walsh Commission," *New York Times.* August 23, 1915.

Ware, Norman J. *Labor in Modern Industrial Society.* New York: D. C. Heath & Co., 1935.

—————. *The Labor Movement in the United States, 1860-1895.* New York: D. Appleton & Co., 1929.

Webb, Sidney and Beatrice. *A Constitution for the Socialist Commonwealth of Great Britain.* London: Longmans, Green & Co., 1920.

—————. *History of Trade Unionism.* London: Longmans, Green & Co., 1894, 1911.

—————. *Industrial Democracy*. London: Longmans, Green & Co., 1897, 1902.

Weber, Gustavus. *Organized Efforts for the Improvement of Methods of Administration in the United States*. New York: D. Appleton & Co., 1919.

Weber, Max. *The Protestant Ethic and the Spirit of Capitalism*. Translated by Talcott Parsons. New York: Charles Scribner's Sons, 1958.

"The Week," *The Nation*, Vol. CI, September 2, 1915, p. 277.

Wells, Oliver E. "The College Anarchist," *The Nation*, Vol. LIX, July 12, 1894.

Werkmeister, W. H. *A History of Philosophical Ideas in America*. New York: Ronald Press Co., 1949.

White, Leonard D. *Trends in Public Administration*. New York: McGraw-Hill Book Co., 1933.

"Why $1,000,000?" *The World*. New York: August 24, 1915.

Wilensky, Harold L., *Intellectuals In Labor Unions*, Glencoe, Ill.: The Free Press, 1956.

Willoughby, W. F. *Principles of Public Administration*. Washington, D. C.: Brookings Institution, 1927.

—————. "Insurance Against Unemployment," in John R. Commons (ed.). *Trade Unionism and Labor Problems*. Boston: Ginn & Co., 1905.

Wilson, Woodrow. *Congressional Government*. Cambridge, Mass.: Riverside Press, 1885.

Witte, Edwin E., "The Development of Unemployment Compensation," *Yale Law Review*, Vol. 55, No. 1, December, 1945.

—————. "Re: Wisconsin As a Leader in Labor Legislation." A Report by the Chief of Legislative Library of Wisconsin, April 26, 1932.

—————. "The Government and Unemployment," *American Labor Legislation Review*. Vol. XXV, March, 1935.

—————. *John B. Andrews Memorial Symposium on Labor Legislation and Social Security*. University of Wisconsin, November 4, 5, 1949.

Wright, David McCord. (ed.). *The Impact of The Union*. New York: Kelley and Millman, October, 1956.

JRC

INDEX